Lecture Notes
and Mathema...

414

Founding Editors:

M. Beckmann
H. P. Künzi

Editorial Board:

H. Albach, M. Beckmann, G. Feichtinger, W. Hildenbrand, W. Krelle
H. P. Künzi, K. Ritter, U. Schittko, P. Schönfeld, R. Selten

Managing Editors:

Prof. Dr. G. Fandel
Fachbereich Wirtschaftswissenschaften
Fernuniversität Hagen
Feithstr. 140/AVZ II, D-58097 Hagen, FRG

Prof. Dr. W. Trockel
Institut für Mathematische Wirtschaftsforschung (IMW)
Universität Bielefeld
Universitätsstr. 25, D-33615 Bielefeld, FRG

Yves Crama Alwin Oerlemans Frits Spieksma

Production Planning in Automated Manufacturing

Springer-Verlag

Berlin Heidelberg New York
London Paris Tokyo
Hong Kong Barcelona
Budapest

Authors

Dr. Yves Crama
Université de Liège
Faculté d' Economie, de Gestion
et de Sciences Sociales
Boulevard du Rectorat 7 (B31)
B-4000 Liège, Belgium

Dr. Alwin G. Oerlemans
Ministerie van Financiën
Korte Voorhout 7
NL-2511 CW The Hague, The Netherlands

Dr. Frits C. R. Spieksma
Rijksuniversiteit Limburg
Department of Mathematics
P. O. Box 616
NL-6200 MD Maastricht, The Netherlands

ISBN 3-540-58082-4 Springer-Verlag Berlin Heidelberg New York
ISBN 0-387-58082-4 Springer-Verlag New York Berlin Heidelberg

Library of congress Cataloging-in-Publication Data

Crama, Yves, 1958- Production planning in automated manufacturing / Yves Crama, Alwin Oerlemans, Frits Spieksma. p. cm. — (Lecture notes in economics and mathematical systems; 414)
ISBN 0-387-58082-4 (Alk. paper)
1. Production planning. 2. Automationl. I. Oerlemans, Alwin III. Title. IV. Series.
TS176.C73   1994   670.42'7—dc20   94-11600

© Springer-Verlag Berlin Heidelberg 1994
Printed in Germany

Typesetting: Camera ready by author
SPIN: 10471075   42/3140-543210 - Printed on acid-free paper

Preface

This monograph is based on the theses of Oerlemans (1992) and Spieksma
(1992). We would like to thank the many individuals, at the University of
Limburg or elsewhere, who have contributed to the genesis of this work.
We are especially indebted to Antoon Kolen, who co-authored Chapters
2 and 8, and who delivered numerous comments on all other parts of the
monograph. We also want to thank Koos Vrieze and Hans-Jürgen Bandelt
for their constructive remarks.

Contents

Chapter 1

Automated manufacturing

1.1   Introduction

During the last two decades, the impact of automation on manufacturing has sharply increased. Nowadays, computers can play a role in every aspect of the production process, ranging from the design of a new product to the inspection of its quality. In some types of industry automated manufacturing has a long history, for instance in chemical or oil-refining industries. However, in the batch-manufacturing industries, like the metalworking industry or the electronics industry, the concept of automated manufacturing was introduced only in the 1970's, causing a profound effect on manufacturing and the way it is organized. So-called flexible manufacturing systems (FMSs) emerged as a critical component in the development towards the "factory of the future". Our focus will be on this type of industry. On the one hand, automated manufacturing has a wide variety of potential benefits to offer to batch-manufacturing industries. One of the most important advantages is the increased ability to respond to changes in demand. This is important in view of today's fast changing demand and short product cycles. Other possible advantages include shorter lead times, lower inventories and higher machine utilization. On the other hand, it is not an easy task to make an efficient use of the newly offered possibilities. In particular, planning the use of a system consisting of a number of connected, complicated machines using limited resources can constitute a formidable challenge.

In this monograph we intend to illustrate the role that quantitative methods, and more specifically combinatorial optimization techniques, can play in the solution of various planning problems encountered in this framework. As a common thread, we concentrate throughout the monograph on models arising in the automated assembly of printed circuit boards (PCBs). Chapter 2 describes a typical production process for PCBs, and some of the planning problems to which this process gives rise. It also presents several optimization models which can be used for handling these problems. Two of these models are studied in more detail in Chapters 3 and 4. Chapters 5 to 8 are devoted to so-called tool-loading problems. This class of problems occupies a very central place in the tactical planning phase for most highly automated, flexible production systems. Chapters 5 to 8 are therefore presented in a rather general setting, and use a terminology pertaining to flexible manufacturing systems rather than to the more particular case of PCB assembly machines. Section 1.3 hereunder contains a more precise, chapter-by-chapter overview of the contents of this monograph. But before going into this, we first propose, in the next section, a very brief review of the literature devoted to production planning for FMSs.

1.2   Production planning for FMSs

In this section we review some of the literature concerning planning and control of FMSs. First, we describe an FMS (Subsection 1.2.1). Next, in Subsection 1.2.2, we review a number of different strategies (or methodologies) proposed in the literature to cope with FMS planning problems. The use of a so-called hierarchical approach is advocated in most papers. Subsections 1.2.3 and 1.2.4 focus on planning problems arising at the tactical and operational level of the decision hierarchy.

1.2.1   What is an FMS?

A flexible manufacturing system is an integrated, computer-controlled complex of numerically controlled machines and automated material handling devices that can simultaneously process medium-sized volumes of a variety of part types (Stecke, 1983). As Gerwin (1982) and Huang and Chen (1986) point out, FMSs are an attempt to solve the production problem of mid-volume (200-20,000 parts per year) and midvariety parts, for which neither the high-production rate transfer lines nor the highly flexible stand-alone numerically controlled machines are suitable. The aim is to achieve the efficiency of mass-production, while utilizing the flexibility of manual job shop production.

   An FMS consists of a number of machines or work stations that are used to perform operations on parts. Each operation requires a number of tools, that can be stored in the limited capacity tool magazine of the machines. An automatic tool interchanging device quickly interchanges the tools during production. This rapid interchange facility enables a machine to perform several operations with virtually no setup time between operations, provided that the tools needed for operations are present in the tool magazine. (We will see in the remainder of this monograph that in PCB assembly systems the so-called feeders, from which electronic components to be mounted on the PCB are fed to the machine, play a very similar role to that of tools in a classical FMS.) Parts are moved automatically to the machines by a transportation system or a Material Handling System (MHS). A number of buffer places or an Automated Storage and Retrieval System (ASRS) are also added to the system, either at a central location or at each machine. In some FMSs, tools are also stored at a central tool store and delivered to machines by a special delivery system (Buzacott and Yao, 1986). Finally, a network of supervisory computers takes care of the control of tools, parts, MHS and machines. The development of FMSs goes along with the other developments in automated manufacturing. The first systems appeared in the 1960's; one of the earliest FMSs, which was designed to process constant speed drive housings for aircraft, was installed by Sunstrand in 1964 (Huang and Chen, 1986). In the late 1970's more systems were developed, while the last decade was mainly devoted to refinement of the systems. Emphasis has shifted from hardware issues to the development of control systems and refinement of the software packages (Huang and Chen, 1986). A number of authors have written excellent books in which detailed descriptions of FMSs are given (Ránky, 1983; Charles Stark Draper Laboratory, 1984; Hartley, 1984; Warnecke and Steinhilper, 1985). Also, several authors have given classifications of FMSs (Groover, 1980; Dupont-Gatelmand, 1982; Browne, Dubois, Rathmill, Sethi and Stecke, 1984).

1.2.2 The hierarchical approach

As already pointed out, substantial benefits can be gained by using FMSs. However, these benefits can only be obtained if the FMS is properly implemented and managed. The successful implementation of an FMS requires effective solutions to the many technical, organizational and planning problems that arise when a manufacturer wants to introduce flexible manufacturing technology. Several authors have presented methodologies for and classification of FMS design, planning, scheduling and control problems (Suri and Whitney, 1984; Kusiak, 1985a; Stecke, 1985; Suri, 1985; Buzacott and Yao, 1986; Kusiak, 1986; Van Looveren, Gelders and Van Wassenhove, 1986; Singhal, Fine, Meredith and Suri, 1987; Stecke, 1988), which are sometimes complementary. Most surveys describe some kind of hierarchical decision structure, relating to a variety of decisions that have to be taken concerning long-term, medium-term or short-term decisions. One of the main reasons for decomposing the general planning problem is that this problem is too complex to be solved globally. In the decomposition schemes, a number of hierarchically coupled subproblems are identified, each of which is easier to solve than the global problem. By solving these subproblems consecutively, a solution to the global problem can be found. Of course, one cannot expect this solution to be globally optimal, even if all subproblems are solved to optimality. Nevertheless, the hierarchical approach seems to be a fertile and appealing way to tackle hard problems. The differences between the different methodologies mentioned before concern the number of levels or the interpretation of a specific level. We now discuss some general classification schemes. In our discussion we basically use the framework of Van Looveren et al. (1986). They rely on the classical three level view of the organization (Holstein, 1968) to identify subproblems, and thus establish three levels of decision making, namely the *strategic, tactical* and *operational* levels. The strategic level relates to long-term decisions taken by the top management, which influence the basic flexibility of the FMS. Problems involved concern the design and selection of the equipment and of the products that have to be manufactured. On the tactical level, the medium-term planning problems are addressed. Decisions taken at this level concern the off-line planning of the production system. Van Looveren et al. (1986) distinguish on this level between the *batching problem* and the *loading problem*. The batching problem is concerned with the splitting of the production orders into batches such that orders are performed on time given the limited available resources. The loading problem takes care of the actual setup of the system given the batches that are formed. Planning on the operational level is concerned with the detailed decision making required for the real-time operation of the system. A release strategy has to be developed, in which one decides which parts are fed into the system (*release problem*). Next the *dispatching problem* has to be solved to decide on the actual use of the production resources like machines, buffers and the MHS. Buzacott and Yao (1986) give a classification of analytical models that can be used for establishing basic design concepts, detailed design, scheduling and control. Suri and Whitney (1984) describe in detail how to integrate the FMS software and hardware in the organizational hierarchy. They emphasize the value of the decision support systems as an integral part of the FMS. Stecke (1985) distinguishes four types of problems: design, planning, scheduling and control. This description closely fits to the decision structure of Van Looveren et al. (1986). Stecke and Solberg (1981), Stecke (1983; 1988) and Berrada and Stecke (1986)) have performed detailed studies on a number of these subproblems. Kusiak (1986) makes a distinction between design and operational problems. The former relate to strategic decisions concerning the economic justification of the system and the design and selection of parts and equipment. The term operational refers to problems on the tactical and operational levels, as defined by Van Looveren et al. (1986). Kusiak (1986) splits the operational problems into four sublevels, that consider aggregate planning, resource grouping, disaggregate planning (batching and loading) and scheduling of equipments. Kiran and Tansel (1986) use a five level decision hierarchy linked to that of

Van Looveren et al. (1986). They distinguish between design, aggregate
planning, system setup, scheduling and control, where design concerns the
strategic level, aggregate planning and system setup take place on the tactical level and scheduling and control are on the operational level. Singhal,
Fine, Meredith and Suri (1987) discuss the problems brought forward by
Buzacott and Yao (1986) and discuss the role of MS/OR techniques in the
design, operation and control of automated manufacturing systems. Zijm
(1988) also discusses problems related to the justification, design and operation of FMSs and gives an overview of related literature. Jaikumar and Van
Wassenhove (1989) give a different outlook on FMS problems. They also
present a three level model for strategic, tactical and operational planning.
But, instead of stressing the complexity of FMS problems, they emphasize
the use of simple models. They argue that scheduling theory and algorithms
are quite sufficient for the task. Several other authors have used the hierarchy presented by Van Looveren et al. (1986) (see Aanen (1988), Van
Vliet and Van Wassenhove (1989) and Zeestraten (1989)). A large number
of mathematical and methodological tools have been used to describe and
solve FMS problems on the strategic, tactical and operational level. The
basic tools and techniques are (see e.g. Kusiak (1986)): (1) Mathematical
programming; (2) Simulation; (3) Queuing networks; (4) Markov processes;
(5) Petri nets; (6) Artificial intelligence; (7) Perturbation analysis.

In this monograph we use mathematical programming techniques to solve
problems arising at the tactical and operational level in planning an FMS.
Let us therefore focus in the next subsection on the specific production
planning problems arising at these levels.

1.2.3   Tactical Planning

A lot of efforts have been devoted to tactical planning problems for FMSs.
In this subsection we review several solution approaches to tactical planning
problems. Special attention is given to the treatment of tooling restrictions,
because these problems are the main focus of chapters 5 - 8 of this monograph.

Van Looveren et al. (1986) split tactical planning into a batching problem and a loading problem. The *batching problem* concerns the partitioning
of the parts that must be produced into batches, taking into account the due
dates of the parts and the availability of fixtures and pallets. The production
resources are also split into a number of batches. Given these batches, the
loading problem is solved, i.e. one decides in more detail how the batches

are to be manufactured. Machines and tools may be pooled in groups that perform the same operations, parts are assigned to machine groups and the available fixtures and pallets are assigned to parts. Stecke (1983) refers to tactical planning as the system setup problem. She considers five subproblems: (1) Part type selection problem; (2) Machine grouping problem; (3) Production ratio (part mix) problem; (4) Resource allocation problem; (5) Loading problem. In the part type selection problem a subset of parts is determined for immediate production. Grouping of the machines into groups of identical machines is pursued to increase system performance (see Stecke and Solberg (1981) and Berrada and Stecke (1986)). The production ratio problem decides on the ratios in which the parts that are selected are produced. Allocation of pallets and fixtures takes place in the resource allocation problem. The loading problem concerns the allocation of operations (that have to be performed on selected parts) and tools among the machines, subject to technological constraints such as the capacity of the tool magazine. A lot of attention has been devoted to the solution of these subproblems; we now review some important contributions in this area.

In Stecke (1983) nonlinear 0-1 mixed-integer models are proposed for the grouping and the loading problems. Linearization techniques are used for solving these problems. Berrada and Stecke (1986) develop a branch-and-bound procedure for solving the loading problem. Whitney and Gaul (1985) propose a sequential decision procedure for solving the batching (part type selection) problem. They sequentially assign part types to batches according to a probabilistic function, which is dependent on the due date of the part, the tool requirements of the part and an index describing whether a part is easy to balance with parts already selected. Chakravarty and Shtub (1984) give several mixed-integer programming models for batching and loading problems. Kusiak (1985c) also uses group technology approaches for grouping parts into families (see also Kumar, Kusiak and Vanelli (1986)). Ammons, Lofgren and McGinnis (1985) present a mixed-integer formulation for a large machine loading problem and propose three heuristics for solving the problem. Rajagopalan (1985; 1986) proposes mixed-integer programming formulations for the part type selection, production ratio and loading problems. The first formulation is used to obtain an optimal part-mix for one planning period. A second formulation is presented to get a production plan for the entire period, which is optimal with respect to the total completion time (including processing and setup time). Two types of sequential heuristics are presented to solve the formulations. Part type priorities are determined by considering either the number of tool slots required or the processing times on the different machines. Hwang (1986) formulates a 0-1 integer programming model for the part type selection problem. A batch is formed by maximizing the number of parts that can be processed given the aggregate tool magazine capacity of the machines. In Hwang and Shogan (1989) this study is extended and lagrangian relaxation approaches are compared to solve the problem. Kiran and Tansel (1986) give an integer programming formulation for the system setup problem. They consider the part type selection, production ratio, resource allocation and loading problems. The objective is to maximize the number of part types produced during the following planning period. All parts of one part type must be processed in one planning period. Kiran and Tansel (1986) propose to solve the integer programming formulation using decomposition techniques. Stecke and Kim (1988) study the part type selection and production ratio problem. They propose a so-called flexible approach. Instead of forming batches, parts 'flow gradually' in the system. Tools can be replaced during production and not only at the start of a planning period. This offers the possibility to replace tools on some machines while production continues on the other machines. The objective is to balance the workloads of the machines. As soon as the production requirements of a part type are reached the model is solved again to determine new production ratios. Simulations are performed to compare the flexible and various batching approaches (Rajagopalan, 1985; Whitney and Gaul, 1985; Hwang, 1986). System utilization appears to be higher for the flexible approach for the types of FMSs considered. Jaikumar and Van Wassenhove (1989) propose a three level model. On the first level the parts selected for production on the FMS and production requirements are set. A mixed-integer program is proposed that is solved by rounding off the solution values of the linear relaxation. The part type selection and loading problems are solved on the second level. The objective is to maximize machine utilization. The scheduling problem is solved at the third level. Feedback mechanisms provide feasibility of the solutions on all levels. Kim and Yano (1992) also describe an iterative approach that solves the part type selection, machine grouping and loading problems.

The most discussed planning problems are the part type selection problem (often solved simultaneously with the production ratio problem) and the loading problem. In the last years, in particular growing attention has been paid to the loading problem and especially to the loading of tools. Therefore, we review some work that has been done in this area.

The importance of *tool management* is stressed by several authors (El-Maraghy, 1985; Gray, Seidmann and Stecke, 1988; Kiran and Krason, 1988;

Gruver and Senninger, 1990). These authors also give an extensive review of the problems involved. Chung (1991) discusses the rough-cut tool planning problem and the tool requirements planning problem. Graver and McGinnis (1989), Daskin, Jones and Lowe (1990) and Jain, Kasilingam and Bhole (1991) discuss the tool provisioning problem, in which is decided on the number and type of tools that must be available in the system. This type of problems can also be seen as strategic problems. Most attention has been focused on the actual tool loading problem. Most of the loading models described above include the tool loading problem. Including the capacity of the tool magazines of the machines in these models prohibits the occurrence of infeasible loadings. De Werra and Widmer (1990) propose four formulations for the tool loading problem. Several authors (Hirabayashi, Suzuki and Tsuchiya, 1984; Bard, 1988; Tang and Denardo, 1988a ; Tang and Denardo, 1988b; Widmer, 1991) have investigated tool loading problems using different objective functions. Ventura, Chen and Leonard (1988) give an overview of more work related to tool loading. Much of the present monograph, in particular chapters 5 - 8, will concentrate on tool loading models; for a further discussion of the topic we refer to these chapters and the references therein.

1.2.4 Operational planning

Operational planning is concerned with short-term decisions and real-time scheduling of the system. Van Looveren et al. (1986) distinguish a *release* and a *dispatching problem*. The release problem decides on the release strategy that controls the flow of parts into the system. This flow is limited for instance by the availability of pallets and fixtures. The dispatching problem relates to decisions concerning the use of machines, buffers and MHS. Procedures that have to be carried out in case of machine or system failure are taken care of within the dispatching problem. Stecke (1983) gives a similar division of operational problems into scheduling and control problems. Scheduling problems concern the flow of parts through the system once it has been set up (at the tactical level). Control problems are associated with monitoring the system and keeping track of production to be sure that requirements and due dates are met.

Due to the huge number of interactions and the possibility of disturbances, the operational problems are complex. Simulation is often used to determine the performance of solution procedures for the release and dispatching problem. Chang, Sullivan, Bagchi and Wilson (1985) describe the dispatching problem as a mixed-integer programming model, which is solved using heuristics (see also Greene and Sadowski (1986) and Bastos (1988)).

The dispatching problem is often solved using (simple) dispatching rules. The purpose of these rules is to generate feasible schedules, not necessarily optimal ones. A lot of attention has been paid to the evaluation of such scheduling rules (see e.g. Panwalker and Iskander (1977), Stecke and Solberg (1981), Akella, Choong and Gershwin (1984), Shanker and Tzen (1985), Zeestraten (1989) and Montazeri and Van Wassenhove (1990)). Zijm (1988) and Blazewicz, Finke, Haupt and Schmidt (1988) give an overview on new trends in scheduling, in particular as they relate to FMS scheduling. A strong interdependence exists between tactical and operational planning. In Spieksma, Vrieze and Oerlemans (1990) a model is presented that can be used for simultaneously formulating the system setup and scheduling problems.

1.3   Overview of the monograph

We have seen that FMS planning problems have a complex nature. In the previous section we presented an overview of hierarchical approaches to the planning process. Using a hierarchical framework may be helpful for identifying and understanding the fundamental underlying problems. In this monograph a number of such subproblems are analyzed. In Chapter 2, a hierarchical procedure is presented to solve a real-world production problem in the electronics industry. Each of Chapters 3 and 4 deals more extensively with a specific subproblem arising in this hierarchy. In chapters 5 - 8 two FMS tool loading problems are studied in detail. The job grouping problem is discussed in Chapters 5, 6 and 7. In Chapter 8 another loading problem is studied, namely the problem of minimizing the number of tool switches. We take now a short walk along these chapters.

In Chapter 2, a throughput rate (production rate) optimization problem for the automated assembly of printed circuit boards (PCBs) is investigated. PCBs are widely applied in consumer electronics (e.g. computers and hi-fi) and the professional industry (e.g. telecommunications). The production of PCBs heavily relies on the use of CNC machines and the technology is continuously updated (Mullins, 1990). As mentioned by Van Laarhoven and Zijm (1993) production preparation for the assembly of PCBs is comparable to the system setup problem in (other) FMSs, although the type of industry is quite different from the metal working industry, which is the main area of

application for FMSs. We assume that the part type selection problem has
been solved (only one part type will be produced), as well as the machine
grouping problem (a line of machines is available). What remains to be
solved is a loading problem, which consists of the assignment of parts and
equipments to the machines, taking some sequencing aspects into account.
A more detailed description is as follows. A line of machines is devoted to
the assembly of one type of PCBs. An automated transport band is used
to carry each PCB from one machine to the next. The assembly of an individual PCB consists of inserting electronic components of prespecified types
into prescribed locations on the board. In order to handle the components,
each machine is equipped with a device called its arm. This arm picks components from so-called feeders, moves to the appropriate locations, inserts
the components into the board and moves back to the feeders to pick new
components. Each feeder delivers components of a certain type (one type
per feeder). Prior to the operation, the feeders are placed in the slots of the
machine; each machine has a row of slots available, of which each feeder occupies 1, 2 or even more adjacent slots. A sequence of operations consisting
of picking components from feeders, moving to the appropriate locations,
and inserting them into the board is called a pick-and-place round. Further,
in the system under study, the arm of each machine has three heads. Each
head can carry one component at the time. Consequently, in one pick-and-
place round three components are inserted in the board. Also, in order to be
able to collect a component from a feeder, a head of the arm of the machine
must be provided with some tools or equipments. Every component type can
only be handled by a restrictive set of alternative equipments. We propose to
decompose the resulting planning problem into the following, hierarchically
coupled, subproblems:

(**A**) determine how many components each machine should insert, and with
what equipment;

(**B**) assign feeder types to machines;

(**C**) determine which components each head should insert into the board;

(**D**) cluster the locations into subsets of size at most three, to be processed
in one pick-and-place round;

(**E**) determine the sequence of pick-and-place operations to be performed
by each machine;

(**F**) assign the feeders to the slots.

Subproblems (A) and (B) determine the workload of each machine. The objective here is to minimize the maximum workload over all machines, since this is equivalent to maximizing the throughput rate. The remaining subproblems (C)-(F) deal with the scheduling of individual machines. In Chapter 2, we model more precisely each of the subproblems (A)-(F) and we develop heuristic approaches for their solution. The performance of our approach is tested on a real-world problem instance: 258 components of 39 types have to be inserted in each PCB by a line of three machines.

Chapter 3 in this monograph deals with subproblem (D) from the decomposition described above. This problem is a special case of the three-dimensional assignment problem (3DA), which can be described as follows (see also Balas and Saltzman (1991)). Given are three disjoint n-sets of points, and nonnegative costs associated with every triple consisting of exactly one point from each set. The problem is to find a minimum-cost collection of n triples covering each point exactly once. In subproblem (D), the three disjoint point-sets correspond to the locations where components have to be inserted by the first, second or third head respectively. The cost of a triple reflects the travel time of the arm between the corresponding locations. Instances of subproblem (D) are specially structured instances of 3DA in the sense that the cost of each triple is determined by a distance defined on the set of all points and satisfying the triangle inequality. We call $T\Delta$ the special case of 3DA where the cost of a triple is equal to the sum of the distances between its points, and $S\Delta$ the case where the cost of a triple is equal to the sum of the two smallest distances between its points. We prove in Chapter 3 that $T\Delta$ as well as $S\Delta$ are $\mathcal{NP}$-hard problems. For both $T\Delta$ and $S\Delta$ we present two polynomial-time heuristics based on the solution of a small number (either two or six) of related two-dimensional assignment problems. We prove that these heuristics always deliver a feasible solution whose cost is at most $\frac{3}{2}$ respectively $\frac{4}{3}$ times the optimal cost. Computational experiments indicate that the performance of these heuristics is excellent on randomly generated instances of $T\Delta$ and $S\Delta$.

Chapter 4 is devoted to the following problem. Given are n jobs which have to be processed on a single machine within a fixed timespan $1, 2, \ldots, T$. The processing time, or length of each job equals p, with p an integer. The processing cost of each job is an arbitrary function of its start-time, and is denoted by $c_{jt}, j = 1, \ldots, n, t = 1, \ldots, T$. The problem is to schedule all jobs so as to minimize the sum of the processing cost. We refer to this problem as problem SEL (Scheduling jobs of Equal Length). It should be noted that SEL is a special case of a very general scheduling problem, say problem S, considered by Sousa and Wolsey (1992), where the jobs may have arbitrary, usually distinct, processing times. It is an easy observation that, if $\{1, \ldots, n\}$ is any subset of the jobs occurring in S, and all jobs in $\{1, \ldots, n\}$ have the same length p, then any valid inequality for SEL is also valid for S. This suggests that the polyhedral description presented in Chapter 4 may prove useful, not only when all jobs have strictly equal length, but also in case where the number of distinct lengths is small. SEL is also strongly related to subproblem (F) in the decomposition described above. This can be seen as follows: each feeder j requires a certain number of slots, say p_j, depending on the feeder type; usually, p_j only takes a small number of values, say $p_j \in \{1, 2, 3\}$. In order to maximize the throughput rate, it is desirable to position the feeders close to the locations where the corresponding components must be inserted. More precisely, for each combination of feeder j and slot t a cost-coefficient can be computed which captures the cost of assigning feeder j to slots $t, t+1, \ldots, t + p_j - 1$. It follows that finding a minimum-cost assignment of feeders to slots is equivalent to solving a scheduling problem where the number of distinct processing times is small. We prove in Chapter 4 that SEL is $\mathcal{NP}$-hard already for $p = 2$ and $c_{jt} \in \{0, 1\}$. On the other hand, if the number of time-units equals $np + c$, where c denotes a constant, then the problem is shown to be polynomially solvable. We also study a 0-1 programming formulation of SEL from a polyhedral point of view. In particular, we show that all facets defined by set-packing inequalities have been previously listed by Sousa and Wolsey (1992). Two more classes of facet-defining inequalities (one of them exponentially large) are derived. The separation problem for these inequalities is solvable in polynomial time.

In Chapter 5 a loading problem is studied, which arises at the tactical level in batch-industries. We present a model which aims at minimizing the number of machine setups. We assume that a number of jobs must processed on a machine. Each job requires a set of tools, which have to be present in the limited capacity tool magazine of the machine when the job is executed. We say that a group (batch) of jobs is feasible if, together, these jobs do not require more tools than can be placed in the tool magazine of the machine. Each tool is assumed to require one slot in the tool magazine. The job grouping problem is to partition the jobs into a minimum number of feasible groups. As noticed for instance by Bard (1988) for a closely related problem (the tool switching problem to be discussed in Chapter 8), an important occurence of the job grouping problem arises in the planning phase of the PCB assembly process. Suppose several types of PCBs are produced by an automated placement machine (or a line of such machines). For each type of PCB, a certain collection of component feeders must be placed on the machine before boards of that type can be produced. As the machine can only hold a limited number of feeders, it is usually necessary to replace some feeders when switching from the production of one type of boards to that of another type. Exchanging feeders is a time-consuming operation and it is therefore important to determine a production sequence which minimizes the number of "feeder-setups". Identifying the feeders with tools and the PCBs with jobs, one can see that this type of situation gives rise to either a job grouping problem or to a tool switching problem (to be discussed below), depending on the characteristics of the production environment. A number of authors have suggested solution approaches for the problem (Hirabayashi et al., 1984; Whitney and Gaul, 1985; Hwang, 1986; Rajagopalan, 1986; Tang and Denardo, 1988b), but no strong lower bounds on the optimal number of groups were obtained until now. We rely on a set covering formulation of the problem (Hirabayashi et al., 1984), and we solve the linear relaxation of this formulation in order to compute tight lower bounds. Since the number of variables is potentially huge, we use a column generation approach. We also describe some fast and simple heuristics for the job grouping problem. The result of our computational experiments on 550 randomly generated instances is that the lower bound is extremely strong: for all instances tested, the lower bound is optimal. The overall quality of the heuristic solutions appears to be very good as well.

Chapter 6 discusses a number of extensions of the previous job grouping model. First we consider the job grouping problem for one machine, where tools have different sizes (i.e., may require several slots in the tool magazine). Then we study the problem in case several machines are needed. The lower and upper bounding procedures described in Chapter 5 are generalized so as to apply to these cases as well. We present the results of computational experiments that were performed on 580 randomly generated instances. It appears that the lower bound is very strong and that the conclusions of Chapter 5 can be largely extended to this broader class of problems.

In Chapter 7 we continue our study of the job grouping problem. Attention is focused on deriving better upper bounds for the problem. A study is performed to determine the possibilities offered by local search approaches. Local search approaches explore the neighbourhood of a current solution in a smart way in order to improve this solution. Four local search approaches, viz. a simple improvement, tabu search, simulated annealing and variable-depth approach are tested. Experiments are conducted to assess the influence of the choice of starting solutions, objective functions, neighbourhood structures and stopping criteria. Computational experiments show that a majority of instances for which other (simple) heuristic procedures (presented in Chapters 5 and 6) do not produce optimal solutions can be solved optimally using a local search approach. The choice of starting solution, objective function and neighbourhood structure seems to have far more impact on the solution quality than the local search approach itself, as long as some kind of local optimum evading strategy is used.

Chapter 8 analyzes another loading problem arising in FMS planning, namely the tool switching problem. A batch of jobs have to be successively processed on a single flexible machine. Each job requires a subset of tools, which have to be placed in the limited capacity tool magazine of the machine before the job can be processed. The total number of tools needed exceed the capacity of the tool magazine. Hence, it is sometimes necessary to change tools between two jobs in a sequence. The tool switching problem is now to determine a job sequence and an associated sequence of loadings for the tool magazine, such that the total number of tool switches is minimized. This problem becomes especially crucial when the time needed to change a tool is significant with respect to the processing times of the parts, or when many small batches of different parts must be processed in succession. These phenomena have been observed in the metal-working industry by several authors. As mentioned above in our overview of Chapter 5, the problem also plays a prominent role in production planning for PCBs. Bard (1988) and Tang and Denardo (1988a) have specifically studied the tool switching problem. In this chapter the problem is revisited, both from a theoretical and from a computational viewpoint. Basic results concerning the computational complexity of the problem are established. For instance, we show that the problem is already $\mathcal{N}P$-hard when the tool magazine capacity is 2, and we provide a new proof of the fact that, for each fixed job sequence, an optimal sequence of tool loadings can be found in polynomial time. Links between the problem and well-known combinatorial optimization problems (traveling salesman, block minimization, interval matrix recognition, etc.) are established and several heuristics are presented which exploit these special structures. Computational results are presented to compare the behaviour of the eight heuristic procedures. Also the influence of local improvement strategies is computationally assessed.

Chapter 2

Throughput rate optimization in the automated assembly of printed circuit boards

2.1 Introduction

The electronics industry relies heavily on numerically controlled machines for the placement of electronic components on the surface of printed circuit boards (PCB). These placement (or mounting, or pick-and-place) machines automatically insert components into PCB's, in a sequence determined by the input program. The most recent among them are characterized by high levels of accuracy and speed, but their throughput rates still appear to be extremely sensitive to the quality of the instructions. On the other hand, the effective programming of the machines becomes steadily more difficult in view of the increasing sophistication of the available technology. The development of optimization procedures allowing the efficient operation of such placement machines therefore provides an exciting challenge for the operations research community, as witnessed by, e.g., the recent papers by Ahmadi, Grotzinger and Johnson (1988), Ball and Magazine (1988), and Leipälä and Nevalainen (1989).

In this chapter we propose a hierarchical approach to the problem of optimizing the throughput rate of a line of several placement machines devoted to the assembly of a single product. As usual in the study of flexible systems, the high complexity of the problem suggests its decomposition into more manageable subproblems, and accepting the solution of each subproblem as the starting point for the next one. Of course, this methodology cannot guarantee the global optimality of the final solution, even assuming that all subproblems are solved to optimality. This is even more true in the present case, where most subproblems themselves turn out to be $\mathcal{N}\mathcal{P}$-hard, and hence can only be approximately solved by heuristic procedures. Nevertheless, such hierarchical approaches have previously proved to deliver good quality solutions to similarly hard problems (e.g. in VLSI-design; see Korte (1989)). They also offer the advantage of providing precise analytical models for the various facets of the global problem (see, for example, Buzacott and Yao (1986) for a discussion of analytical models in FMS).

Our approach has been tested on some industrial problems, but more experimentation would be required in order to precisely assess the quality of its performance and its range of applicability. In particular, as pointed out by one of the referees, the validity of some of our models is conditioned by the validity of some exogenous assumptions about the nature of instances "coming up in practice" (see, for instance, Subsection 2.4.1). Even though these assumptions were fulfilled in the industrial settings that motivated our study, they may well fail to be satisfied in other practical situations. This would then invalidate the use of the corresponding models. However, we believe that the hierarchical scheme and most of the techniques presented in this chapter would nevertheless remain applicable for a wide range of problem instances.

We now give a brief outline of the chapter. The next section contains a more detailed description of the technological environment, and Section 2.3 provides a precise statement of the problem and a brief account of previous related work. Sections 2.4 and 2.5 present our approach to the solution of the throughput rate optimization problem. Section 2.4 addresses the workload balancing problem for the line of machines, and Section 2.5 deals with the optimal sequencing of operations for individual machines. Both sections present mathematical models and heuristic solution methods for the various subproblems arising in our decomposition of the global problem. Finally, in Section 2.6 we describe the results supplied by our approach on a practical problem instance.

2.2   Technological environment

In this chapter, we are concerned with the automated assembly of a number of identical PCB's. For our purpose, the assembly of a PCB consists of the insertion of electronic components of prespecified *types* (indexed by $1, \ldots, T$) into prespecified *locations* (indexed by $1, \ldots, N$) on a board. Prior to operations, the components of different types are collected on different *feeders* (one type per feeder). Feeders are used by the placement machines as described below. We denote by N_t the number of components of type t $(t = 1, \ldots, T)$. So, $N = \sum_{t=1}^{T} N_t$.

We assume that a line of M placement machines is devoted to the assembly of the PCB's. The machines we have in mind are of the CSM (Component Surface Mounting) family. They feature a *worktable*, a number S of *feeder slots*, and three *pick-and-place heads* (see Figure 2.1).

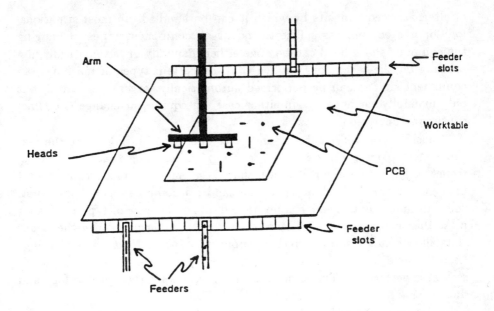

Figure 2.1 Schematic representation of a placement machine.

The PCB is carried from one machine to the next by an automatic transportband until it comes to rest on the worktable. It stays motionless during the mounting operations.

The feeder slots are fixed to two opposite sides of the worktable, $S/2$ of them on each side. The feeders containing the components to be placed by the machine must be loaded in the slots before the mounting begins. Depending on its type, each feeder may require 1, 2, or even more adjacent slots.

The pick-and-place heads are numbered from 1 to $3M$, with heads $3m-2$, $3m-1$ and $3m$ on machine m (but, for short, we shall also refer to heads 1, 2 and 3 of each machine). They are fixed along a same *arm* which always remains parallel to the side of the worktable supporting the feeder slots. The arm can move in a horizontal plane above the worktable. It can perform vertical moves to allow the heads to pick components from the feeders or to insert components into the board.

Each head can carry at most one component at a time. It must be equipped with certain tools (chucks and nozzles) before it can handle any components. The collection of tools necessary to process a given component we call *equipment*. With every component type is associated a restricted set of alternative equipments by which it can be handled. In most situations, four or five equipments suffice to mount all component types. Changing the equipment of a head can be done either manually or automatically, depending on the technology (notice that, on certain types of machines, an equipment change can be performed automatically for heads 1 and 2, but only manually for head 3). In either case, an equipment change is a time-consuming operation.

Consider now a typical pick-and-place operation, during which the machine must place components of types i, j and k using heads 1, 2 and 3, respectively. Suppose, for instance, that these components are to be placed in the order j, i, k. Such an operation can be decomposed as follows. First, the arm moves until head 1 is positioned above a feeder of type i. Head 1 picks then a component i. Two more moves of the arm between the feeder slots allow heads 2 and 3 to pick components j and k. Next, the arm brings head 2 above the location where component j is to be placed, and the insertion is performed. The same operation is subsequently repeated for i and finally for k.

Some remarks are in order concerning such a pick-and-place round. Notice that the picking of the components must always be performed by head 1 first, then by head 2, then by head 3 (of course, we may decide in some rounds to use only one or two heads), whereas an arbitrary sequence may be selected for their placement. Once a head has been positioned by the arm above the required feeder slot or location, the time needed to pick or to place the corresponding component depends on the type of the component, but is otherwise constant. Thus, on one machine, the only opportunities for a reduction of the total pick-and-place time reside in a clever sequencing of the operations and assignment of the feeders to feeder slots.

We have intentionally omitted many details in this brief description of the placement machines and of their functionning. For example, the insertion heads have to rotate to a predetermined angle before picking or placing components; some feeder slots or board locations are unreachable for certain heads; heads may be unavailable (e.g. broken) or may be assigned fixed equipments; the arm can only move in a limited number of directions; etc.

Some of these features (unreachable locations, unavailable heads, etc.) can be easily introduced in our models by setting variables to fixed values, thus resulting in a simplification of these models. Others will be implicitly incorporated in the models. For instance, parameters of the models such as the pick-and-place time or the travel time between board locations will be assumed to take into account the rotation of the heads and the restricted moves of the arm. Of course, there remains a possibility that these characteristics could be exploited explicitly to improve the performance of the machines, but we did not attempt to do so.

2.3 The throughput rate optimization problem

With this description of the technological constraints, we can now state a *global throughput rate optimization* problem as follows. Given the specifications of a PCB and of M placement machines, determine:

(1) an assignment of the components to the M machines;

(2) for each machine, an assignment of feeders to feeder slots;

(3) for each machine, a sequence of pick-and-place rounds, each round consisting itself of a sequence of at most three component locations among those assigned to the machine in step (1);

(4) for each machine and for each pick-and-place round, an assignment of equipment to heads.

These decisions are to be made so that the PCB can be mounted using all M machines, and so as to minimize the processing time on the *bottleneck machine* (i.e., the machine with the longest processing time).

In our solution of this problem, we shall also take into account a secondary criterion, dictated by cost considerations. Because feeders are rather expensive, it appears desirable (at least, in the practical situations that we encountered) to minimize the total number of feeders used. Ideally, thus, all components of a same type should be processed by one machine. We shall show in Subsection 2.4.2 how this criterion can be accomodated.

This formulation of the throughput rate optimization problem is patterned after a (confidential) report of the Philips Center for Quantitative Methods (CQM (1988); see also Van Laarhoven and Zijm (1993)). This report proposes a hierarchical decomposition of the problem, and heuristics for the resulting subproblems. Our decomposition, as well as all heuristics presented in the next two sections, are different from CQM's. Our heuristics, in particular, rely more explicitly on the precise mathematical modeling of the subproblems.

The throughput rate optimization problem is also mentioned by Ball and Magazine (1988), under somewhat simpler technological conditions. In particular, each machine has but one pick-and-place head. The authors investigate in detail only the sequencing of pick-and-place operations over one machine (i.e., our step (3) above).

Leipälä and Nevalainen (1989) discuss our steps (2) and (3), for a different type of one-head machines.

Ahmadi et al. (1988) consider the case of one machine featuring two heads. They address subproblems (2), (3) and (4), but their technological constraints are very different from ours, and their models do not seem to be directly applicable in our framework.

In the next two sections we describe our approach to the throughput rate optimization problem. This approach is based on a decomposition of the global problem into the following list of subproblems (which thus refines the original formulation (1)–(4) given before):

(A) determine how many components each machine must mount, and with what equipments;

(B) assign feeder types to machines;

(C) determine what components each head must mount;

(D) cluster the locations into subsets of size at most three, to be processed in one pick-and-place round;

(E) determine the sequence of pick-and-place operations to be performed by each machine;

(F) assign the feeders to feeder slots.

Subproblems (A) and (B) in this list answer together question (1) and part of question (4) above. Our main concern in solving these two subproblems will be to achieve an approximate balance of the workload over the line of machines. This will be done in Section 2.4.

Subproblems (C), (D), (E), (F) address the scheduling of individual machines, and are dealt with in Section 2.5.

In our computer experiments, the sequence of subproblems (A)–(F) is solved hierarchically in a single pass (except for (E) and (F); see Section 2.5). It may be possible to use an iterative solution procedure, and to exploit the solution of certain subproblems in order to revise previous ones. We have not further explored these possibilities.

2.4   Workload balancing

2.4.1   Subproblem (A)

The model

We proceed in this phase to a preliminary distribution of the workload over the machine line, based on the number of equipment changes for each head and on a rough estimate of the time needed to mount each component. The latter estimate is computed as follows.

In Section 2.1, we have seen that the time needed to mount a component of type t $(t = 1, \ldots, T)$ consists of two terms: a variable term measuring the travel time of the head, and a constant term p_t representing the total time spent to pick the component when the head is directly above feeder t, plus the time to place the component when the head is above the desired location.

Let now v_t be an estimate of the first variable term; then, $v_t + p_t$ is an estimate of the mounting time required by each component of type t. Notice that, in practice, a reasonable value for v_t does not appear too difficult to come by, e.g. by evaluating the average time required for the arm to travel from feeder slots to mounting locations. The solution of the model given below does not appear to be very sensitive to the exact value of v_t. (In our computer experimentations, we used a constant value v for all v_t, $t = 1, \ldots, T$.) Otherwise, solving the model for a few alternative values of v_t $(t = 1, \ldots, T)$ provides different initial solutions for the subsequent phases of the procedure. If necessary, after all subproblems (A)–(F) have been solved, a solution to the global problem can be used to adjust the values v_t and reiterate the whole solution procedure.

Define now two component types to be *equivalent* if the quantity $v_t + p_t$ is the same for both types, and if both types can be handled by precisely the same equipment. This relation induces a partition of the set of components into C *classes*, with each class containing components of equivalent types.

We are now almost ready to describe our model. We first introduce a few more parameters:

Q = number of available equipments;
      for $c = 1, \ldots, C$,
B_c = number of components in class c;
w_c = common value of $v_t + p_t$ for the types represented in class c;
$Q(c)$ = set of equipments which can handle the components in class c;

for $h = 1, \ldots, 3M$,

E_h = time required by an equipment change for head h.

The decision variables are: for $c = 1, \ldots, C$, for $m = 1, \ldots, M$, for $h = 1, \ldots, 3M$, for $q = 1, \ldots, Q$:

x_{cm} = number of components of class c to be mounted by machine m;
z_{mq} = 1 if machine m uses equipment q;
       = 0 otherwise;
r_h = number of equipment changes required for head h;
W = estimated workload of the bottleneck machine.

The optimization model for subproblem (A) is:

(M_A) minimize W

subject to
$$\sum_{m=1}^{M} x_{cm} = B_c \qquad\qquad c = 1, \ldots, C, \qquad (2.1)$$

$$x_{cm} \leq B_c \sum_{q \in Q(c)} z_{mq} \qquad c = 1, \ldots, C;$$
$$m = 1, \ldots, M, \qquad (2.2)$$

$$\sum_{q=1}^{Q} z_{mq} \leq \sum_{h=3m-2}^{3m} r_h + 3 \qquad m = 1, \ldots, M, \qquad (2.3)$$

$$W \geq \sum_{c=1}^{C} w_c x_{cm} + \sum_{h=3m-2}^{3m} E_h r_h \quad m = 1, \ldots, M, \qquad (2.4)$$

$$x_{cm} \geq 0 \text{ integer} \qquad\qquad c = 1, \ldots, C;$$
$$m = 1, \ldots, M, \qquad (2.5)$$

$$z_{mq} \in \{0,1\} \qquad\qquad m = 1, \ldots, M;$$
$$q = 1, \ldots, Q, \qquad (2.6)$$

$$r_h \geq 0 \text{ integer} \qquad\qquad h = 1, \ldots, 3M. \qquad (2.7)$$

Constraints (2.1) express that all components must be mounted. Constraints (2.2) ensure that machine m is assigned at least one of the equipments in $Q(c)$ when x_{cm} is nonzero. Constraints (2.3) together with (2.4), (2.7) and the minimization objective, impose that the number of equipment changes on each machine be equal to the number of equipments used minus three, or to zero if the latter quantity becomes negative. The right-handside of (2.4) evaluates the processing time on machine m (we assume here that the time needed to bring a new PCB on the worktable, after completion of the previous one, is always larger than the time required for an equipment change). Thus, at the optimum of (M_A), W is equal to the maximum of these processing times.

Two comments are in order concerning this model. First, we could have formulated a similar model using variables x_{km} instead of x_{cm}, with the index k running over all component locations, from 1 to N. The advantage of aggregating the components into classes is that the number of variables is greatly reduced, and that some flexibility remains for the exact assignment of operations to heads. This flexibility will be exploited in the solution of further subproblems. Second, observe that we do not impose any constraint on the number of feeder slots required by a solution of (M_A). This could, in principle, be done easily, e.g. as in the partitioning model of Ahmadi et al. (1988), but requires the introduction of a large number of new variables, resulting again from the disaggregation of classes into types. From a practical point of view, since we always allocate at most one feeder of each type per machine (remember the secondary criterion expressed in Section 2.3), the number of feeder slots never appears to be a restrictive factor; hence the solutions of (M_A) are implementable.

In practice, the number of equipments needed to mount all components is often smaller than the number of heads available. When this is the case, we can in general safely assume that no change of equipments will be performed in the optimal solution of (M_A) (since E_h is very large). We may then replace (M_A) by a more restrictive model, obtained by fixing $r_h = 0$ for $h = 1, \ldots, 3M$.

Complexity and solution of model (M_A)

Every instance of the well-known set-covering problem can be polynomially transformed to an instance of (M_A) with $M = 1$, which implies that model (M_A) is already $\mathcal{N}\mathcal{P}$-hard when only one machine is available (we assume the familiarity of the reader with the basic concepts of complexity theory; see, for example, Garey and Johnson (1979) or Nemhauser and Wolsey (1988); the proofs of all the complexity results can be found in Crama, Kolen, Oerlemans and Spieksma (1989)).

In spite of this negative result, obtaining solutions of good quality for (M_A) turns out to be easy in practical applications. To understand this better, notice that the number of variables in these applications is usually small. The real-world machine line which motivated our study features three machines. A typical PCB may require the insertion of a few hundred components, but these fall into five to ten classes. The number of equipments needed to mount the board (after deletion of a few clearly redundant ones) seems rarely to exceed five. So, we have to deal in (M_A) with about 10 to 30 zero-one variables and 15 to 50 integer variables.

In view of these favorable conditions, we take a two-phase approach to the solution of (M_A). In a first phase, we consider the relaxation of (M_A) obtained by omitting the integrality requirement on the x-variables (in constraints (2.5)). The resulting mixed-integer program is easily solved by any commercial branch-and-bound code (one may also envision the development of a special code for this relaxed model, but this never appeared necessary in this context).

In the second phase, we fix all r- and z-variables of (M_A) to the values obtained in the optimal solution of the first phase.
In this way we obtain a model of the form:

(M_A') minimize W

$$\text{subject to} \quad \sum_{m=1}^{M} x_{cm} = B_c \qquad c = 1, \ldots, C,$$

$$W \geq \sum_{c=1}^{C} w_c x_{cm} + W_m \quad m = 1, \ldots, M,$$

$$x_{cm} \geq 0 \text{ integer} \qquad c = 1, \ldots, C;$$
$$m = 1, \ldots, M,$$

where some variables x_{cm} are possibly fixed to zero (by constraints (2.2) of (M_A)), and W_m is the total time required for equipment changes on machine m $(m = 1, \ldots, M)$.

In practice, model (M_A') is again relatively easy to solve (even though one can show by an easy argument that (M_A') is $\mathcal{N}P$-hard). If we cannot solve it optimally, then we simply-round up or down the values assumed by the x-variables in the optimal solution of the first phase, while preserving equality in the constraints (2.1).

In our implementation of this solution approach, we actually added a third phase to the procedure. The goal of this third phase is twofold: 1) to improve the heuristic solutions found in the first two phases; 2) to generate alternative "good" solutions of (M_A), which can be used as initial solutions for the subsequent subproblems of our hierarchical approach.

Two type of ideas are applied in the third phase. On the one hand, we modify "locally" the solutions delivered by phase 1 or 2, e.g. by exchanging the equipments of two machines, or by decreasing the workload of one machine at the expense of some other machine. On the other hand, we slightly modify model (M_A) by imposing an upperbound on the number of components assigned to each machine, and we solve this new model.

Running the third phase results in the generation of a few alternative solutions associated with reasonable low estimates of the bottleneck workload.

2.4.2   Subproblem (B)

The model

At the beginning of this phase, we know how many components of each class are to be mounted on each machine, i.e. the values of the variables x_{cm} in model (M_A). Our goal is now to disaggregate these figures and to determine how many components of each type must be handled by each machine. The criterion to make this decision will be the minimization of the number of feeders required (this is the secondary criterion discussed in Section 2.3).

So, consider now an arbitrary (but fixed) class c. Reorder the types of the components so that the types of the components contained in class c are indexed by $t = 1, \ldots, R$. Recall that N_t is the total number of components of type t to be placed on the board for all t. To simplify our notations, we also let $X_m = x_{cm}$ denote the number of components of class c to be mounted by machine m. So, $\sum_{t=1}^{R} N_t = \sum_{m=1}^{M} X_m = B_c$. We define the following decision variables: for $t = 1, \ldots, R$, for $m = 1, \ldots, M$;

u_{tm} = number of components of type t to be mounted by machine m;
v_{tm} = 1 if a feeder of type t is required on machine m;
$\quad\quad$ = 0 otherwise.

Our model for subproblem (B) is:

$$(M_B) \quad \text{minimize} \quad \sum_{t=1}^{R} \sum_{m=1}^{M} v_{tm}$$

$$\text{subject to} \quad \sum_{t=1}^{R} u_{tm} = X_m \quad\quad m = 1, \ldots, M,$$

$$\sum_{m=1}^{M} u_{tm} = N_t \quad\quad t = 1, \ldots, R,$$

$$u_{tm} \leq \min(X_m, N_t)v_{tm} \quad t = 1, \ldots, R;$$
$$m = 1, \ldots, M,$$
$$u_{tm} \geq 0 \text{ integer} \quad t = 1, \ldots, R;$$
$$m = 1, \ldots, M,$$
$$v_{tm} \in \{0, 1\} \quad t = 1, \ldots, R;$$
$$m = 1, \ldots, M.$$

Model (M_B) is a so-called pure fixed-charge transportation problem (see Fisk and McKeown (1979), Nemhauser and Wolsey (1988)).

Another way of thinking about model (M_B) is in terms of machine scheduling. Consider R jobs and M machines, where each job can be processed on any machine. Job t needs a processing time N_t ($t = 1, \ldots, R$) and machine m is only available in the interval $[0, X_m]$ ($m = 1, \ldots, M$). Recall that $\sum_{t=1}^R N_t = \sum_{m=1}^M X_m$. So, if preemption is allowed, there exists a feasible schedule requiring exactly the available time of each machine. Model (M_B) asks for such a schedule minimizing the number of preempted jobs (in this interpretation, $v_{tm} = 1$ if and only if job t is processed on machine m).

Complexity and solution of model (M_B)

The well-known partition problem can be polynomially transformed to model (M_B), which implies that (M_B) is $\mathcal{N}\mathcal{P}$-hard.

Model (M_B) can be tackled by a specialized cutting-plane algorithm for fixed-charge transportation problems (Nemhauser and Wolsey (1988)), but we choose to use instead a simple heuristic. This heuristic consists in repeatedly applying the following rule, until all component types are assigned:

Rule:
Assign the type (say t) with largest number N_t of components to the machine (say m) with largest availability X_m; if $N_t \leq X_m$, delete type t from the list, and reduce X_m to $X_m - N_t$; otherwise, reduce N_t to $N_t - X_m$, and X_m to 0.

Clearly, this heuristic always delivers a feasible solution of (M_B), with value exceeding the optimum of (M_B) by at most $M - 1$ (since, of all the component types assigned to a machine, at most one is also assigned to another machine). In other words, for a class c containing R component types, the heuristic finds an assignment of types to machines requiring at most $R + M - 1$ feeders. This performance is likely to be quite satisfactory, since R is usually large with respect to M.

In situations where duplication of feeders is strictly ruled out, i.e. where *all* components of one type *must* be mounted by the same machine, we replace the heuristic rule given above by:

Modified rule:
Assign the type (say t) with largest number N_t of components to the machine with largest availability X_m; delete type t from the list; reduce X_m to $\max(0, X_m - N_t)$.

Of course, this modified rule does not, in general, produce a feasible solution of (M_B). In particular, some machine m may have to mount more components of class c than the amount X_m determined by subproblem (A), and the estimated workload W of the bottleneck machine may increase. In such a case, we continue with the solution supplied by the modified rule. A possible increase in estimated workload is the price to be paid for imposing more stringent requirements on the solution.

Before proceeding to the next phase, i.e. the scheduling of individual machines, we still have to settle one last point concerning the distribution of the workload over the machines. Namely, the solution of model (M_B) tells us how many components of each type must be processed by each machine (namely, u_{tm}), but not which ones. Since the latter decision does not seem to affect very much the quality of our final solution, we neglect to give here many details about its implementation. Let us simply mention that we rely on a model aiming at an even dispersion of the components over the PCB for each machine. The dispersion is measured as follows: we subdivide the PCB into cells, and we sum up the discrepancies between the expected number of components in each cell and their actual number. It is then easy to set up an integer linear programming problem, where the assignment of components to machines is modelled by 0-1 variables, and the objective corresponds to dispersion minimization. The optimal solution of this problem determines completely the final workload distribution.

2.5   Scheduling of individual machines

In this section we concentrate on one individual machine (for simplicity, we henceforth omit the machine index). Given by subproblem (B) are the locations (say $1, \ldots, N$) of the components to be mounted by this machine and their types $(1, \ldots, T)$. Given by subproblem (A) are the equipments $(1, \ldots, Q)$ to be used by the machine, and the number r_h of equipment changes per head.

2.5.1   Subproblem (C)

The model

Our current goal is to determine the distribution of the workload over the three heads of the machine (a similar "partitioning" problem is treated by Ahmadi et al. (1988), under quite different technological conditions). This will be done so as to minimize the number of trips made by the heads between the feeder slots and the PCB. In other words, we want to minimize the maximum number of components mounted by a head. In general, this criterion will only determine how many components each head must pick and place, but not which ones. The latter indeterminacy will be lifted by the introduction of a secondary criterion, to be explained at the end of this subsection.

Here, we are going to use a model very similar to (M_A). Since we are only interested in the number of components mounted by each head, let us redefine two components as *equivalent* if they can be handled by the same equipments (compare with the definition used in Subsection 2.4.1). This relation determines C classes of equivalent components. As for subproblem (M_A), we let, for $c = 1, \ldots, C$:

B_c = number of components in class c;
$Q(c)$ = set of equipments which can handle the components in class c.

We use the following decision variables: for $c = 1, \ldots, C$, for $h = 1, 2, 3$, for $q = 1, \ldots, Q$:

x_{ch} = number of components of class c to be mounted by head h;
z_{hq} = 1 if head h uses equipment q;
         = 0 otherwise;
V = number of components mounted by the bottleneck head.

The model for subproblem (C) is:

(M_C) minimize V

$$
\text{subject to} \quad \sum_{h=1}^{3} x_{ch} = B_c \qquad c = 1, \ldots, C,
$$

$$
x_{ch} \leq B_c \sum_{q \in Q(c)} z_{hq} \qquad c = 1, \ldots, C; h = 1, 2, 3,
$$

$$
\sum_{q=1}^{Q} z_{hq} = r_h + 1 \qquad h = 1, 2, 3,
$$

$$V \geq \sum_{c=1}^{C} x_{ch} \qquad h = 1, 2, 3,$$

$$x_{ch} \geq 0 \text{ integer} \qquad c = 1, \ldots, C; \ h = 1, 2, 3,$$

$$z_{hq} \in \{0, 1\} \qquad h = 1, 2, 3; \ q = 1, \ldots, Q.$$

(Recall that $r_h + 1$ is the number of equipments allocated to head h by model (M_A)).

Complexity and solution of model (M_C)

Again, the partition problem is easily transformed to model (M_C), implying that the problem is $\mathcal{NP}$-hard.

Moreover, as was the case for (M_A), model (M_C) is actually easy to solve in practice, due to the small number of variables. Here, we can use the same type of two-phase approach outlined for (M_A).

As mentioned earlier, the solution of (M_C) does not identify which components have to be mounted by each head. To answer the latter question, we considered different models taking into account the dispersion of the components over the board. However, it turned out empirically that a simple assignment procedure performed at least as well as the more sophisticated heuristics derived from these models. We describe now this procedure.

Consider a coordinate axis parallel to the arm along which the three heads are mounted. We orient this axis so that the coordinates of heads 1, 2 and 3 are of the form X, $X + k$ and $X + 2k$ respectively, where k is the distance between two heads ($k > 0$). Notice that X is variable, whereas k is fixed, since the arm cannot rotate.

The idea of our procedure is to assign the component locations with smallest coordinates to head 1, those with largest coordinates to head 3, and the remaining ones to head 2. Since this must be done within the restrictions imposed by (M_C), let us consider the values x_{ch} obtained by solving (M_C). Then, for each c, the components of class c to be mounted by head 1 are chosen to be the x_{c1} components with smallest coordinates among all components of class c. Similarly, head 3 is assigned the x_{c3} components with largest coordinates among the components of class c, and head 2 is assigned the remaining ones.

As mentioned before, this heuristic provided good empirical results. The reason for this good performance may be sought in the fact that the inter-head distance k is of the same order of magnitude as the length of a typical

PCB. Thus, our simple-minded procedure tends to minimize the distance travelled by the heads.

2.5.2 Subproblem (D)

The model

For simplicity, we first consider the case where every head has been assigned exactly one piece of equipment (i.e., $r_1 = r_2 = r_3 = 0$ in model (M_C)). Thus, at this point, the components have been partitioned into three *groups*, with group h containing the G_h components to be mounted by head h ($h = 1, 2, 3$). Let us further assume that $G_1 = G_2 = G_3 = G$ (if this is not the case, then we add a number of "dummy" components to the smaller groups). We know that G is also the minimum number of pick-and-place rounds necessary to mount all these components. We are now going to determine the composition of these rounds, with a view to minimizing the total travel time of the arm supporting the heads.

Suppose that the components in each group have been (arbitrarily) numbered $1, \ldots, G$. Consider two components i and j belonging to different groups, and assume that these components are to be mounted succesively, in a same round. We denote by d_{ij} the time necessary to reposition the arm between the insertions of i and j. For instance, if i is in group 1, j is in group 2, and i must be placed before j, then d_{ij} is the time required to bring head 2 above the location of j, starting with head 1 above i.

For a pick-and-place round involving three components i, j, k, we can arbitrarily choose the order in which these components are mounted (see Section 2.2). Therefore, an underestimate for the travel time of the arm between the first and the third placements of this round is given by:

(i) $d_{ijk} = \min\{d_{ij} + d_{jk}, d_{ik} + d_{kj}, d_{ji} + d_{ik}\}$ if none of i, j, k is a dummy;

(ii) $d_{ijk} = d_{ij}$ if k is a dummy;

(iii) $d_{ijk} = 0$ if at least two of i, j, k are dummies.

Let us introduce the decision variables u_{ijk}, for $i, j, k \in \{1, \ldots, G\}$, with the interpretation:

u_{ijk} $= 1$ if components i, j and k, from groups 1,2 and 3, respectively, are mounted in the same round;
$= 0$ otherwise.

Then, our optimization model for subproblem (D) is:

(M_D) minimize $\displaystyle\sum_{i=1}^{G}\sum_{j=1}^{G}\sum_{k=1}^{G} d_{ijk} u_{ijk}$

subject to $\displaystyle\sum_{i=1}^{G}\sum_{j=1}^{G} u_{ijk} = 1 \qquad k = 1,\ldots,G,$

$$\sum_{i=1}^{G}\sum_{k=1}^{G} u_{ijk} = 1 \qquad j = 1,\ldots,G,$$

$$\sum_{j=1}^{G}\sum_{k=1}^{G} u_{ijk} = 1 \qquad i = 1,\ldots,G,$$

$$u_{ijk} \in \{0,1\} \qquad i,j,k = 1,\ldots,G.$$

An optimal solution of (M_D) determines G clusters, of three components each, such that the sum of the (underestimates of the) travel times "within clusters" is minimized.

In cases where some or all of the heads have been assigned more'than one piece of equipment in model (M_A), we adapt our approach as follows. Let q_h be the first piece of equipment to be used by head h and G_h be the number of components which can be handled by q_h among those to be mounted by head h $(h = 1,2,3)$. Say for instance that $G_1 \leq G_2 \leq G_3$. We can now set up a model similar to (M_D) for the clustering of these $G_1 + G_2 + G_3$ components. Any feasible solution of this model determines exactly G_1 clusters containing no dummy components. These clusters correspond to our first G_1, pick-and-place rounds, to be performed by equipments q_1, q_2 and q_3. Next, q_1 is replaced by a new equipment q_4, and the process can be repeated with q_4, q_2 and q_3.

Complexity and solution of (M_D)

Model (M_D), with arbitrary coefficients d_{ijk}, has been studied in the literature under the name of three-dimensional assignment problem. The problem is known to be $\mathcal{N}P$-hard (see Garey and Johnson (1979)). However, observe that, in our case, the coefficients d_{ijk} are of the very special type defined by (i)–(iii). Moreover, the travel times d_{ij} $(i,j = 1,\ldots,G)$ are themselves far from arbitrary; in particular, they satisfy the triangle inequality: $d_{ij} \leq d_{ik} + d_{kj}$ for $i,j,k = 1,\ldots,G$. However, even under these added restrictions, model (M_D) remains $\mathcal{N}P$-hard (Chapter 3 of this monograph).

A number of heuristic and exact algorithms have been proposed to solve the three-dimensional assignment problem (see, for example, Frieze and Yadegar (1981) and the references therein). In view of the role of (M_D) as a subproblem in the hierarchy (A)–(F), and of the special structure of its cost coefficients, we opt here for a specialized heuristic procedure.

Our heuristic works in two phases. We start by solving an (ordinary) assignment problem, obtained by disregarding the components of the third group. Thus, we solve:

$$(AP1) \quad \text{minimize} \quad \sum_{i=1}^{G} \sum_{j=1}^{G} d_{ij} u_{ij}$$

$$\text{subject to} \quad \sum_{j=1}^{G} u_{ij} = 1 \qquad i = 1, \ldots, G,$$

$$\sum_{i=1}^{G} u_{ij} = 1 \qquad j = 1, \ldots, G,$$

$$u_{ij} \in \{0, 1\} \qquad i, j, k = 1, \ldots, G,$$

where $d_{ij} = 0$ if either i or j is dummy. An optimal solution u^* of (AP1) can be computed in time $O(G^3)$ (Papadimitriou and Steiglitz (1982)).

Let now $A = \{(i, j) : u_{ij}^* = 1\}$. Thus, A is the set of pairs (i, j) matched by the solution of (AP1). The second phase of our heuristic consists in assigning the (previously disregarded) components of the third group to the pairs in A. Formally, we solve:

$$(AP2) \quad \text{minimize} \quad \sum_{(i,j) \in A} \sum_{k=1}^{G} d_{ijk} u_{ijk}$$

$$\text{subject to} \quad \sum_{k=1}^{G} u_{ijk} = 1 \qquad (i, j) \in A,$$

$$\sum_{(i,j) \in A} u_{ijk} = 1 \qquad k = 1, \ldots, G,$$

$$u_{ijk} \in \{0, 1\} \qquad (i, j) \in A; \ k = 1, \ldots, G.$$

The optimal solution of (AP2) can be obtained in time $O(G^3)$ and provides a heuristic solution of (M_D). Frieze and Yadegar (1981) proposed a closely related heuristic for general 3-dimensional assignment problems, and observed its good empirical performance.

Let β_3 denote the optimal value of (AP2). The notation β_3 is a reminder that, in the first phase of our heuristic, we arbitrarily decided to disregard the components from the third group. Of course, similar procedures could be defined, and corresponding bounds β_1 and β_2 would be derived, by initially disregarding the components from either group 1 or group 2.

In our computer implementations, we compute the three bounds, β_1, β_2, β_3, and we retain the clustering of the components corresponding to the smallest bound. In Chapter 3 of this monograph it is proven that this bound is never worse than $\frac{4}{3}$ times the optimal value for any instance of (M_D). The computer experiments reported in there indicate that the practical performance of this heuristic is excellent.

2.5.3   Subproblem (E)

The solution of subproblem (D) has supplied a list $C_1, \ldots, C_G$ of clusters, with each cluster containing (at most) three components to be placed in the same round (if some heads must use more than one piece of equipment, then we successively consider several such lists, where each list consists of clusters which can be processed without equipment changes). Subproblem (E) asks for the sequence of pick-and-place operations to be performed by the machine, given this list of clusters.

This problem has been studied by Ball and Magazine (1988) and Leipälä and Nevalainen (1989), for machines featuring only one insertion head. In both papers, the authors observed that the decisions to be made in subproblem (E) are highly dependent on the assignment of feeders to feeder slots (i.e. on the solution of our subproblem (F)), and conversely. On the other hand, a model simultaneously taking into account both subproblems is far too complicated to be of any practical value.

We therefore choose an approach already suggested by Leipälä and Nevalainen (1989). Namely, we first solve subproblem (E); using this solution as input, we compute a solution of subproblem (F), which in turn is used to revise the solution of subproblem (E), and so on. This process is iterated until some stopping condition is verified.

The models

According to the previous discussion, we need two models for subproblem (E): the first one to be used when no feeder assignment is yet known, and the second one taking into account a given feeder assignment. In either case, we reduce (E) to the solution of a shortest Hamiltonian path problem (see Lawler, Lenstra, Rinnooy Kan and Shmoys (1985)) over the set of clusters

$\{C_1, \ldots, C_G\}$: for $i, j = 1, \ldots, G$, we define a cost (travel time) $c(i, j)$ for processing C_i immediately before C_j; the problem is then to find a permutation $\sigma = (\sigma_1, \ldots, \sigma_G)$ of $\{1, \ldots, G\}$ which minimizes

$$c(\sigma) = \sum_{i=1}^{G-1} c(\sigma_i, \sigma_{i+1}) \tag{2.8}$$

The definition of $c(i, j)$ depends on the given feeder assignment (if any), as explained hereunder.

Consider first the situation where feeders are already assigned to feeder slots, and let C_i, C_j be two arbitrary clusters. In this case, the appropriate definition of $c(i, j)$ is given by CQM (1988) as follows. Denote by l_1, l_2, l_3 the component locations in C_i, where l_h is to be processed by head h ($h = 1, 2, 3$). We assume that the feeder needed for l_h is in slot s_h ($h = 1, 2, 3$). Similarly, l_4 is the location to be processed by head 1 in cluster C_j, and slot s_4 contains the corresponding feeder (for simplicity, we assume that C_i and C_j consist of exactly three locations; obvious modifications of our description are required when this is not the case).

Suppose now for a moment that l_1, l_2 and l_3 are to be mounted in the order $\pi = (\pi_1, \pi_2, \pi_3)$, where (π_1, π_2, π_3) is a permutation of $\{1, 2, 3\}$. For this fixed order, we can easily compute the time (say, $c_{ij}(\pi)$) required to carry out the following operations: starting with head 1 above slot s_1, sequentially pick one component from each of s_1, s_2, s_3 using heads $1, 2, 3$ respectively; mount $l_{\pi_1}, l_{\pi_2}, l_{\pi_3}$, in that order; bring head 1 above slot s_4.

Obviously, in an optimal pick-and-place sequence, we would select the permutation π^* of $\{1, 2, 3\}$ which minimizes $c_{ij}(\pi)$. We accordingly define: $c(i, j) = c_{ij}(\pi^*)$.

Now, if σ is any permutation of $\{1, \ldots, G\}$, then $c(\sigma)$ (given by (2.8)) is the time required by a complete pick-and-place sequence processing the clusters in the order $(\sigma_1, \ldots, \sigma_G)$. The shortest Hamiltonian path problem with costs c_{ij} thus provides a natural model for subproblem (E). As a last remark on this model, notice that the computation of $c_{ij}(\pi)$ can be simplified by omitting from its definition those elements which are independent of π or σ. Namely, we can use a "modified $c_{ij}(\pi)$" defined as the time needed, starting with head 3 above s_3, to bring successively head π_1 above l_{π_1}, head π_2 above l_{π_2}, head π_3 above l_{π_3} and finally head 1 above s_4.

Let us return now to the initial solution of (E), when the feeder positions are still unknown. Since this initial sequence will be modified by the subsequent iterations of our procedure, it does not seem necessary at this stage to look for a solution of very high quality (actually, one may even argue that an initial sequencing of lower quality is desirable since it provides more flexibility in the next phases of the procedure; see, for example, Leipälä and Nevalainen (1989) for more comments along this line). Accordingly, we define the coefficients $c(i, j)$ for our initial traveling salesman problem as rough estimates of the actual travel times. We experimented with some possible definitions, which seem to lead to comparable results (in terms of the final solution obtained). One such definition is as follows. Let g_i and g_j be the centers of gravity of the clusters C_i and C_j, respectively. Let s be the feeder slot minimizing the total distance from g_i to s to g_j. Then, $c(i, j)$ is the time needed for the arm to travel this total distance.

Complexity and solution of the models

The shortest Hamiltonian path problem is closely related to the traveling salesman problem, and is well-known to be NP-hard, even when the costs $c(i, j)$ satisfy the triangle inequality (Lawler et al. (1985)). Many heuristics have been devised for this problem, and we have chosen to experiment with two of the simplest: nearest neighbor (with all possible starting points) and farthest insertion, which respectively run in $O(G^3)$ and $O(G^2)$ steps (we refer to Lawler et al. (1985) for details on these procedures). Both heuristics produced results of comparable quality.

2.5.4 Subproblem (F)

The model

As input to this subproblem, we are given the types $(1, \ldots, T)$ and the locations $(1, \ldots, N)$ of the components to be mounted, where $(1, \ldots, N)$ is the mounting sequence determined by the previous solution of subproblem (E). Our problem is now to allocate each feeder $1, \ldots, T$ to one of the feeder slots $1, \ldots, S$, so as to minimize the total mounting time (for the sake of clarity, we first assume that every feeder can be loaded in exactly one slot; we indicate later how our model can be modified when some feeders require two or more slots).

We use the decision variables v_{ts} $(t = 1, \ldots, T;\ s = 1, \ldots, S)$ with the interpretation:

$$v_{ts} \quad = 1 \text{ if feeder } t \text{ is loaded in slot } s;$$
$$= 0 \text{ otherwise.}$$

These variables must obey the following restrictions, expressing that every feeder occupies exactly one slot, and no slot contains two feeders:

$$\sum_{s=1}^{S} v_{ts} = 1 \qquad t = 1, \ldots, T, \tag{2.9}$$

$$\sum_{t=1}^{T} v_{ts} \leq 1 \qquad s = 1, \ldots, S, \tag{2.10}$$

$$v_{ts} \in \{0, 1\} \qquad t = 1, \ldots, T; \ s = 1, \ldots, S. \tag{2.11}$$

Before describing the other elements of our model, we first introduce some terminological conventions. We say that a movement of the arm is a *feeder-board* movement if it occurs between the last picking and the first placing of the same round, or between the last placing of a round and the first picking of the next one. By contrast, a *feeder-feeder* movement takes place between two pickings of a same round.

Consider now a fixed solution v_{ts} $(t = 1, \ldots, T; \ s = 1, \ldots, S)$ of (2.9)–(2.11). For the corresponding assignment of feeders to slots, the total mounting time of the PCB can be broken up into three terms:

1) a term $\sum_{t=1}^{T} \sum_{s=1}^{S} a_{ts} v_{ts}$, where a_{ts} is the total time spent in feeder-board movements from or to feeder t, when feeder t is loaded in slot s; this term represents the total feeder-board travel time; notice that the value of each coefficient a_{ts} is completely determined by the technological features of the machine, and by the sequence of pick-and-place operations to be performed by the machine (i.e., by the solution of subproblem (E));

2) a term $\sum_{p,t=1}^{T} \sum_{r,s=1}^{S} b_{prts} v_{pr} v_{ts}$, where b_{prts} is the total time spent in feeder-feeder movements between feeders p and t, when feeder p is in slot r and feeder t is in slot s; this term gives the total feeder-feeder travel time; here again, the coefficients b_{prts} are easily computed;

3) a term accounting for all other operations (picking and placing of all components, and travel time between placements of the same round); for a fixed pick-and-place sequence, this term is independent of v_{ts}.

According to this discussion, our model for subproblem (F) can be formulated as:

$$(M_F) \quad \text{minimize} \quad \sum_{t=1}^{T} \sum_{s=1}^{S} a_{ts} v_{ts} + \sum_{p,t=1}^{T} \sum_{r,s=1}^{S} b_{prts} v_{pr} v_{ts}$$

$$\text{subject to} \quad (2.9), (2.10), (2.11).$$

Problem (M_F) is a quadratic assignment problem (see Burkard (1984)). As mentioned earlier, this formulation can easily be modified to accomodate additional restrictions. For instance, if feeder t must occupy two slots, we reinterpret:

v_{ts} = 1 if feeder t is loaded in slots s and $s + 1$;
= 0 otherwise.

Straightforward restrictions must then be added to (2.9)–(2.11) to preclude the assignment of any feeder to slot $s + 1$ when $v_{ts} = 1$. This can also be achieved while preserving the quadratic assignment structure of (M_F), by raising all coefficients $b_{p,s+1,t,s}$ to very high values.

As a last remark on (M_F), let us observe that this model boils down to a linear assignment problem for machines featuring only one insertion head. On the other hand, Leipälä and Nevalainen (1989) proposed a quadratic assignment formulation of the feeder assignment subproblem (F) for another type of one-head machines. This discrepancy is obviously due to the different technologies.

Complexity and solution of (M_F)

The quadratic assignment problem is well-known to be NP-hard, and to be particularly difficult to solve exactly for values of T and S larger than twenty (Burkard (1984)). A typical instance of (M_F) may involve as many as twenty feeder types and sixty slots, and hence must be tackled by heuristic methods.

For (M_F), we have used a local improvement method, based on pairwise exchanges of feeders (see Burkard (1984)). This procedure starts with an initial solution of (2.9)–(2.11), and applies either of the following steps, as long as they improve the objective function value in (M_F):

Step 1 : move a feeder from its current slot to some empty slot;
Step 2 : interchange the slot assignments of two feeders.

To determine an initial assignment of feeders to slots, we proceed in two phases. First, we solve the assignment problem (M_F') obtained by setting all coefficients b_{prts} to zero in (M_F) (this amounts to disregarding the feeder-feeder movements of the arm). Let v^* be an optimal solution of (M_F').

Next, we consider those feeders (say $1, \ldots, P$) whose components are only picked by head 2. Observe that the associated variables v_{ts} ($t = 1, \ldots, P$; $s = 1, \ldots, S$) do not appear in the objective function of (M_F'), since there are no feeder-board movements to or from these feeders (i.e., $a_{ts} = 0$ for $t = 1, \ldots, P$; $s = 1, \ldots, S$). Consequently, the value of these variables in v^* is conditioned only by the constraints (2.9)–(2.11), and may as well be random. In order to determine more meaningful values for these variables, we solve the restriction of (M_F) obtained by setting $v_{ts} = v_{ts}^*$ for $t = P+1, \ldots, T$ and $s = 1, \ldots, S$. It is easy to see that this again is a linear assignment problem, aiming at the minimization of the total feeder-feeder travel time under the partial assignment v_{ts}^* $(t = P+1, \ldots, T; s = 1, \ldots, S)$. The optimal solution of this problem together with the values v_{ts}^* $(t = P+1, \ldots, T; s = 1, \ldots, S)$, provides the initial solution for the improvement procedure described above.

2.6   An example

In this section, we discuss the performance of our heuristics on a problem instance described in CQM (1988). The placement line under consideration consists of three machines. The third head is broken and unavailable on machine 3. The 258 components to be mounted on the PCB are grouped in 39 types (actually, the PCB is partitioned into three identical blocks, of 86 components each; we shall make use of this peculiarity in the solution of subproblem (A)). Three distinct pieces of equipments suffice to handle all the component types; moreover, each type can be handled by exactly one of these three pieces of equipments.

For the sake of comparison, let us mention that CQM (1988) evaluates to 74, 65 and 81 seconds, respectively, the mounting times required by the three machines for the actual operations sequence implemented by the plant (notice that this sequence is not known in full detail, and that these "plant times" appear to be underestimates). The hierarchical decomposition and the heuristics developed in CQM (1988) produce a solution with mounting times 68.41, 66.52 and 68.88 seconds for the three machines. A still better solution is obtained in CQM (1988) after imposing that the equipments used remain fixed as in the plant situation. Under these conditions, production times of 66.12, 65.25 and 65.47 are achieved on the three machines, i.e. an improvement of at least 18 percent of the bottleneck time with respect to the plant solution. To fully appreciate these figures, one should also know that a constant time of 106 seconds is needed for the pick-and-place operations alone, independently of the production sequence (see Section 2.2). These unavoidable 106 seconds represent more than half of the total mounting time required by the CQM solutions.

Subproblem (A)

We now take up our subproblem (A). With a constant estimate of $v = 0.3$ (secs) for the travel time of the heads between two insertions, the components fall into five classes, characterized by the parameters in Table 2.1.

Class	1	2	3	4	5
B_c	201	27	24	3	3
w_c	0.6	1.35	0.75	1.65	1.15
$Q(c)$	{1}	{2}	{3}	{3}	{3}

Table 2.1 Parameters for subproblem (A).

We set up model (M_A) with these parameters and $E_h = 2$ $(h = 1, \ldots, 8)$ (and the obvious modifications implied by the unavailability of head 9). This model is easily solved by the approach described in Subsection 2.4.1. Notice that the relaxation of (M_A) obtained by omitting the integrality requirement for the x-variables has several alternative optima. As expected, $r_h = 0$ $(h = 1, \ldots, 8)$ in all these optimal solutions, i.e. equipment changes are ruled out.

As explained in Subsection 2.4.1, the solutions found for subproblem (A) can be considered as alternative inputs for the subsequent subproblems in the decomposition. In the present case, most of these solutions led us to production plans with processing times of 66 to 68 seconds. To illustrate the next steps of our approach, we shall concentrate now on a specific solution of (M_A), derived as follows.

We mentioned before that our PCB consists of three identical blocks. So, rather than solving (M_A) for the complete board, we can solve first the model corresponding to one of the blocks, and eventually multiply all figures by 3. A workload distribution obtained in that way is displayed in Table 2.2.

Machine	1	2	3
Equipments	1	1,3	1,2
x_{cm} = number of components	$x_{11} = 102$	$x_{12} = 57$	$x_{13} = 42$
of class c on		$x_{32} = 24$	$x_{23} = 27$
machine m		$x_{42} = 3$	
		$x_{52} = 3$	

Table 2.2 Workload distribution.

Subproblem (B)

Since all components of class 2 are to be handled by machine 3, and all components of classes 3, 4, 5 by machine 2, we see that the distribution shown in Table 2.3 need only be further refined for class 1. Specifically, 28 components types are represented in class 1. The number of components of each type $(1, \ldots, 28)$ is given in Table 2.3.

Type	1	2	3	4	5	6	7	8	9	10	11	12	13	14
N_t	24	18	18	15	12	9	9	9	9	6	6	6	6	6
Type	15	16	17	18	19	20	21	22	23	24	25	26	27	28
N_t	6	6	3	3	3	3	3	3	3	3	3	3	3	3

Table 2.3 Number of components of each type for subproblem (B).

The heuristic rule described in Subsection 2.4.2 produces the assignment shown in Table 2.4. Observe that each type is assigned to exactly one machine, and hence exactly one feeder of each type will be needed in the final solution (in particular, the heuristic delivers here an optimal solution of (M_B)).

Machine	Types
1	1,2,3,5,10,11,14,17,20,23,26
2	4,6,8,12,15,18,21,24,27
3	7,9,13,16,19,22,25,28

Table 2.4 Assignment of component types to machines.

Subproblem (C)

Since model (M_C) attempts to minimize the maximum workload of the heads (per machine), in this case we obviously find an assignment of the type given in Table 2.5.

Head	1	2	3	4	5	6	7	8
Equipment	1	1	1	1	1	3	1	2
Number of components	34	34	34	29	28	30	42	27

Table 2.5 Assignment for subproblem (C).

The components to be mounted by heads 1,2,3,4,5 are further identified as explained at the end of Subsection 2.5.2. In the present case, this amounts to assigning to head 1 all components of block 1, to head 2 all components of block 2, and to head 3 all components of block 3, among those previously assigned to machine 1.

Subproblem (D)

We now solve the three-dimensional assignment model (M_D) for each of the three machines. Since machine 3 only has two heads, (M_D) actually reduces to the assignment problem (AP1) for this machine, and hence can be solved exactly (optimal value: 3.26 secs).

For machines 1 and 2, we solve (M_D) using the heuristics described in Subsection 2.5.2. For machine 1, these heuristics supply a very good clustering of the components (value: 4.95 secs), where each cluster simply contains corresponding components from each block of the PCB. For machine 2 we obtain a clustering with value 8.95 secs.

Subproblems (E) and (F)

These two subproblems are solved alternately and iteratively for each machine.

On machine 2, for instance, the first Hamiltonian path (corresponding to travel times between centers of gravity of the clusters) has value 13.16 secs. An initial feeder assignment is obtained as in Subsection 2.5.4. The pick-and-place sequence determined by this assignment and the first Hamiltonian path corresponds to a total feeder-board time of 14.10 secs and a total feeder-feeder time of 11.63 secs, for a total travel time of 25.73 secs.

The local improvement procedure is next applied to this initial solution. In *each iteration* of this procedure, we sequentially consider *all feeders*, and we attempt to perform one of the exchange steps 1 and 2 on each of them. After four iterations of the procedure, no more improving steps are found. The corresponding feeder-board and feeder-feeder times are respectively 14.68 secs and 8.62 secs, and hence the previous total travel time is improved to 23.30 secs.

Taking this feeder assignment into account, a revised Hamiltonian path with value 14.07 secs is computed. The feeder assignment is in turn modified, resulting in (after three iterations of the local improvement procedure) a total travel time of 22.94 secs. No better Hamiltonian path or assignment are found in the next solutions of subproblems (E) and (F). Therefore, we adopt this solution for machine 2.

Similar computations are carried out for the other machines. The pick-and-place sequences obtained in this way correspond to processing times of 63.83, 66.27 and 65.82 secs on machines 1, 2 and 3 respectively. These times are comparable to the best ones obtained by CQM.

Acknowledgements
We are grateful to P. van Laarhoven and H. Zijm for introducing us to the problem, and for providing us with the data (CQM, 1988).

Chapter 3

Approximation algorithms for three-dimensional assignment problems with triangle inequalities

3.1 Introduction

Consider the following classical formulation of the (*axial*) *three-dimensional assignment problem* (3DA) (see e.g. Balas and Saltzman (1989)). Given is a complete tripartite graph $K_{n,n,n} = (I \cup J \cup K, (I \times J) \cup (I \times K) \cup (J \times K))$, where I, J, K are disjoint sets of size n, and a cost c_{ijk} for each triangle $(i, j, k) \in I \times J \times K$. The problem 3DA is to find a subset A of n triangles, $A \subseteq I \times J \times K$, such that every element of $I \cup J \cup K$ occurs in exactly one triangle of A, and the total cost $c(A) = \sum_{(i,j,k) \in A} c_{ijk}$ is minimized. Some recent references to this problem are Balas and Saltzman (1989), Frieze (1974), Frieze and Yadegar (1981), Hansen and Kaufman (1973).

When one formulates 3DA in graph-theoretic terms, as we just did it, it is natural to assume that the costs c_{ijk} are not completely arbitrary, but are rather defined in terms of costs attached to the edges of the graph. More precisely, we shall restrict our attention in this chapter to the special cases of 3DA where each edge $(u, v) \in (I \times J) \cup (I \times K) \cup (J \times K)$ is assigned a nonnegative *length* d_{uv}, and where the cost of a triangle $(i, j, k) \in I \times J \times K$ is defined either by its total length t_{ijk}:

$$t_{ijk} = d_{ij} + d_{ik} + d_{jk}, \tag{3.1}$$

or by s_{ijk}, the sum of the lengths of its two shortest edges:

$$s_{ijk} = \min\{d_{ij} + d_{ik}, \ d_{ij} + d_{jk}, \ d_{ik} + d_{jk}\} \tag{3.2}$$

(notice that the lengths d_{uv} are symmetric: $d_{uv} = d_{vu}$ for all (u, v)).

We refer to the problem 3DA with cost coefficients $c_{ijk} = t_{ijk}$, or $c_{ijk} = s_{ijk}$, as problem T or S, respectively.

Instances of problem T arise in the scheduling of teaching practices at colleges of education (Frieze and Yadegar (1981)).

Either T or S can also be used to model a situation encountered in the production of printed circuit boards by numerically controlled machines featuring three placement heads (see Chapter 2 of this monograph).

In the latter application (which motivated the present study), the lengths d_{uv} represent travel times of the arm of the machine between locations u and v, where electronic components are to be inserted. In particular, and even though the exact definition of these travel times may be quite intricate, the lengths d_{uv} define a distance, i.e. they satisfy the *triangle inequalities*:

$$d_{uv} \leq d_{uw} + d_{vw} \text{ for all } u, v, w \in I \cup J \cup K. \tag{3.3}$$

In the remainder of this chapter, we concentrate on problems $T\Delta$ and $S\Delta$, i.e., on the special cases of T and S for which the triangle inequalities (3.3) hold. We show in Section 3.2 that $T\Delta$ and $S\Delta$ are $\mathcal{N}P$-hard. In Section 3.3, we describe some heuristics for $T\Delta$ and $S\Delta$, and establish tight bounds on their worst-case performance. The results of computational experiments with these heuristics are presented in Section 3.4.

Finally, in Bandelt, Crama and Spieksma (1991) heuristics are proposed and investigated for generalizations of $T\Delta$ and $S\Delta$ to multidimensional assignment problems with so-called decomposable costs.

3.2   Complexity of $T\Delta$ and $S\Delta$

The problem 3DA is well-known to be $\mathcal{N}P$-hard, even when the costs c_{ijk} can only take two distinct values (see e.g. Garey and Johnson (1979) for a proof). We show now that its special cases $T\Delta$ and $S\Delta$ remain $\mathcal{N}P$-hard too.

Theorem 3.1 *Problem $T\Delta$ is $\mathcal{N}P$-hard.*

Proof:
We use the argument presented by Garey and Johnson (1979) to establish the $\mathcal{N}P$-hardness of the problem Partition into Triangles. Consider an instance I of 3DA, defined by three sets I_0, J_0, K_0 of size n, and $c_{ijk} \in \{0, 1\}$ for all $(i, j, k) \in I_0 \times J_0 \times K_0$.

With I, we associate an instance of $T\Delta$, as follows. Let $M = \{(i, j, k) : c_{ijk} = 0\}$, $|M| = m$, and

$$
\begin{aligned}
I &= I_0 \cup \{i_l(e) : e \in M, \ l = 1, 2, 3\}, \\
J &= J_0 \cup \{j_l(e) : e \in M, \ l = 1, 2, 3\}, \\
K &= K_0 \cup \{k_l(e) : e \in M, \ l = 1, 2, 3\},
\end{aligned}
$$

where $i_l(e)$, $j_l(e)$, $h_l(e)$ ($e \in M$, $l = 1, 2, 3$) are $9m$ new elements.

In order to conveniently define the lengths of the edges of the complete tripartite graph G on $I \cup J \cup K$, we first introduce m subgraphs of G. For each $e = (i, j, k) \in M$, $G(e)$ is the graph represented in Figure 3.1.

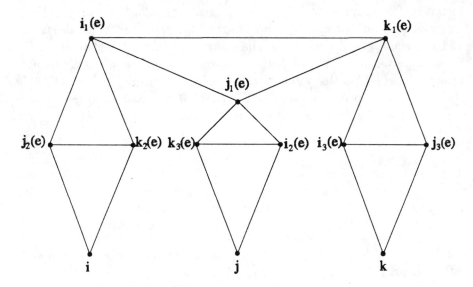

Figure 3.1

Now for each $(u,v) \in (I \times J) \cup (I \times K) \cup (J \times K)$, we let: $d_{uv} = 1$ if (u,v) is an edge in some graph $G(e)$ $(e \in M)$, and $d_{uv} = 2$ otherwise. Clearly, the triangle inequalities (3.3) are satisfied by this assignment, so that I, J, K and the lengths d_{uv} together define an instance $\mathcal{T}$ of $T\Delta$.

Observe that every feasible solution of $\mathcal{T}$ contains exactly $n + 3m$ triangles, each with cost at least 3. We claim that $\mathcal{T}$ has an optimal solution with value $3n + 9m$ if and only if I has a solution with value 0. We leave details to the reader (see Garey and Johnson (1979), pp. 68-69). □

Theorem 3.2 *Problem $S\Delta$ is NP-hard.*

Proof:
The proof is similar to the previous one: simply delete from each subgraph $G(e)$ the edges $(i_1(e), j_2(e))$, $(i, j_2(e))$, $(j_1(e), k_3(e))$, $(j, k_3(e))$, $(i_3(e), k_1(e))$, $(i_3(e), k)$, for all $e \in M$. The resulting instance of $S\Delta$ has an optimal solution with value $2n + 6m$ if and only if I has a solution with value 0. □

3.3   Approximation algorithms

In this section, we present approximation algorithms for $T\Delta$ and $S\Delta$. First, we recall a definition from Papadimitriou and Steiglitz (1982) (see also Garey and Johnson (1979)). Consider a minimization problem P, and an algorithm H which, given any instance I of P, returns a feasible solution $H(I)$ of I. Denote by $c(H(I))$ the value of this heuristic solution, and by $\text{OPT}(I)$ the value of an optimal solution of I. Then, H is called an ε-*approximate algorithm* for P, where ε is a nonnegative constant, if:

$$c(H(I)) \leq (1+\varepsilon)\,\text{OPT}\,(I)$$

for all instances I of P.

We will show that $\frac{1}{3}$-approximate polynomial-time algorithms exist for problems $T\Delta$ and $S\Delta$. As indicated by our next theorem, the triangle inequalities (3.3) play an instrumental role in the proof of such results:

Theorem 3.3 *Unless $P = \mathcal{N}P$, there is no ε-approximate polynomial algorithm for problems T and S, for any $\varepsilon \geq 0$.*

Proof:
We establish the statement for problem T (the other case being similar). Assume that there is an ε-approximate algorithm for T, say H.
As in the proof of Theorem 3.1, consider an instance I of 3DA with $c_{ijk} \in \{0,1\}$ for all (i,j,k), the corresponding sets I, J, K, and the subgraphs $G(e)(e \in M)$.
For $(u,v) \in (I \times J) \cup (I \times K) \cup (J \times K)$, let: $d_{uv} = 1$ if (u,v) is an edge of $G(e)(e \in M)$, and $d_{uv} = (3n+9m)\varepsilon + 2$ otherwise. This defines an instance T of problem T, with the property that T has an optimal solution with value $3n + 9m$ if and only if I has a solution with value 0.

Now, it is easy to see that the ε-approximate algorithm H always returns a solution of T with value $3n + 9m$, if there is one (because the second best solution has value at least $(1+\varepsilon)(3n+9m)+1$). Hence, unless $P = \mathcal{N}P$, H cannot be a polynomial-time algorithm.   □

We describe now informally a polynomial-time heuristic H_{IJ} for problems T and S. This heuristic was proposed in Chapter 2 of this thesis. The input to H_{IJ} is the set of edge-lengths d_{uv}, where $(u,v) \in (I \times J) \cup (I \times K) \cup (J \times K)$, and $|I| = |J| = |K| = n$.
The heuristic proceeds in two phases, first matching the elements of I and J,

and next assigning the elements of K to the pairs thus formed (Frieze and Yadegar (1981) propose a similar heuristic for the general 3DA problem). More precisely:

<u>Phase 1.</u> Find an optimal solution x^* of $(P1)$:

$(P1)$ minimize $\displaystyle\sum_{i \in I} \sum_{j \in J} d_{ij} x_{ij}$

   subject to $\displaystyle\sum_{i \in I} x_{ij} = 1 \qquad j \in J$

   $\displaystyle\sum_{j \in J} x_{ij} = 1 \qquad i \in I$

   $x_{ij} \in \{0,1\} \qquad i \in I, j \in J.$

Let $M = \{(i,j) : x_{ij}^* = 1\}$.

<u>Phase 2.</u> Find an optimal solution y^* of $(P2)$:

$(P2)$ minimize $\displaystyle\sum_{(i,j) \in M} \sum_{k \in K} c_{ijk} y_{ijk}$

   subject to $\displaystyle\sum_{(i,j) \in M} y_{ijk} = 1 \qquad k \in K$

   $\displaystyle\sum_{k \in K} y_{ijk} = 1 \qquad (i,j) \in M$

   $y_{ijk} \in \{0,1\} \qquad (i,j) \in M, \ k \in K,$

where $c_{ijk} = t_{ijk}$ (respectively $c_{ijk} = s_{ijk}$) if the problem to be solved is an instance of T (respectively S).

The feasible solution of T (or S) returned by the heuristic H_{IJ} is $A = \{(i,j,k) : y_{ijk}^* = 1\}$, and its cost is denoted by c_{IJ}.

Notice that both $(P1)$ and $(P2)$ are instances of the classical (two-dimensional) assignment problem, or weighted bipartite matching problem, and hence can be solved in $O(n^3)$ operations (Papadimitriou and Steiglitz (1982)). It follows that H_{IJ} also runs in time $O(n^3)$.

We leave it as an easy exercise to verify that, as suggested by Theorem 3.3, H_{IJ} is not an ε-approximate algorithm for either T or S, for any $\varepsilon \geq 0$.

On the other hand, when the lengths d_{uv} satisfy the triangle inequalities, we get:

Theorem 3.4 H_{IJ} *is a $\frac{1}{2}$-approximate algorithm for problem $T\Delta$. Moreover, there exist arbitrary large instances T of $T\Delta$ such that $c_{IJ} = \frac{3}{2} OPT(T)$.*

Proof:

Let T be an instance of $T\Delta$. Let M be the matching of $I \cup J$ found by the first phase of H_{IJ}, and A be the assignment returned by H_{IJ}.

Consider now an optimal solution of T, say F. With F, we associate another feasible solution $B = \{(i,j,k) : (i,j) \in M, \text{ and } (u,j,k) \in F \text{ for some } u \in I\}$.

We obtain successively:

$$c_{IJ} = \sum_{(i,j,k)\in A} t_{ijk}$$

$$\leq \sum_{(i,j,k)\in B} t_{ijk} \tag{3.4}$$

$$= \sum_{(i,j,k)\in B} (d_{ij} + d_{ik} + d_{jk}) \tag{3.5}$$

$$\leq 2 \sum_{(i,j,k)\in B} (d_{ij} + d_{jk}) \tag{3.6}$$

$$= 2 \sum_{(i,j,k)\in A} d_{ij} + 2 \sum_{(i,j,k)\in F} d_{jk} \tag{3.7}$$

$$\leq 2 \sum_{(i,j,k)\in F} (d_{ij} + d_{jk}) \tag{3.8}$$

((3.4) holds because A is optimal for $(P2)$, (3.5) is by definition of t_{ijk}, (3.6) uses the triangle inequality, (3.7) is by definition of B, and (3.8) follows from optimality of M for $(P1)$).

By symmetry with (3.8), we can also derive:

$$c_{IJ} \leq 2 \sum_{(i,j,k)\in F} (d_{ij} + d_{ik}) \tag{3.9}$$

Now, (3.8) and (3.9) together entail:

$$c_{IJ} \leq \sum_{(i,j,k)\in F} (2d_{ij} + d_{ik} + d_{jk})$$

$$= \sum_{(i,j,k)\in F} (\frac{3}{2}d_{ij} + \frac{1}{2}d_{ij} + d_{ik} + d_{jk}) \tag{3.10}$$

and, using the triangle inequalities to bound $\frac{1}{2}d_{ij}$:

$$c_{IJ} \leq \frac{3}{2} \sum_{(i,j,k) \in F} t_{ijk} = \frac{3}{2} \text{ OPT}(\mathcal{T}). \tag{3.11}$$

To see that equality may hold in (3.11), consider first the graph G represented in Figure 3.2.

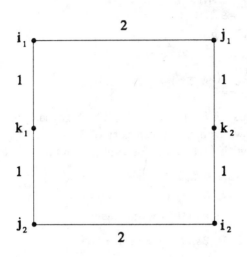

Figure 3.2

Also indicated in Figure 3.2 are the costs $c_{uv} \in \{1,2\}$ of the edges of G.

Now, we define an instance $\mathcal{T}$ of $T\Delta$ as follows. We let $I = \{i_1, i_2\}$, $J = \{j_1, j_2\}$, $K = \{k_1, k_2\}$. For $(u, v) \in (I \times J) \cup (I \times K) \cup (J \times K)$, d_{uv} is the length of a shortest path from u to v in G, with respect to the costs c_{uv}.

It is easy to see that an optimal solution for this instance is $F = \{i_1, j_2, k_1\}$, $(i_2, j_1, k_2)\}$, with $\text{OPT}(\mathcal{T}) = 8$.

But H_{IJ} can pick (in Phase 1) $M = \{(i_1, j_1), (i_2, j_2)\}$, and next (in Phase 2) $A = \{(i_1, j_1, k_1), (i_2, j_2, k_2)\}$, with cost $c_{IJ} = 12 = \frac{3}{2} \text{ OPT}(\mathcal{T})$. Arbitrary large instances of $T\Delta$ can be obtained by taking several copies of G, with very large distances between points in different copies. $\quad\square$

The previous result also holds mutatis mutandis for problem $S\Delta$:

Theorem 3.5 H_{IJ} *is a $\frac{1}{2}$-approximate algorithm for problem $S\Delta$. Moreover, there exist arbitrary large instances S of $S\Delta$ such that $c_{IJ} = \frac{3}{2} \text{ OPT}(S)$.*

Proof:

Let S be an instance of $S\Delta$. Define M, A, F and B in the same way as for the proof of Theorem 3.4. We derive the following inequalities:

$$c_{IJ} = \sum_{(i,j,k) \in A} s_{ijk}$$

$$\leq \sum_{(i,j,k) \in B} s_{ijk} \tag{3.12}$$

$$\leq \sum_{(i,j,k) \in A} d_{ij} + \sum_{(i,j,k) \in F} d_{jk} \tag{3.13}$$

$$\leq \sum_{(i,j,k) \in F} (d_{ij} + d_{jk}) \tag{3.14}$$

((3.12) holds because A is optimal for $(P2)$, (3.13) is by definition of B and of s_{ijk}, (3.14) follows from the optimality of M for $(P1)$).

By symmetry with (3.14), the following inequality is also valid:

$$c_{IJ} \leq \sum_{(i,j,k) \in F} (d_{ij} + d_{ik}). \tag{3.15}$$

Using the triangle inequalities, one easily checks:

$$2d_{ij} + d_{ik} + d_{jk} \leq 3s_{ijk} \quad \text{for all } i, j, k. \tag{3.16}$$

Hence, (3.14), (3.15) and (3.16) together imply:

$$c_{IJ} \leq \frac{3}{2} \sum_{(i,j,k) \in F} s_{ijk} = \frac{3}{2} \text{OPT}(S). \tag{3.17}$$

The example presented in the proof of Theorem 3.4 also achieves equality in (3.17), and can be used to build arbitrary large instances.   □

Of course, one can define in a natural way two more $\frac{1}{2}$-approximate algorithms for problems $T\Delta$ and $S\Delta$, namely the heuristics H_{IK} and H_{JK} obtained by permuting the roles of I, J and K in the description of H_{IJ}. We denote by c_{IK} and c_{JK} the values of the solutions delivered by H_{IK} and H_{JK}, respectively.

Consider now the heuristic H, which consists in applying all three heuristics H_{IJ}, H_{IK} and H_{JK} to the given instance of $T\Delta$ or $S\Delta$, and in retaining the best feasible solution thus produced. We denote by γ the value of the solution returned by H : $\gamma = \min\{c_{IJ}, c_{IK}, c_{JK}\}$.

Clearly, H can again be implemented to run in time $O(n^3)$, and H is a $\frac{1}{2}$-approximate algorithm for $T\Delta$ and $S\Delta$. But even more is true:

Theorem 3.6 *H is a $\frac{1}{3}$-approximate algorithm for problem $T\Delta$. Moreover, there exist arbitrary large instances T of $T\Delta$ such that $\gamma = \frac{4}{3}$ $OPT(T)$.*

Proof:
Let T be an instance of $T\Delta$, and F an optimal solution of T. As in the proof of Theorem 3.4, we obtain inequalities (3.8), (3.9), as well as the symmetric inequality:

$$c_{IK} \leq 2 \sum_{(i,j,k) \in F} (d_{ik} + d_{jk}). \tag{3.18}$$

Summing up (3.8), (3.9) and (3.18) yields:

$$3\gamma \leq 2c_{IJ} + c_{IK} \leq 4 \sum_{(i,j,k) \in F} t_{ijk} = 4 \, OPT(T), \tag{3.19}$$

which proves that H is a $\frac{1}{3}$-approximate algorithm.

Equality in (3.19) is achieved by the instance T depicted in Figure 3.3.

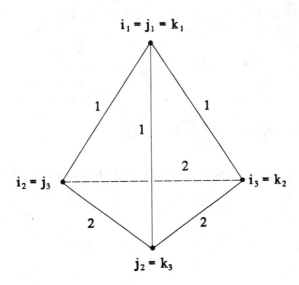

Figure 3.3

Here, $I = \{i_1, i_2, i_3\}$, $J = \{j_1, j_2, j_3\}$, $K = \{k_1, k_2, k_3\}$. The lengths d_{uv} are indicated next to the edges of the "pyramid", with $d_{uv} = 0$ if $u = v$. It is easy to see that T is an instance of $T\Delta$. Moreover, because T is symmetric on I, J and K, we can assume that $\gamma = c_{IJ} = c_{IK} = c_{JK}$.

An optimal solution of $\mathcal{T}$ is given by $F = \{(i_1, j_2, k_3), (i_2, j_3, k_1), (i_3, j_1, k_2)\}$ with $\mathrm{OPT}(\mathcal{T}) = 6$. But H_{IJ} can return a solution with cost $c_{IJ} = 8$, by picking $M = \{(i_1, j_1), (i_2, j_3), (i_3, j_2)\}$ in the first phase, and $A = \{(i_1, j_1, k_1), (i_2, j_3, k_2), (i_3, j_2, k_3)\}$ in the second phase. $\square$

Notice that we actually proved a little bit more than announced by the statement of Theorem 3.6. Indeed, inequality (3.19) shows that the minimum of *any two* of the bounds c_{IJ}, c_{IK} and c_{JK} is already bounded by $\frac{4}{3} \mathrm{OPT}(\mathcal{T})$. On the other hand, one can exhibit examples for which $c_{IJ} = c_{IK} = \frac{4}{3}\mathrm{OPT}(\mathcal{T})$, and $c_{JK} = \mathrm{OPT}(\mathcal{T})$. Thus, heuristic H is in general better than the strategy which consists in computing only two of the bounds c_{IJ}, c_{IK}, c_{JK}, and retaining the best one.

The same remarks apply to our next result:

Theorem 3.7 *H is a $\frac{1}{3}$-approximate algorithm for problem $S\Delta$. Moreover, there exist arbitrary large instances S of $S\Delta$ such that $\gamma = \frac{4}{3} OPT(S)$.*

Proof:
Let S be an instance of $S\Delta$, and F be an optimal solution of S. Summing up inequalities (3.14), (3.15) and

$$c_{IK} \leq \sum_{(i,j,k) \in F} (d_{ik} + d_{jk}),$$

we get:

$$3\gamma \leq 2c_{IJ} + c_{IK} \leq 2 \sum_{(i,j,k) \in F} (d_{ij} + d_{ik} + d_{jk}). \tag{3.20}$$

Using the triangle inequalities to bound the right-hand side of (3.20) yields:

$$3\gamma \leq 4 \sum_{(i,j,k) \in F} s_{ijk} = 4 \, \mathrm{OPT}(S). \tag{3.21}$$

A worst-case instance S is represented in Figure 3.4.

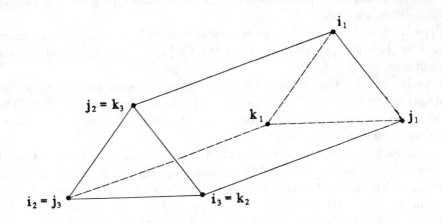

Figure 3.4

All edges of this prism have length 1, and the distances are Euclidean.

The optimal solution $\{(i_1, j_2, k_3), (i_2, j_3, k_1), (i_3, j_1, k_2)\}$ has cost $\text{OPT}(S)$ $= 3$. The heuristic H_{IJ} may return $M = \{(i_1, j_1), (i_2, j_3), (i_3, j_2)\}$ in phase 1, and $A = \{(i_1, j_1, k_1), (i_2, j_3, k_2), (i_3, j_2, k_3)\}$ in phase 2, for a total cost $c_{IJ} = 4$. Hence, by symmetry, $\gamma = 4$ is possible. $\qquad\Box$

3.4 Computational results

Of course, the quality of a heuristic cannot only be judged by its worst-case performance. Very often, it is the case that this worst-case performance is determined by pathological instances of the problem. With this in mind, we conducted some numerical experiments to better assess the quality of the various approximation algorithms discussed in Section 3.3.

For fixed $n = |I| = |J| = |K|$, we considered random problems of three different types.

<u>Type I</u> The elements of $I \cup J \cup K$ are generated at random, uniformly in the square $[0, 1] \times [0, 1]$. For each pair of points $(u, v), d_{uv}$ is the Euclidean distance from u to v (we also used for d_{uv} the Manhattan distance from u to v, with results similar to those displayed below).

Instances of type I form a "natural" class of random instances for problems $T\Delta$ or $S\Delta$. But, due to their high degree of uniformity, one may expect these instances to be easy to solve for most heuristics when n grows large. The next two types of instances are meant to be more "irregular", and hence more difficult to solve.

<u>Type II</u> The elements of I are generated uniformly in $[0, \frac{1}{3}] \times [0, 1]$, those of J in $[\frac{1}{3}, 1] \times [0, \frac{1}{2}]$, those of K in $[\frac{1}{3}, 1] \times [\frac{1}{2}, 1]$. The distances d_{uv} are Euclidean.

<u>Type III</u> We fix a parameter $p \in [0, 1]$. Then, for each pair (u, v), we let $d(u, v) = 1$ with probability p, and $d(u, v) = 2$ with probability $1 - p$. The value of p was empirically adjusted so as to produce rather difficult problem instances for our heuristics.

For each problem type, we report in Tables 3.1, 3.2 on the solution of three instances with $n = 33$ and three instances with $n = 66$ (more instances were actually tested, but the results displayed here are representative). The problems of type III were generated with $p = \frac{1}{17}$ for $n = 33$ and $p = \frac{1}{50}$ for $n = 66$. Table 3.1 deals with problem $T\Delta$ and Table 3.2 with problem $S\Delta$.

For the sake of comparison, we also give in Table 3.1 and 3.2 a lower-bound lb on the optimal value of each instance, as well as the value of the ratio $\frac{z}{lb}$. The bound lb was computed using a Lagrangean relaxation scheme and subgradient optimization, as proposed by Frieze and Yadegar (1981).

Type	n	c_{IJ}	c_{IK}	c_{JK}	γ	lb	γ/lb
I	33	16.18	16.36	16.55	16.18	16.07	1.007
	33	14.16	14.16	14.11	14.11	13.95	1.011
	33	16.09	16.33	16.32	16.09	16.04	1.003
	66	26.92	26.87	26.68	26.68	26.54	1.005
	66	25.00	24.81	24.69	24.69	24.33	1.015
	66	28.13	27.75	27.91	27.75	27.48	1.010
II	33	48.83	48.61	48.75	48.61	47.72	1.019
	33	51.72	51.42	51.49	51.42	50.35	1.021
	33	43.52	43.83	44.01	43.52	42.60	1.022
	66	98.09	97.80	99.15	97.80	96.33	1.015
	66	91.47	91.60	91.42	91.42	88.31	1.035
	66	99.39	98.88	99.57	98.88	96.70	1.023
III	33	140	135	136	135	133	1.015
	33	141	137	139	137	130	1.054
	33	135	136	137	135	130	1.038
	66	295	293	296	293	283	1.035
	66	294	298	294	294	281	1.046
	66	295	296	293	293	280	1.046

Table 3.1 Problem $T\Delta$.

Type	n	c_{IJ}	c_{IK}	c_{JK}	γ	lb	γ/lb
I	33	8.57	8.69	8.64	8.57	8.45	1.014
	33	7.61	7.54	7.53	7.53	7.39	1.019
	33	8.43	8.55	8.58	8.43	8.37	1.007
	66	14.23	14.31	14.09	14.09	13.90	1.014
	66	13.38	13.13	13.13	13.13	12.84	1.023
	66	14.70	14.53	14.46	14.46	14.20	1.018
II	33	26.54	26.65	27.32	26.54	25.96	1.022
	33	28.62	28.73	28.98	28.62	27.81	1.029
	33	23.78	23.79	24.21	23.78	23.11	1.029
	66	53.86	54.05	55.90	53.86	53.12	1.014
	66	49.29	49.47	50.43	49.29	47.88	1.029
	66	54.70	54.84	56.19	54.70	53.52	1.022
III	33	75	71	71	71	69	1.029
	33	75	72	73	72	67	1.075
	33	71	72	72	71	67	1.060
	66	163	161	165	161	151	1.066
	66	163	167	164	163	152	1.072
	66	163	165	161	161	147	1.095

Table 3.2 Problem $S\triangle$.

The results exhibited in these tables indicate that, from a practical viewpoint, the heuristics presented in Section 3.3 perform quite satisfactorily. In particular, heuristic H solved all randomly generated instances within 10 % of optimality, and often came within 3 % of the optimal value (or, more precisely, of the lower-bound lb).

Acknowledgements

The authors wish to thank Koos Vrieze for his insightful suggestions, which led to the discovery of the worst-case examples presented in the proofs of Theorems 3.6 and 3.7, and Hans-Jürgen Bandelt for his comments on this chapter.

Chapter 4

Scheduling jobs of equal length: complexity and facets

4.1 Introduction

The following problem is studied in this chapter. Given are n jobs, which have to be processed on a single machine within a fixed timespan $\{1, 2, \ldots, T\}$. The *processing time*, or *length*, of each job equals p, $p \in I\!N$. The *processing cost* of each job is an arbitrary function of its start-time: we denote by c_{jt} the cost of starting job j at time t. The problem is to schedule all jobs so as minimize the sum of the processing costs. We refer to this problem as problem SEL (*Scheduling jobs of Equal Length*).

Mathematically, SEL can be formulated as follows:

$$\text{minimize} \quad \sum_{j=1}^{n} \sum_{t=1}^{T-p+1} c_{jt} x_{jt}$$

$$\text{subject to} \quad \sum_{t=1}^{T-p+1} x_{jt} = 1 \qquad j = 1, \ldots, n, \tag{4.1}$$

$$\sum_{j=1}^{n} \sum_{t=s}^{s+p-1} x_{jt} \leq 1 \qquad s = 1, \ldots, T - 2p + 2, \tag{4.2}$$

$$x_{jt} \in \{0, 1\} \qquad j = 1, \ldots, n; t = 1, \ldots, T - p + 1, \tag{4.3}$$

where $x_{jt} = 1$ if job j starts at time t, and $x_{jt} = 0$ otherwise.

In Section 4.2, this problem is shown to be strongly $\mathcal{N}P$-hard, even when all jobs have length $p = 2$. Section 4.3 introduces some facets and valid inequalities for the solution set of (4.1)-(4.3). Section 4.4 describes some computational experiments.

Notice that SEL is a special case of a very general scheduling problem (say, problem S) considered by Sousa and Wolsey (1992). In problem S, the jobs may have arbitrary, usually distinct, processing times. Sousa and Wolsey propose several classes of facets and valid inequalities for S. It is an easy observation that, if $\{1, \ldots, n\}$ is any subset of the jobs occurring in S, and all the jobs in $\{1, \ldots, n\}$ have the same length p, then any valid inequality for (4.1)–(4.3) is also valid for S. This suggests that the polyhedral description presented in Section 4.3 may prove useful, not only when all jobs strictly have equal length, but also in situations where the number of distinct lengths is small, or where most of the jobs have the same length. We now proceed to describe an interesting application in which the latter assumptions are fulfilled, and which originally motivated our study.

The electronics industry relies on numerically controlled machines for the automated assembly of printed circuit boards (PCBs). Prior to the start of operations, a number n of feeders, containing the electronic components to be mounted on the PCBs, are positioned alongside the machine, in some available slots $1, 2, \ldots, T$. Each feeder j requires a certain number of slots, say p_j, depending on the feeder type; usually, p_j only takes a small number of values, say $p_j \in \{1, 2, 3\}$. In order to minimize the production makespan, it is desirable to position the feeders "close" to the locations where the corresponding components must be inserted. More precisely, for each combination of feeder j and slot t, a coefficient c_{jt} can be computed which captures the cost of assigning feeder j to slots $t, t + 1, \ldots, t + p_j - 1$. It should now be clear that finding a minimum-cost assignment of feeders to slots is equivalent to solving a scheduling problem with "small number of distinct processing times" (see e.g. Ball and Magazine (1988) for a description of this model with $p_j = 1$ for all j, and Ahmadi, Ahmadi, Matsuo and Tirupati (1990), Chapter 2 of this monograph, and Van Laarhoven and Zijm (1993) for a more general discussion).

Let us finally mention that SEL may be regarded as a discrete analogue of scheduling problems with unit-length tasks and arbitrary rational start-times (see e.g. Garey, Johnson, Simons and Tarjan (1981)). SEL is also superficially related to an assignment problem with side constraints investigated by Aboudi and Nemhauser (1990, 1991).

4.2   Complexity of SEL

It is obvious that, when each job has length 1 (the case $p = 1$), SEL reduces to an assignment problem, and hence is solvable in polynomial time. The following theorem shows that SEL is already strongly $\mathcal{NP}$-hard for $p = 2$:

Theorem 4.1 *SEL is $\mathcal{NP}$-hard, even for $p = 2$ and $c_{jt} \in \{0, 1\}$ for all j, t.*

Proof:
An instance of SEL, with $p = 2$ and processing costs equal to 0 or 1, can be described by a bipartite graph $G = (V_1 \cup V_2, E)$. Each job is represented by a vertex in V_1, each time-unit is represented by a vertex in V_2, and there is an edge $(j, t) \in E$, with $j \in V_1$ and $t \in V_2$, if and only if starting job j at time-unit t has processing cost $c_{jt} = 0$. The instance of SEL admits a schedule with zero cost if and only if there exists a set of edges $A \subseteq E$ such that:

i) each vertex in V_1 is incident to precisely one edge in A;

ii) each vertex in V_2 is incident to at most one edge in A;

iii) if vertex $t \in V_2$ is incident to an edge in A, then vertex $t + 1$ is not incident to any edge in A, for all $t = 1, \ldots, |V_2| - 1$.

We use a reduction from the $\mathcal{NP}$-hard 3-dimensional matching problem (see Garey and Johnson(1979)). An instance I of 3-dimensional matching is specified by three mutually disjoint sets K_1, K_2 and K_3 with $|K_i| = n$, for $i = 1, 2, 3$, and a set $Q \subseteq K_1 \times K_2 \times K_3$, with $|Q| = m$. The instance is feasible if there exists a set $Q' \subseteq Q$ such that every element of $K_1 \cup K_2 \cup K_3$ occurs in exactly one element of Q'.

With I, we associate an instance of SEL as follows. Let

$$V_1 = K_1 \cup K_2 \cup K_3 \cup \{a_1, \ldots, a_{m-n}\} \cup \{b_1, \ldots, b_{m-n}\},$$
$$V_2 = \{d_1, \ldots, d_{6m}\}.$$

In order to define the edge-set E, denote by $Q_r = \{k_r^1, k_r^2, k_r^3\}$ the r-th triple in Q, where

$$k_r^1 \in K_1, \ k_r^2 \in K_2 \text{ and } k_r^3 \in K_3 \ (r = 1, \ldots, m).$$

Now, let E consist of the following edges:

$$(k_r^1, d_{6(r-1)+1}), \ (k_r^2, d_{6(r-1)+3}) \text{ and } (k_r^3, d_{6(r-1)+5})$$

for $r = 1, \ldots, m$ and

$$(a_s, d_{6(r-1)+2}) \text{ and } (b_s, d_{6(r-1)+4})$$

for $s = 1, \ldots, m - n$, and $r = 1, \ldots, m$.

A typical piece of the graph is shown in Figure 4.1.

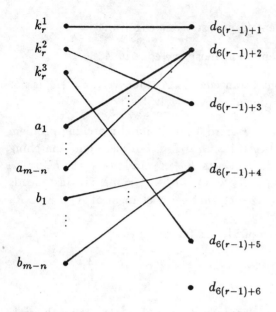

Figure 4.1

When the instance I of 3-dimensional matching has a feasible solution, it is straightforward to find a set of edges $A \subseteq E$ which defines a zero-cost schedule. Conversely, assume that SEL has a feasible solution specified by an edge set A. Define $D_r = \{d_{6(r-1)+1}, \ldots, d_{6r}\}$ for $r = 1, \ldots, m$ and let

$R_0 = \{r : \text{neither } d_{6(r-1)+2} \text{ nor } d_{6(r-1)+4} \text{ is incident to any edge in } A\}$,

$R_1 = \{r : \text{exactly one of } d_{6(r-1)+2}, d_{6(r-1)+4} \text{ is incident to an edge in } A\}$,

$R_2 = \{r : \text{both } d_{6(r-1)+2} \text{ and } d_{6(r-1)+4} \text{ are incident to edges in } A\}$.

Since each of a_s, b_s $(s = 1, \ldots, m - n)$ is incident to an edge in A,

$$2(m - n) = |R_1| + 2|R_2| \tag{4.4}$$

and, since $\{R_0, R_1, R_2\}$ is a partition of $\{1, \ldots, m\}$,

$$m = |R_0| + |R_1| + |R_2|. \tag{4.5}$$

Now, we claim that $|R_1| = 0$. Indeed, if $|R_1| > 0$, then (4.4) implies

$$m - n < |R_1| + |R_2|. \tag{4.6}$$

However, for each $r \in R_0$, at most three vertices of D_r are incident to some edge of A, and for each $r \in R_1 \cup R_2$, at most two vertices of D_r are incident

to an edge of A.
This implies:

$$
\begin{aligned}
|A| = |V_1| \ &= \ 2m + n \\
&\leq \ 3|R_0| + 2|R_1| + 2|R_2| \\
&= \ 3m - |R_1| - |R_2| & \text{(by (4.5))} \\
&< \ 2m + n. & \text{(by (4.6))}
\end{aligned}
$$

This contradiction proves $|R_1| = 0$. Then, it follows easily by (4.4) and (4.5) that $|R_0| = n$, and $\{Q_r : r \in R_0\}$ defines a feasible solution of the 3-dimensional matching problem. $\qquad\Box$

Notice that the proof of Theorem 4.1 is easily adapted to show that a related problem, in which n_1 jobs have length 1, n_2 jobs have length 2, and $T = n_1 + 2 \cdot n_2$, is $\mathcal{N}P$-hard too. This is to be contrasted with the following statement:

Theorem 4.2 *If $T = n \cdot p + c$, where c denotes a constant, $c \in \mathbb{N}$, then SEL is polynomially solvable.*

Proof:
We claim that, in this case, it is sufficient to solve $\begin{pmatrix} n + c \\ n \end{pmatrix} = O(n^c)$ assignment problems, where each assignment problem corresponds to a set of starting times allowing a feasible solution to SEL. The proof is by induction on n.

If $n = 1$, then it is easy to see that $c + 1$ trivial assignment problems need to be solved, since each of the first $T - p + 1 = c + 1$ time-units is a feasible starting time for the job. Assuming that the induction hypothesis is true for $n = k$, consider now the case $T = (k + 1) \cdot p + c$. Let the smallest starting time in a feasible set of starting times be denoted by i, with $1 \leq i \leq c + 1$. The remaining k starting times have to be chosen from the set $\{i + p, \ldots, T\}$. By the induction hypothesis, and since $T - (i + p) + 1 = k \cdot p + c - i + 1$, there are $\begin{pmatrix} k + c - i + 1 \\ k \end{pmatrix}$ feasible sets of starting times, for $i = 1, \ldots, c + 1$.

As $\displaystyle\sum_{i=1}^{c+1} \begin{pmatrix} k + c - i + 1 \\ k \end{pmatrix} = \sum_{i=0}^{c} \begin{pmatrix} k + i \\ k \end{pmatrix} = \begin{pmatrix} k + c + 1 \\ k + 1 \end{pmatrix}$, the theorem is proven. $\qquad\Box$

4.3   A partial polyhedral description of SEL

Let us first recall some fundamental definitions from polyhedral theory (for
a thorough introduction, the reader is referred to Nemhauser and Wolsey
(1988)). Consider a polyhedron $P = \{x \in I\!\!R^k : Ax \leq b\}$. The *equality set* of
(A, b) is the set of rows of (A, b), say $(A^=, b^=)$, such that: $A^= x = b^=$ for all
x in P. The *dimension* of P is given by: $dim(P) = k - rank(A^=, b^=)$. The
inequality $\alpha x \leq \alpha_0$ is *valid* for P if it is satisfied by all points in P. For a
valid inequality $\alpha x \leq \alpha_0$, the set $F = \{x \in P : \alpha x = \alpha_0\}$ is called a *facet* of
P if $dim(F) = dim(P) - 1$. Equivalently, when $\emptyset \neq F \neq P$, F is a facet if
and only if the following condition holds: if all points in F satisfy $\pi x = \pi_0$,
for some $(\pi, \pi_0) \in I\!\!R^{k+1}$, then (π, π_0) is a linear combination of $(A^=, b^=)$ and
(α, α_0) (see Nemhauser and Wolsey (1988), p. 91).

Consider now the formulation in Section 4.1, and let P denote the convex
hull of the feasible solutions to constraints (4.1), (4.2) and (4.3). Furthermore, assume from now on that $T \geq p \cdot (n + 1)$. (Notice that $\dim(P) \leq$
$n \cdot (T - p + 1) - n = n \cdot (T - p)$. If $T < p \cdot (n + 1)$, then it is easy to see
that $\dim(P) < n \cdot (T - p)$; for instance $\sum_{j=1}^{n}\sum_{t=1}^{p} x_{jt} = 1$ is implied by (4.1) and
(4.2)). To avoid trivialities, assume also $n > 2$, $p \geq 2$.

Sousa and Wolsey (1992) established the dimension of P. For the sake
of completeness, we also include a proof of this result:

Theorem 4.3 $dim(P) = n \cdot (T - p)$.

Proof:

We just noticed that $\dim(P) \leq n \cdot (T - p)$. Suppose $\sum_{j=1}^{n} \sum_{t=1}^{T-p+1} \pi_{jt} x_{jt} = \pi_0$ for
all $x \in P$; we want to show that this equality is implied by constraints (4.1).

To see this, fix j and t, $t \leq T - p$, and consider a solution with job j
starting at time-unit t, while the other jobs start arbitrarily at time-units in
$[1, t - p] \cup [t + p + 1, T - p + 1]$. Note that this is always possible; e.g. let
$t = k \cdot p + q$, with $1 \leq q \leq p$; then, a feasible schedule can be found using
only start-times in

$$S_t = \{j \cdot p + q : j = 0, \ldots k\} \cup \{j \cdot p + q + 1 : j = k + 1, \ldots, m\},$$

where m is the largest index such that $m \cdot p + q + 1 \leq T - p + 1$. Indeed,
since $T \geq p \cdot (n + 1)$, S_t contains at least n time periods.

Consider now a second schedule, obtained by starting job j at time-unit
$t + 1$, while all other jobs remain untouched. Comparing the two schedules,

it follows easily that $\pi_{jt} = \pi_{j,t+1}$ for all $j = 1, \ldots, n$, $t = 1, \ldots, T - p$. (This construction will be used in subsequent proofs.) Thus, with $\pi_{jt} = \pi_j$ for all $j = 1, \ldots, n$, $t = 1, \ldots, T - p + 1$, we get $\displaystyle\sum_{j=1}^{n} \sum_{t=1}^{T-p+1} \pi_{jt} x_{jt} = \sum_{j=1}^{n} \pi_j \sum_{t=1}^{T-p+1} x_{jt} = \pi_0$, which is a linear combination of the equalities (4.1). $\square$

With the dimension of P established, we now can proceed to show that some inequalities define facets of P. First, we prove that the inequalities in the LP-relaxation of (4.1)-(4.3) are facet-defining.

Theorem 4.4 *The inequalities $x_{jt} \geq 0$ define facets of P, for all $j = 1, \ldots, n$, $t = 1, \ldots, T - p + 1$.*

Proof:
Let $F = \{x \in P \colon x_{is} = 0\}$ for any i, s with $1 \leq i \leq n$, $1 \leq s \leq T - p + 1$ and suppose $\displaystyle\sum_{j=1}^{n} \sum_{t=1}^{T-p+1} \pi_{jt} x_{jt} = \pi_0$ for all $x \in F$.

To prove $\pi_j = \pi_{jt}$ for all $j = 1, \ldots, n$, $j \neq i$, $t = 1, \ldots, T - p + 1$, we refer to the construction used in the proof of Theorem 4.3 (it is obvious that it is always possible to ensure that job i is not placed at s, for any s). Moreover, we can use this construction for job i and starting-time t for all $t \leq s - 2$ and $t \geq s + 1$, proving that $\pi_{i1} = \pi_{i2} = \ldots = \pi_{i,s-1}$ and $\pi_{i,s+1} = \pi_{i,s+2} = \ldots = \pi_{i,T-p+1}$.

If $s \neq 1$ and $s \neq T - p + 1$, consider a solution with job i at time-unit 1 and the other jobs at time-units $1+p, 1+2p, \ldots, 1+(n-1)\cdot p$, and a solution with job i at $T - p + 1$, and all other jobs at the same time-units as before (again, note that this is always possible, since we assumed $T \geq p \cdot (n + 1)$). Comparing these solutions, it follows that $\pi_{i1} = \pi_{i,T-p+1}$ and thus $\pi_i = \pi_{it}$ for all $t \neq s$. So:

$$\sum_{j=1}^{n} \sum_{t=1}^{T-p+1} \pi_{jt} x_{jt} = \sum_{j=1}^{n} \pi_j \sum_{t=1}^{T-p+1} x_{jt} + \rho x_{is},$$

which shows that the equality $\displaystyle\sum_{j=1}^{n} \sum_{t=1}^{T-p+1} \pi_{jt} x_{jt} = \pi_0$ is a linear combination of (4.1) and of $x_{is} = 0$. $\square$

Theorem 4.5 *The inequalities (4.2) define facets of P.*

Proof:

Let $F = \{x \in P : \sum\limits_{j=1}^{n} \sum\limits_{t=s}^{s+p-1} x_{jt} = 1\}$, for any $1 \leq s \leq T - 2p + 2$, and suppose

$\sum\limits_{j=1}^{n} \sum\limits_{t=1}^{T-p+1} \pi_{jt} x_{jt} = \pi_0$ for all $x \in F$.

For any j and any t, consider a schedule using only start-times in S_t (as in Theorem 4.3) and with $x_{jt} = 1$. There is always such a schedule corresponding to a point in F, unless $t = s - 1$. Also, the schedule obtained by delaying the start-time of job j until $t + 1$ is in F, unless $t = s + p - 1$. From this, one easily concludes that, for all $j = 1, \ldots, n$,

$$
\begin{aligned}
\pi_{j1} &= \pi_{j2} = \ldots = \pi_{j,s-1} = \alpha_j, \\
\pi_{js} &= \pi_{j,s+1} = \ldots = \pi_{j,s+p-1} = \beta_j, \\
\pi_{j,s+p} &= \pi_{j,s+p+1} = \ldots = \pi_{j,T-p+1} = \gamma_j.
\end{aligned}
\tag{4.7}
$$

If $2 \leq s \leq T - 2p + 1$, then one can also show as in Theorem 4.4 that $\pi_{j1} = \pi_{j,T-p+1}$ for all $j = 1, \ldots, n$, or, more generally:

$$
\gamma_j = \alpha_j \text{ for all } j = 1, \ldots, n.
\tag{4.8}
$$

Furthermore, simple interchange arguments yield:

$$
\beta_j + \alpha_i = \alpha_j + \beta_i \text{ for all } i, j \in \{1, 2, \ldots, n\},
\tag{4.9}
$$

or equivalently $\delta = \beta_j - \alpha_j$ for all $j = 1, \ldots, n$.

So, (4.7), (4.8) and (4.9) together imply:

$$
\begin{aligned}
&\sum_{j=1}^{n} \sum_{t=1}^{T-p+1} \pi_{jt} x_{jt} \\
&= \sum_{j=1}^{n} \alpha_j \left(\sum_{t=1}^{s-1} x_{jt} + \sum_{t=s+p}^{T-p+1} x_{jt} \right) + \sum_{j=1}^{n} \beta_j \sum_{t=s}^{s+p-1} x_{jt} \\
&= \sum_{j=1}^{n} \alpha_j \sum_{t=1}^{T-p+1} x_{jt} + \delta \sum_{j=1}^{n} \sum_{t=s}^{s+p-1} x_{jt},
\end{aligned}
$$

which proves the theorem. $\square$

Now, let us consider the following inequalities:

$$\sum_{t=s}^{s+p+l-1} x_{it} + \sum_{j=1 \atop j \neq i}^{n} \sum_{t=s+l}^{s+p-1} x_{jt} \leq 1$$

for $1 \leq i \leq n$, $1 \leq l \leq p-1$ and $1 \leq s \leq T - 2p - l + 2$. (4.10)

These inequalities are introduced in Sousa and Wolsey (1992). Notice that the inequalities (4.2) are the special case of (4.10) for $l = 0$. However, for reasons of convenience, we maintain the distinction between these two classes. It is not difficult to see that the inequalities (4.10) are valid, but they are also facet-defining, as witnessed by the next theorem (due to Sousa and Wolsey (1992)).

Theorem 4.6 *The inequalities (4.10) define facets of P.*

The validity of this theorem will also follow from the validity of the more general Theorem 4.8.

Observe that all (in)equalities (4.1), (4.2) and (4.10) are of the set-packing type, i.e. they only involve coefficients 0 or 1, and their right-hand side equals 1. In fact, the following holds if $T \geq p \cdot (n+2) - 2$:

Theorem 4.7 *All facets of P defined by set-packing inequalities are given by (4.2) and (4.10).*

Proof:
Consider an arbitrary valid set-packing inequality I and define

$$t^* = \max_{j} \max_{t_2 \geq t_1} \{t_2 - t_1 : x_{jt_2} \text{ and } x_{jt_1} \text{ occur with coefficient 1 in } I\}.$$

Let i be the job which realizes t^*. We will make use of the following observation: no two variables x_{jt} and x_{ks}, with $k \neq j$, and $|s - t| \geq p$, can simultaneously occur with coefficient 1 in I.

Let us first consider the case $t^* \geq 2p - 1$. Then, it is easy to verify that no variable x_{it}, $i \neq j$, for any t, can occur in the inequality; thus I is implied by equalities (4.1), and cannot represent a facet.

Next, suppose $p \leq t^* \leq 2p - 2$, i.e. $t^* = p + l - 1$ for some $1 \leq l \leq p - 1$. More specifically, suppose that x_{is} and $x_{i,s+p+l-1}$ have coefficient 1 in I. From our previous observation, it easily follows that, for any $j \neq i$, x_{jt} cannot occur in I if either $t \leq s + l - 1$ or $t \geq s + p$. Hence, I is implied by (4.10).

Finally, when $t^* \leq p - 1$, let s be the smallest index such that, for some k, x_{ks} occurs in I with coefficient 1. It follows again from our observation that , for all j and for all $t \geq s + p$, x_{jt} does not occur in I. Hence, I is implied by (4.2).   □

(M. van den Akker has independently established that, for the more general scheduling problem S mentioned in Section 4.1, all facet-defining set-packing inequalities are given by Sousa and Wolsey (1992) (private communication). Theorem 4.7 does not hold if $p \cdot (n + 1) \leq T < p \cdot (n + 2) - 2$, as pointed out to us by H.-J. Bandelt (private communication)).

In the following we investigate generalizations of (4.10). To start with, (4.10) can be generalized to the following inequalities:

$$\sum_{j \in J} \sum_{t=s}^{s+k \cdot p + l - 1} x_{jt} + \sum_{j \notin J} \sum_{r=0}^{k-1} \sum_{t=s+l}^{s+p-1} x_{j,t+r \cdot p} \leq k,$$

for $J \subset \{1, \ldots, n\}$ with $|J| = k > 0$,

$$1 \leq l \leq p - 1 \text{ and } 1 \leq s \leq T - (k + 1) \cdot p - l + 2. \tag{4.11}$$

Notice that for $J = \{i\}$, (4.11) is equivalent to (4.10). The inequalities (4.11) are valid and even facet-defining as witnessed by the following theorem:

Theorem 4.8 *The inequalities (4.11) define facets of P.*

Proof:
To facilitate the proof, we define subsets of time-units which occur in (4.11). Let:

$$A = [s, s + k \cdot p + l - 1] \text{ and}$$
$$B = \{t + r \cdot p : r = 0, \ldots, k - 1; t = s + l, \ldots, s + p - 1\}$$
$$= [s + l, s + p - 1] \cup [s + p + l, s + 2p - 1] \cup \ldots$$
$$\ldots \cup [s + (k - 1) \cdot p + l, s + k \cdot p - 1].$$

(see Figure 4.2 for an illustration of the case $p = 5$, $k = 3$, $l = 2$). With these notations, (4.11) can be rewritten as

$$\sum_{j \in J} \sum_{t \in A} x_{jt} + \sum_{j \notin J} \sum_{t \in B} x_{jt} \leq k. \tag{4.12}$$

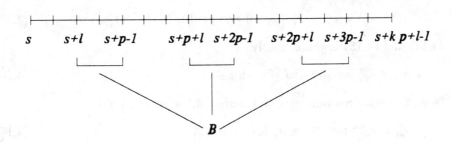

Figure 4.2

First we show that these inequalities are valid. Suppose that $k+1$ jobs start in the interval $[s, \; s + k \cdot p + l - 1]$. The only way to achieve this is to start exactly one job in each of the intervals $[s, \; s + l - 1]$, $[s + p, \; s + p + l - 1]$, $\ldots , [s + k \cdot p, \; s + k \cdot p + l - 1]$ (this is easily checked by induction on k), i.e. to start the jobs in $A \backslash B$. However, the time-units in $A \backslash B$ only occur in (4.12) for the k jobs in J. This implies that (4.12) is valid. Let us show now that (4.12) is facet-defining.

Let $F = \{x \in P \colon \sum_{j \in J} \sum_{t \in A} x_{jt} + \sum_{j \notin J} \sum_{t \in B} x_{jt} = k\}$ and suppose $\sum_{j=1}^{n} \sum_{t=1}^{T-p+1} \pi_{jt} x_{jt} = \pi_0$ for all $x \in F$.

Now, let $j \in J$ and $t \in A \backslash \{s + k \cdot p + l - 1\}$. Consider a solution with job j started at time-unit t, and other jobs started at $t - p, t - 2p, \ldots$ and $t + p + 1$, $t + 2\,p + 1, \ldots$, in such a way that jobs in J are started in A (thus ensuring that $x \in F$). Shifting job j one time-unit towards $t + 1$ proves

$$\pi_{jt} = \pi_j^{\text{in}} \text{ for all } j \in J, \text{ for all } t \in A. \tag{4.13}$$

Let now $i \notin J$ and $t \in [s + r \cdot p + l, s + (r+1) \cdot p - 2]$, where $r \in \{0, \ldots, k-1\}$ (this is assuming $l \leq p - 2$; else this step of the proof is not required). Consider the following solution: start job i at time t, start $k - 1$ jobs from J in A, at time-units $t - p, t - 2p, \ldots$, and $t + p + 1, t + 2p + 1, \ldots$, and start all other jobs outside A. Shifting job i one time-unit proves

$$\pi_{it} = \pi_i^r \text{ for all } i \notin J, \; t \in [s + r \cdot p + l, \; s + (r + 1) \cdot p - 1],$$
$$r \in \{0, \ldots, k - 1\}. \tag{4.14}$$

Also, interchanging job $i \notin J$ and job $j \in J$ proves (for any $l \in \{1, \ldots, p-1\}$):

$$\pi_j^{\text{in}} + \pi_i^{r_1} = \pi_j^{\text{in}} + \pi_i^{r_2} \text{ for all } r_1, r_2 \in \{0, \ldots, k-1\}. \tag{4.15}$$

(4.14) and (4.15) together imply:

$$\pi_{it} = \pi_i^{\text{in}} \text{ for all } i \notin J, \text{ for all } t \in B. \tag{4.16}$$

Now, a similar reasoning as in Theorem 4.5 ensures that

$$\pi_{it} = \pi_i^{\text{out}} \text{ for all } i \notin J, \text{ for all } t \notin A. \tag{4.17}$$

Furthermore, consider a solution with the jobs from J at s, $s + p, \ldots, s + (k-1) \cdot p$ and job i, $i \notin J$ at $s + k \cdot p$. Simple interchange arguments imply, together with (4.12) and (4.17),

$$\pi_{it} = \pi_i^{\text{out}} \text{ for all } i \notin J, \ t \notin B. \tag{4.18}$$

Also, similar arguments imply

$$\pi_{jt} = \pi_j^{\text{out}} \text{ for all } j \in J, \ t \notin A. \tag{4.19}$$

Moreover, it is easy to see that

$$\pi_j^{\text{in}} + \pi_i^{\text{out}} = \pi_j^{\text{out}} + \pi_i^{\text{in}} \text{ for all } i, j \in \{1, 2, \ldots, n\}, \tag{4.20}$$

or equivalently $\beta = \pi_j^{\text{in}} - \pi_j^{\text{out}}$ for all $j = 1, \ldots, n$.

Now (4.12), (4.16), (4.18), (4.19) and (4.20) imply:

$$\sum_{j=1}^{n} \sum_{t=1}^{T-p+1} \pi_{jt} x_{jt}$$

$$= \sum_{j \in J} \sum_{t \in A} \pi_j^{\text{in}} x_{jt} + \sum_{j \in J} \sum_{t \notin A} \pi_j^{\text{out}} x_{jt} + \sum_{j \notin J} \sum_{t \in B} \pi_j^{\text{in}} x_{jt} + \sum_{j \notin J} \sum_{t \notin B} \pi_j^{\text{out}} x_{jt}$$

$$= \sum_{j=1}^{n} \pi_j^{\text{out}} \sum_{t=1}^{T-p+1} x_{jt} + \beta \cdot \left(\sum_{j \in J} \sum_{t \in A} x_{jt} + \sum_{j \notin J} \sum_{t \in B} x_{jt} \right),$$

proving the theorem. $\qquad\qquad\qquad\qquad\qquad\qquad\qquad\qquad\qquad\qquad \Box$

Even though there is an exponential number of inequalities of type (4.11), the separation problem for this class of inequalities is polynomially solvable. Indeed, notice that (4.11) can be rewritten as:

$$\sum_{j=1}^{n}\sum_{r=0}^{k-1}\sum_{t=s+l}^{s+p-1} x_{j,t+r\cdot p} + \sum_{j\in J}\sum_{r=0}^{k}\sum_{t=s}^{s+l-1} x_{j,t+r\cdot p} \leq k. \tag{4.21}$$

We want to check whether a given x^* violates one of these inequalities. Fix s, l and k (there are only $O(pnT)$ choices for these three values). Then, the first term of (4.21) is a constant. Pick the k values of j which maximize the second term and put them in a set J^*. If x^* violates (4.21) for any J, then it does so for J^*.

Another way of generalizing the inequalities (4.10) is the following. Choose a non-empty set $J \subset \{1,\ldots,n\}$ and a non-empty set $S \subset \{1,\ldots,T-2p+2\}$. For each $s \in \{1,\ldots,T-p+1\}$, define $q_s = 1$ if $s \in S$ and $q_s = 0$ otherwise. Then, by adding the constraints (4.1) for $j \in J$ and the constraints (4.2) for $s \in S$, each with coefficient $\frac{1}{2}$, we obtain the following valid inequality:

$$\sum_{j\in J}\sum_{t=1}^{T-p+1} \left\lfloor \left(\frac{1}{2}+\frac{1}{2}\cdot\sum_{s=t-p+1}^{t} q_s\right)\right\rfloor \cdot x_{jt}$$

$$+\sum_{j\notin J}\sum_{t=1}^{T-p+1} \left\lfloor \frac{1}{2}\cdot\sum_{s=t-p+1}^{t} q_s\right\rfloor \cdot x_{jt} \leq \left\lfloor \frac{1}{2}(|J|+|S|)\right\rfloor \tag{4.22}$$

We refer to these inequalities as (J,S) inequalities. The inequalities (4.10) are the special case of (4.22) obtained for $J = \{i\}$ and $S = \{s,\ s+l\}$. Of course, a more sophisticated choice for S could lead to other valid inequalities. Indeed, it is possible to generalize inequalities (4.10) by choosing S as k couples of time-units in the following way: for some $k \geq 2$ and $l \in \{1,\ldots,p-1\}$,

$$S = \{s,\ s+l,\ s+p,\ s+p+l,\ldots,s+(k-1)\cdot p, s+(k-1)\cdot p+l\}.$$

However, the resulting (J,S) inequalities do not define facets of P. In fact, (when $k \geq 2$ of course), they can be strengthened by lifting certain coefficients to 2. The following inequalities result:

$$\sum_{j\neq i}\sum_{t=s+l}^{s+k\cdot p-1} x_{jt} + \sum_{t=s}^{s+k\cdot p+l-1} x_{it} + \sum_{r=1}^{k-1}\sum_{t=s}^{s+l-1} x_{i,t+r\cdot p} \leq k,$$

for i,k,l,s with $1 \leq i \leq n, 1 \leq k \leq n, 1 \leq l \leq p-1$ and

$$1 \leq s \leq T-(k+1)\cdot p-l+2 \tag{4.23}$$

(observe that, when $k \geq 2$, then some variables occur with coefficient 2 in (4.23)). The following holds:

Theorem 4.9 *The inequalities (4.23) define facets of P.*

Proof:
We first introduce some notation. With i, k, l, s as in (4.23), let

$$
\begin{aligned}
A &= [s, s + k \cdot p + l - 1], \\
C &= [s + l, s + k \cdot p - 1], \\
D &= \{t + r \cdot p : r = 1, \ldots, k - 1; t = s, \ldots, s + l - 1\} \\
&= [s + p, s + p + l - 1] \cup [s + 2p, s + 2p + l - 1] \cup \ldots \\
&\quad \ldots \cup [s + (k - 1) \cdot p, s + (k - 1) \cdot p + l - 1].
\end{aligned}
$$

We can rewrite (4.23) as

$$
\sum_{j \neq i} \sum_{t \in C} x_{jt} + \sum_{t \in A \setminus D} x_{it} + 2 \cdot \sum_{t \in D} x_{it} \leq k \tag{4.24}
$$

Let us first show that (4.24) is valid for P. Consider any feasible schedule. It is easy to see that the only way to start k jobs in C is to start them in $C \setminus D = [s + l, s + p - 1] \cup \ldots \cup [s + (k - 1) \cdot p + l, s + k \cdot p - 1]$ (one job in each subinterval). But, if this is the case, then there is no room left to start job i in A, and hence (4.24) is satisfied. So, the only way to violate (4.24) is to start $k - 1$ jobs in C, and job i in D. Let us suppose job i starts at $s + r \cdot p + q$, $r \in \{1, \ldots, k - 1\}$, $q \in \{0, \ldots, l - 1\}$. Then two intervals of consecutive time-units remain for placing $k - 1$ jobs in C:

$$
[s + l, \; s + (r - 1) \cdot p + q] \text{ and } [s + (r + 1) \cdot p + q, \; s + k \cdot p - 1].
$$

But it is easy to check that no $k - 1$ jobs can start in these intervals. This establishes the validity of (4.24). Let us show now that (4.24) is facet-defining.

Let $F = \{x \in P : \sum_{j \neq i} \sum_{t \in C} x_{jt} + \sum_{t \in A \setminus D} x_{it} + 2 \sum_{t \in D} x_{it} = k\}$, and suppose $\sum_{j=1}^{n} \sum_{t=1}^{T-p+1} \pi_{jt} x_{jt} = \pi_0$ for all $x \in F$.

Consider a solution with job j, $j \neq i$, starting at time-unit $t \in C \setminus \{s + k \cdot p - 1\}$. Let the other jobs start at $t - p$, $t - 2\,p, \ldots$, and at $t + p + 1$, $t + 2\,p + 1, \ldots$, while ensuring that $x \in F$ (this is always possible). Shifting job j towards time-unit $t + 1$ proves that

$$
\pi_{jt} = \pi_j^{\text{in}} \text{ for all } j \neq i, \text{ for all } t \in C. \tag{4.25}
$$

Now, consider a solution with job i placed at t, with $t \in [s, \ s+l-1]$, and all other jobs at $t - p, t - 2\,p, \ldots$, and $t+p+1, t+2\,p+1, \ldots$. This can be done in such a way that $x \in F$, since $t+p+1, t+2p+1, \ldots, t+(k-1)\cdot p+1$ are $k-1$ time-units in C. Now, shifting job i from t to $t+1$ proves that

$$\pi_{it} = \pi_i^{\text{in}1} \text{ for all } t \in [s, \ s+l]. \tag{4.26}$$

A similar argument shows:

$$\pi_{it} = \pi_i^{\text{in}2} \text{ for all } t \in [s + k \cdot p, \ s + k \cdot p + l - 1]. \tag{4.27}$$

Consider next a schedule x with job i starting at t, $t \in [s + r \cdot p + l, s + (r+1) \cdot p - 2]$, for some $0 \le r \le k - 1$, and $k - 1$ other jobs starting at $t - r \cdot p, t - (r-1) \cdot p, \ldots, t - p, t + p + 1, \ldots, t + (k - r - 1) \cdot p + 1$. Notice that the latter time-units are all in $C \backslash D$, and hence $x \in F$. Comparing x with another schedule in which job i starts at $t+1$ shows that $\pi_{it} = \pi_{i,t+1}$ for all $t \in [s + r \cdot p + l, s + (r-1) \cdot p - 2]$. Also exchanging job i with one of the other jobs which start in $C \backslash D$ shows, in combination with our previous observations (4.25), (4.26) and (4.27) that:

$$\pi_{it} = \pi_i^{\text{in}1} = \pi_i^{\text{in}2} = \pi_i^1 \text{ for all } t \in A \backslash D. \tag{4.28}$$

Now, consider a solution with job i starting at t, $t \in D$ and place the other jobs at $t - p, t - 2\,p, \ldots$ and $t + p, t + 2\,p, \ldots$, ensuring that the solution is in F (notice that exactly $k - 2$ of these time-units are in D, and hence in C). Interchanging job i and job $j \ne i$ leads easily to

$$\pi_{it} = \pi_i^2 \text{ for all } t \in D. \tag{4.29}$$

To prove $\pi_{jt} = \pi_j^{\text{out}}$ for all j, for all $t \notin C$, we refer to the construction used in Theorem 4.5. Moreover, simple interchange arguments imply:

$$\pi_{j_1}^{\text{out}} + \pi_{j_2}^{\text{in}} = \pi_{j_1}^{\text{in}} + \pi_{j_2}^{\text{out}} \text{ for all } j_1, j_2 \ne i,$$
$$\pi_i^1 + \pi_j^{\text{out}} = \pi_i^{\text{out}} + \pi_j^{\text{in}} \text{ for all } j \ne i, \text{ and}$$
$$\pi_i^2 + \pi_j^{\text{out}} = \pi_i^{\text{in}} + \pi_j^{\text{in}} \text{ for all } j \ne i.$$

With these last equalities established and together with (4.25), (4.28) and (4.29) the theorem follows easily. $\qquad \square$

Notice that there are $O(pn^2T)$ inequalities in the class (4.23). Hence, the separation problem for this class of inequalities can be solved in polynomial time.

4.4 A cutting-plane algorithm for SEL

In this section, we describe an (unsophisticated) cutting-plane algorithm for SEL, based on the results of Section 4.3, and we report on its performance on a few randomly generated problems. The algorithm works as follows. We start with a model consisting solely of the constraints (4.1). This model is solved to optimality (we used the LP-package LINDO). Then the following four classes of inequalities are searched successively in order to find violated inequalities:

- constraints (4.2);

- constraints (4.10) with $l = 1$;

- constraints (4.11) and (4.23) with $k > 1$;

- constraints (4.22) with $|J| = 2$, and $S = \{s_1, s_2, s_2 + 1\}$ for $1 \leq s_1 \leq T - 2p + 3$ and $1 \leq s_2 \leq T - 2p + 2$.

When violated inequalities are found, they are added to the model, the extended model is solved to optimality and the whole process is repeated. When no violated inequalities are detected or if an integral solution is found, the algorithm stops.

A few implementation issues are worth mentioning. First, if violated inequalities in one of the four classes are found, then subsequent classes are not checked. Secondly, at each iteration, only those inequalities are maintained whose slack is smaller than 0.1; all other inequalities are removed from the model. Observe also that, for all classes of valid inequalities used in this algorithm, the separation problem is polynomially solvable.

We generated 35 problem instances distributed over 7 categories. For each category, values of n, p and T are specified as well as a range from which the cost-coefficients are randomly drawn (using a uniform distribution); see the first column of Table 4.1. Notice that all cost-coefficients are integer, so that all lowerbounds computed can validly be rounded-up to the next integer. Regarding the choice of T, preliminary experiments indicated that for relatively large values of T ($T \geq (p + 1) \cdot n$) as well as for minimal values of T ($T = p \cdot (n + 1)$), the LP-relaxation of model (4.1) - (4.3) almost always has an integral optimal solution. So, we tried to choose T in such a way that fractional LP-relaxations arise.

In Table 4.1, LP denotes the value of the LP-relaxation of model (4.1) - (4.3). CPA denotes the value found by the cutting-plane algorithm described earlier and (i) indicates that the solution found is integral.

		LP	CPA
$p = 2$	1	4 (i)	4 (i)
$n = 20$	2	7 (i)	7 (i)
$T = 46$	3	6.50	7 (i)
[0–25]	4	12.33	12.5
	5	9 (i)	9 (i)
$p = 2$	1	7	7
$n = 30$	2	10.5	10.5
$T = 66$	3	9	9.2
[0–25]	4	11.11	11.29
	5	7.33	7.68
$p = 2$	1	18.63	20.20
$n = 40$	2	22.05	22.67
$T = 86$	3	21.86	22.36
[0–40]	4	20.00	20.33
	5	20.67	21.11
$p = 3$	1	4.88	5 (i)
$n = 20$	2	8.17	9 (i)
$T = 67$	3	11.27	11.38
[0–25]	4	8 (i)	8 (i)
	5	9.67	10 (i)

		LP	CPA
$p = 3$	1	14.25	14.28
$n = 30$	2	14.00	14.15
$T = 102$	3	15.21	15.33
[0–40]	4	9 (i)	9 (i)
	5	10.00	10.28
$p = 4$	1	15.00	15.00
$n = 20$	2	19.50	21.87
$T = 93$	3	20.08	21.20
[0–60]	4	23.00	24.00
	5	23.43	24.83
$p = 5$	1	12.62	14.5
$n = 20$	2	11.00	11 (i)
$T = 114$	3	21.17	22.54
[0–60]	4	22.14	22.25
	5	15.90	16 (i)

Table 4.1

The cutting-plane algorithm finds 11 times an integral solution (compared to six times for the LP-relaxation of (4.1) - (4.3)). In the other cases, it improves the (rounded-up) value of the lower bound 13 times.

Not surprisingly, the results indicate that the problems get harder when p and/or n increase. For the "easier" problems ($n = 20$, $p = 2, 3$), the cutting-plane algorithm often finds integral optimal solutions. For the "hard" problems ($p = 2$, $n = 40$ and $p = 4, 5$) the algorithm usually improves the lower bound obtained from the LP-relaxation of (4.1) - (4.3). For the remaining problems ($n = 30$, $p = 2, 3$) neither did the algorithm find integral solutions nor could it noticeably improve the lower bounds.

Acknowledgements

We are grateful to Antoon Kolen for pointing out the inequalities (4.22) to us.

Chapter 5

A column generation approach to job grouping

5.1 Introduction

Several authors have stressed the influence of *tool management* on the overall performance of automated manufacturing facilities in general, and of flexible manufacturing systems (FMS) in particular (Gray, Seidmann and Stecke, 1988; Kiran and Krason, 1988). An FMS consists of a number of numerically controlled machines, linked by automated material handling devices, that perform the operations required to manufacture parts. The tools required by these operations are stored in a limited capacity tool magazine attached to each machine. An automated tool interchanging device enables the machine to interchange tools very quickly (in seconds). This fast tool interchanging capability avoids costly setups while producing with the tools available in the magazine, and is an essential feature of FMSs. When it becomes necessary to add tools to the tool magazine to allow new operations, the machine sometimes has to be shutdown while the tools are interchanged, after which the machine may resume production. The latter type of setup is time-consuming (it may take up to two hours). The performance of an FMS may therefore be considerably boosted by reducing the occurrences of these setups.

In this chapter we study a model which aims at minimizing the number of setups. We assume that a number of jobs must be processed on a single machine. The *job grouping problem* asks for a partition of the jobs into a minimum number of groups (batches), such that the jobs in each group do not require more tools than can be stored in the tool magazine (see Section 5.2 for a precise formulation of the model). This is equivalent to minimizing the number of setups in the situation described above.

The job grouping problem has been studied by different authors, who largely ignore each other. Hirabayashi, Suzuki and Tsuchiya (1984) refer to it as the 'optimal parts grouping problem' and propose a set covering formulation of it. They mention the possibility to solve this set covering formulation using a column generation approach, but concentrate in their paper on developing a branch-and-bound procedure for the column generation subproblem (see Section 5.2). Hwang (1986) investigates the equivalent 'optimal part type grouping problem'. He proposes to solve it approximately by sequentially creating groups that consist of a maximum number of jobs (this is in fact equivalent to solving the set covering formulation of the problem by a greedy heuristic; see Section 5.3). Hwang and Shogan (1989) use branch-and-bound to solve the sequence of subproblems. Hwang (1986) remarks that other sequential approaches (Whitney and Gaul, 1985) and group technology approaches (Chakravarty and Shtub, 1984) exist for part grouping problems, although the latter are inapplicable to FMS because they disregard tool magazine capacity limitations. In Hwang and Shogan (1989) the approach of Hwang (1986) is extended to allow the consideration of due dates. Rajagopalan (1985; 1986) gives a general model, which incorporates the job grouping problem as a special case. He presents a number of heuristic procedures for its solution (some of these will be presented in Section 5.3). Stecke and Kim (1988) have extended and made comparisons between the procedures of Rajagopalan (1985), Whitney and Gaul (1985) and Hwang (1986). Rajagopalan (1985; 1986) and Tang and Denardo (1988b) observe that partitioning jobs into a minimum number of batches can be seen as packing the jobs into a minimum number of bins with fixed capacity. It follows that the bin packing problem is a special case of the job grouping problem, and hence, that the latter is $\mathcal{N}P$-hard (Tang and Denardo, 1988b). Tang and Denardo (1988b) present a non-LP based branch-and-bound procedure for job grouping. They propose non-trivial lower bounds (see Section 5.2), and heuristics similar to Rajagopalan's (see Section 5.3). Kuhn (1990) has developed and tested more heuristics for job grouping. Related problems in process planning are also studied by Kusiak (1985b), Finke and Kusiak (1987) and Bard and Feo (1989).

In this chapter, we implement a column generation approach to solve the linear relaxation of the set covering formulation of the job grouping problem. We demonstrate experimentally that this approach leads to the derivation of extremely strong lower bounds (always equal, in our experiments, to the optimal value of the problem). The column generation scheme is presented in Section 5.2. In Section 5.3, heuristic solution procedures are suggested. The implementation of our procedures is described in Section 5.4. Section 5.5 reviews our computational experiments with these procedures. Section 5.6 contains some conclusions.

5.2   Lower bounds

In this section, we present formulations for the job grouping problem and explain the column generation approach we used to derive lower bounds on its optimal value. Some easier, but weaker lower bounds are also discussed.

5.2.1 The job grouping problem

The job grouping problem can be described by the following model (Hirabayashi et al., 1984; Hwang, 1986; Tang and Denardo, 1988b). Assume there are N jobs and M tools. The basic data are the capacity C of the tool magazine and the tool requirements for the jobs. These tool requirements are represented by a so-called tool-job matrix A of dimension $M \times N$, with:

$$a_{ki} = 1 \quad \text{if job } i \text{ requires tool } k$$
$$= 0 \quad \text{otherwise,}$$

for $k = 1, \ldots, M$ and $i = 1, \ldots, N$. We call a subset (group) S of jobs (or of columns of A) *feasible* if these jobs together require at most C tools, i.e. if $|\{k : \sum_{i \in S} a_{ki} \geq 1\}| \leq C$. The job grouping problem consists in finding a minimum set of feasible groups such that each job is contained in (at least) one group. To formulate this as a set covering problem, let us suppose that there exist P feasible groups, and let

$$q_{ij} = 1 \quad \text{if job } i \text{ is contained in the feasible group } j,$$
$$= 0 \quad \text{otherwise,}$$

for $i = 1, \ldots, N$ and $j = 1, \ldots, P$. The job grouping problem is:

$$\text{minimize} \quad \sum_{j=1}^{P} y_j \tag{5.1}$$

$$\text{subject to} \quad \sum_{j=1}^{P} q_{ij} y_j \geq 1 \qquad i = 1, \ldots, N, \tag{5.2}$$

$$y_j \geq 0 \qquad j = 1, \ldots, P, \tag{5.3}$$

$$y_j \text{ integer} \qquad j = 1, \ldots, P, \tag{5.4}$$

where $y_j = 1$ if group j is part of the optimal covering (notice that $y_j \in \{0, 1\}$ for $j = 1, \ldots, P$ in any optimal solution of (5.1) - (5.4)). Notice that an equivalent set covering model would be obtained if we restricted the set $\{1, \ldots, P\}$ to the subset of *maximal feasible* groups, i.e. to those feasible groups of jobs to which no more job can be added without destroying feasibility.

The main drawback of the formulation (5.1) - (5.4) is the possibly huge number of columns that it involves. Several authors report on efficient algorithms for solving large set covering problems to optimality (e.g. Balas and Ho (1980)), or for finding good heuristic solutions to such problems (e.g.

Nemhauser and Wolsey (1988) and Vasko and Wolf (1988)). Here, however, even generating the complete set covering formulation is a tedious task for larger instances (see Section 5.5, Table 5.6). In spite of this, we shall see in the next sections that it is possible to solve efficiently the LP-relaxation of (5.1) - (5.4), and that the optimal value of this relaxation provides a very strong lower bound on the optimal value of the set covering problem. The latter observation can only be seen as an empirical one, without theoretical basis. Indeed, it is known that the LP-relaxation of arbitrary set covering problems can be rather weak. On the other hand:

Theorem 5.1 *Any instance of the set covering problem can be interpreted as an instance of the job grouping problem, for some suitable choice of the tool-job incidence matrix and of the capacity.*

Proof:
Consider an arbitrary instance (SC) of the set covering problem, in the form (5.1) - (5.4). We associate with this instance the $P \times N$ tool-job matrix A defined by

$$a_{ji} = 1 - q_{ij} \qquad j = 1, \ldots, P; i = 1, \ldots, N,$$

and the capacity $C = P - 1$ (we assume without loss of generality that $Q = (q_{ij})$ has no zero row, so that A has no column involving $C + 1$ ones). We claim that the set covering formulation of the job grouping instance described by A and C is exactly (SC). Indeed, a subset S of jobs ($S \subseteq N$) is feasible for the instances described by (A, C) if and only if there exists a row j of A ($j \in \{1, \ldots, P\}$) such that $a_{ji} = 0$ for all $i \in S$, or, equivalently, if and only if there is a column j of (q_{ij}) such that $q_{ij} = 1$ for all $i \in S$. But this also means that the (maximal) columns of (q_{ij}) exactly correspond to the maximal feasible sets of jobs.   □

Notice, however, that the value of the tool magazine capacity occurring in this proof (namely, the total number of tools minus one) is not very realistic from the viewpoint of the job grouping problem. From a computational complexity viewpoint, Theorem 5.1 may be seen as a proof that the job grouping problem is $\mathcal{N}P$-hard (see also Tang and Denardo (1988b)). As a matter of fact, we can prove that the problem is $\mathcal{N}P$-hard even when $C = 3$ (transformation from the problem edge partition into triangles; Holyer (1981)) and that deciding whether there exists a partition of the jobs into two feasible groups is $\mathcal{N}P$-complete (this is equivalent to the block folding problem discussed in Möhring (1990)).

5.2.2 Column generation

To find a lower bound for the set covering problem, we want to solve the LP-relaxation of (5.1) - (5.4), i.e. the problem (5.1) - (5.3). We avoid the difficulty of explicitly generating all columns of this problem, by working with only a subset of the columns and adding new columns as needed. This approach was suggested by Gilmore and Gomory (1961) for solving cutting stock problems. It can also be seen as an essential part of the Dantzig-Wolfe decomposition (Dantzig and Wolfe, 1960). For a thorough discussion of column generation we point to Chvátal (1983), and we only briefly recall here the main features of the approach. At each iteration of the column generation procedure, we solve the LP obtained by restricting (5.1) - (5.3) to some subset T of columns, i.e. we solve a problem of the form:

$$\text{minimize} \quad \sum_{j \in T} y_j \tag{5.5}$$

$$\text{subject to} \quad \sum_{j \in T} q_{ij} y_j \geq 1 \qquad i = 1, \ldots, N, \tag{5.6}$$

$$y_j \geq 0 \qquad j \in T, \tag{5.7}$$

for some $T \subseteq \{1, \ldots, P\}$ (we shall indicate in Section 5.4 how an initial set T may be chosen). Let y^* be an optimal solution to (5.5) - (5.7) and λ^* be an optimal solution to the dual of (5.5) - (5.7). Consider also the dual of (5.1) - (5.3), in the form

$$\text{maximize} \quad \sum_{i=1}^{N} \lambda_i \tag{5.8}$$

$$\text{subject to} \quad \sum_{i=1}^{N} q_{ij} \lambda_i \leq 1 \qquad j = 1, \ldots, P, \tag{5.9}$$

$$\lambda_i \geq 0 \qquad i = 1, \ldots, N. \tag{5.10}$$

Observe that y^* satisfies the constraints (5.2), (5.3) and that $\sum_{j=1}^{P} y_j^* = \sum_{i=1}^{N} \lambda_i^*$ (we suppose here that y_j^* is extended to a vector of $\mathbb{R}^P$ by letting $y_j^* = 0$ for $j \notin T$). Hence, if λ^* satisfies all constraints (5.9), it follows from the duality theorem of linear programming theory (see Chvátal (1983)) that y^* is an optimal solution to the LP relaxation (5.1) - (5.3). In such a case, the column generation procedure does not need to proceed further. On the other hand, if λ^* does not satisfy (5.9), that is if there exists a column $j \in \{1, \ldots, P\}$ such that $\sum_{i=1}^{N} q_{ij} \lambda_i^* > 1$, then the current set T can be extended by this new index j, and a new iteration of the column generation

procedure can be started (alternatively, j can be seen as a column with
negative reduced cost for the relaxation (5.1) - (5.3)). Classical LP theory
ensures again that this procedure can be made to converge in a finite number
of iterations. In the next subsection, we discuss the question of finding a
violated constraint among (5.9).

5.2.3   The generation subproblem

The efficiency of column generation procedures is to a large extend determined by the complexity of the so-called *generation subproblem*, that is, in
our case of the subproblem:

given $\lambda_1^*, \ldots, \lambda_N^*$, is there $j \in \{1, \ldots, P\}$ such that $\displaystyle\sum_{i=1}^{N} q_{ij}\lambda_i^* > 1$?   (5.11)

In many successful applications of column generation, the subproblem is
relatively easy, e.g. solvable in polynomial or pseudo-polynomial time (see
e.g. Gilmore and Gomory (1961), Desrosiers, Soumis and Desrochers (1984),
Ribeiro, Minoux and Penna (1989), and Minoux (1987) for a general discussion). Other applications exist, however, where the subproblem itself turns
out to be hard (see e.g. Kavvadias and Papadimitriou (1989), Jaumard,
Hansen and Poggi de Aragão (1991)). In order to determine the complexity
of our subproblem, notice first that (5.11) can be rephrased as:

given $\lambda_1^*, \ldots, \lambda_N^*$, is there a feasible group S such that $\displaystyle\sum_{i \in S} \lambda_i^* > 1$?   (5.12)

Now, (5.12) could certainly be answered if we could find a feasible group
S which maximizes the expression $\sum_{i \in S} \lambda_i^*$ over all feasible groups. We may
express this reformulation of the subproblem as follows. Introduce variables

$$x_i = 1 \qquad \text{if job } i \text{ is in group } S$$
$$\quad= 0 \qquad \text{otherwise,}$$

for $i = 1, \ldots, N$, and

$$z_k = 1 \qquad \text{if tool } k \text{ is required by some job in } S,$$
$$\quad= 0 \qquad \text{otherwise,}$$

for $k = 1, \ldots, M$. The maximization version of (5.12) becomes (Hirabayashi
et al., 1984):

$$\text{maximize} \quad \sum_{i=1}^{N} \lambda_i^* x_i \tag{5.13}$$

subject to $a_{ki}x_i \leq z_k$ $i = 1, \ldots, N; k = 1, \ldots, M,$ (5.14)

$$\sum_{k=1}^{M} z_k \leq C \tag{5.15}$$

$$x_i \in \{0, 1\} \qquad i = 1, \ldots, N, \tag{5.16}$$

$$z_k \in \{0, 1\} \qquad k = 1, \ldots, M, \tag{5.17}$$

This problem is known to be $\mathcal{N}\mathcal{P}$-hard, even when $\lambda_1^* = \ldots = \lambda_N^* = 1$ (Gallo, Hammer and Simeone, 1980). Notice that, when $\lambda_1^* = \ldots = \lambda_N^* = 1$, (5.13) -(5.17) boils down to determining a feasible group that contains as many jobs as possible; this subproblem has been considered by Hwang (1986) and Hwang and Shogan (1989). Problem (5.13) - (5.17) (and generalizations thereof) has been investigated by a number of authors. Hirabayashi et al. (1984) developed a branch-and-bound procedure for it. To obtain an upper bound, they solve the linear relaxation of the problem by a specialized primal-dual algorithm. Mamer and Shogan (1987) use a Lagrangian method with the help of subgradient optimization to solve the relaxation of (5.13) - (5.17). This approach has been developed further by Gallo and Simeone (1988) (see also Chaillou, Hansen and Mahieu (1989)). Dietrich, Lee and Lee (1991) present a heuristic procedure for the problem (see Section 5.4). They also use the LP-relaxation for obtaining an upper bound, and present some valid inequalities to improve this bound and to fasten up the branch-and-bound search. From a practical viewpoint, (5.13) - (5.17) remains a hard problem to solve. In particular, experimental results of Dietrich et al. (1991) show a large gap between the LP-relaxation value and the optimal value of (5.13) - (5.17). Our own experience also indicates that the LP-relaxation is generally weak. Especially in the case where optimality in the column generation procedure is nearly reached (i.e. where the generation subproblem has an optimal value close to 1), the gap between LP- and IP-formulation is considerable (often larger than 2). This results in large search trees when attacking (5.13) - (5.17) by branch-and-bound. Another drawback of solving (5.13) - (5.17) to optimality is that this only allows one new column of the set covering problem to be generated in each iteration (i.e., we find only one violated inequality of type (5.9)). This may lead to a large number of iterations of the column generation procedure. Because we are using the LP package LINDO in our experiments, and this package does not allow to add columns to a model in a dynamic fashion, one new LP problem has to be reoptimized from scratch in each such iteration, a rather costly operation. In view of all these considerations, we decided to use a complete enumeration procedure for the solution of the generation subproblem. Thus, in terms of the formulation (5.12), we are not only interested in finding one group S for which $\sum_{i \in S} \lambda_i^* > 1$, but in finding all (or many) such groups. All the corresponding columns may enter the set covering formulation, and this tends to reduce the number of iterations of the column generation procedure. The enumeration procedure works as follows. First, we sort the dual variables by nonincreasing values, say e.g. $\lambda_1^* \geq \lambda_2^* \geq \ldots \geq \lambda_N^*$. Then we grow a binary tree, by successively attempting to include or not to include each of the jobs $1, 2, \ldots, N$ in a feasible group. Early on in the column generation procedure, the λ_i^*'s are bad estimates of the optimal dual variables, and hence the enumeration procedure produces very quickly a large number of feasible groups S with $\sum_{i \in S} \lambda_i^* > 1$. Therefore, the total number of columns that is generated in one iteration is limited to a fixed arbitrary number (100 in our implementation). For the instance sizes which we considered in our experiments, the enumeration procedure always remained manageable (see Section 5.5).

5.2.4 Computation of lower bounds via column generation

The column generation procedure can be summarized as follows (see Section 5.4 for details about its implementation):

Initialization: Generate an initial set T of columns of the set covering formulation (5.1) - (5.3).

LP Solution: Solve the LP (5.5)-(5.7); let y^* and λ^* be optimal primal and dual solutions of (5.5)-(5.7).

Column Generation: Generate new columns by solving the generation subproblem: that is, find indices $j \in \{1, \ldots, P\}$ such that $\sum_{i=1}^{N} q_{ij} \lambda_i^* > 1$, and let $T \leftarrow T \cup \{j\}$ for each such j. If no such new columns can be found then STOP: y^* is an optimal solution of (5.1) - (5.3); otherwise return to LP Solution.

When the column generation procedure stops we have an optimal solution y^* for the LP relaxation (5.1) - (5.3). Rounding up the solution value $\sum_{j \in T} y_j^*$ to the next integer gives a lower bound for the job grouping problem. We will refer to the bound $\lceil \sum_{j \in T} y_j^* \rceil$ as LB_{CG}.

It is also possible to compute weaker lower bounds on the optimal value of the job grouping problem before the column generation procedure terminates. To see this, let Z denote the optimal value of the generation subproblem (5.13) - (5.17), as computed for instance in some iteration of the column generation step (for the results below to be valid, the λ_i^* may actually be arbitrary numbers in $[0,1]$, and do not necessarily need to arise from the LP solution step). Farley (1990) observed the following:

Theorem 5.2 *If $Z \geq 1$, then $\sum_{i=1}^{N} \lambda_i^*/Z$ is a lower bound on the optimal value of (5.1) - (5.3).*

Proof:
By definition, Z is the maximum value of $\sum_{i=1}^{N} q_{ij}\lambda_i^*$ over j (see (5.11)). Thus, λ^*/Z is a feasible solution for the dual (5.8) - (5.10) of (5.1) - (5.3), and it follows that $\sum_{i=1}^{N} \lambda_i^*/Z$ is a valid lower bound for (5.1) - (5.3).   □

Another lower bound can also be derived as follows:

Theorem 5.3 *If $Z \geq 1$, then $\sum_{i=1}^{N} \lambda_i^* + N \cdot (1 - Z)$ is a lower bound on the optimal value of (5.1) - (5.3).*

Proof:
Let y^* be an optimal solution of (5.1) - (5.3). Notice that $\sum_{i=1}^{N} q_{ij} y_j^* \geq 1$ $(i = 1, \ldots, N)$ and $\sum_{j=1}^{P} y_j^* \leq N$. Hence,

$$\sum_{j=1}^{P} y_j^* \geq \sum_{j=1}^{P} y_j^* + \sum_{i=1}^{N}(1 - \sum_{j=1}^{P} q_{ij} y_j^*)\lambda_i^*$$
$$= \sum_{i=1}^{N} \lambda_i^* + \sum_{j=1}^{P}(1 - \sum_{i=1}^{N} q_{ij}\lambda_i^*)y_j^*$$
$$\geq \sum_{i=1}^{N} \lambda_i^* + (1 - Z)\sum_{j=1}^{P} y_j^*$$
$$\geq \sum_{i=1}^{N} \lambda_i^* + N(1 - Z).$$
□

Theorem 5.4 *If $Z > 1$, then $\sum_{i=1}^{N} \lambda_i^*/Z > \sum_{i=1}^{N} \lambda_i^* + N \cdot (1 - Z)$.*

Proof:
Trivial.   □

Theorem 5.4 shows that the bound given in Theorem 5.3 is strictly better than the bound in Theorem 5.2 whenever $Z > 1$. When $Z = 1$, both bounds coincide with the optimal value of (5.1) - (5.3). Thus, we will only consider from now on the stronger bound $\sum_{i=1}^{N} \lambda_i^*/Z$. More precisely, we define

$$LB_{Farley} = \lceil \sum_{i=1}^{N} \lambda_i^* / Z \rceil$$

LB_{Farley} is obviously a valid lower bound on the optimal value of the job grouping problem. As the column generation proceeds, Z approaches 1 and LB_{Farley} approaches the lower bound LB_{CG} (see Farley (1990)).

5.2.5 Lagrangian relaxation

In this subsection, we present an alternative integer programming model for the job grouping problem and we discuss the quality of the bounds that it yields, either by continuous relaxation or by Lagrangian relaxation. In this model, a variable x_{ij} is used to denote the assignment of job i to one of N groups, indexed by j $(i = 1, \ldots, N; j = 1, \ldots, N)$ (one may best think of the N groups as being initially empty). We use the following notation

$$
\begin{aligned}
x_{ij} &= 1 \quad \text{if job } i \text{ is assigned to group } j, \\
&= 0 \quad \text{otherwise,} \\
y_j &= 1 \quad \text{if group } j \text{ is non-empty,} \\
&= 0 \quad \text{otherwise,} \\
z_{kj} &= 1 \quad \text{if tool } k \text{ is used for the production of group } j, \\
&= 0 \quad \text{otherwise,}
\end{aligned}
$$

for $i = 1, \ldots, N, j = 1, \ldots, N, k = 1, \ldots, M$.
The model is now:

$$\text{minimize} \quad \sum_{j=1}^{N} y_j \tag{5.18}$$

$$\text{subject to} \quad \sum_{j=1}^{N} x_{ij} = 1 \qquad i = 1, \ldots, N, \tag{5.19}$$

$$a_{ki} x_{ij} \leq z_{kj} \qquad i = 1, \ldots, N; j = 1, \ldots, N; k = 1, \ldots, M, \tag{5.20}$$

$$\sum_{k=1}^{M} z_{kj} \leq C y_j \qquad j = 1, \ldots, N, \tag{5.21}$$

$$y_j \in \{0, 1\} \qquad j = 1, \ldots, N, \tag{5.22}$$

$$x_{ij} \in \{0, 1\} \qquad i = 1, \ldots, N; j = 1, \ldots, N, \tag{5.23}$$

$$z_{kj} \in \{0, 1\} \qquad j = 1, \ldots, N; k = 1, \ldots, M. \tag{5.24}$$

The objective function (5.18) minimizes the number of nonempty groups. Restrictions (5.19) make sure that each job is assigned to some group. Restrictions (5.20) assure that the tools needed for a job are available for the production of the group to which the job is assigned. Restrictions (5.21) describe the tool magazine capacity constraints for each group. The continuous relaxation of this model yields a weak lower bound on the optimal value. Indeed, the solution $x_{ij} = 1/N, z_{kj} = 1/N$ and $y_j = M/CN$, $(i = 1, \ldots, N; j = 1, \ldots, N; k = 1, \ldots, M)$ is feasible, with an objective function value of M/C (which is trivially a valid lower bound; see Section 5.2.6). Lagrangian relaxation could be used to compute a stronger bound. For instance, if we dualize restrictions (5.19) with multipliers $\lambda_1^*, \ldots, \lambda_N^*$, we obtain a lower bound $LB_{lr}(\lambda)$ by solving:

$$LB_{LR}(\lambda) = \quad \text{minimize} \quad \sum_{j=1}^{N} y_j + \sum_{i=1}^{N} \lambda_i \left(1 - \sum_{j=1}^{N} x_{ij}\right) \qquad (5.25)$$
$$\text{subject to} \quad (5.20) - (5.24).$$

Up to deletion of an additive constant, $\sum_{i=1}^{N} \lambda_i$, this problem can be equivalently rewritten as

$$\text{minimize} \quad \sum_{j=1}^{N} \left(y_j - \sum_{i=1}^{N} \lambda_i x_{ij}\right) \qquad (5.26)$$
$$\text{subject to} \quad (5.20) - (5.24).$$

Now problem (5.26), (5.20) - (5.24) can be decomposed into N identical subproblems, one for each value of $j = 1, \ldots, N$. Deleting the index j, the generic form of each subproblem is:

$$\text{minimize} \quad y - \sum_{i=1}^{N} \lambda_i x_i \qquad (5.27)$$
$$\text{subject to} \quad a_{ki} x_i \le z_k \qquad i = 1, \ldots, N; k = 1, \ldots, M, \qquad (5.28)$$
$$\sum_{k=1}^{M} z_k \le C \cdot y \qquad (5.29)$$
$$y \in \{0, 1\} \qquad (5.30)$$
$$x_i \in \{0, 1\} \qquad i = 1, \ldots, N, \qquad (5.31)$$
$$z_k \in \{0, 1\} \qquad k = 1, \ldots, M. \qquad (5.32)$$

If $y = 0$ in the optimal solution of (5.27) - (5.32), then also $z_k = 0$ for $k = 1, \ldots, M, x_i = 0$ for $i = 1, \ldots, N$, and the optimal value is 0. If

$y = 1$ at optimality, then minimizing the objective function (5.27) becomes equivalent to maximizing $\sum_{i=1}^{N} \lambda_i x_i$. Therefore, we conclude that the subproblem arising via this Lagrangian relaxation is essentially equivalent to the subproblem (5.13) - (5.17) arising via column generation. Denote by Z, as usual, the maximum of $\sum_{i=1}^{N} \lambda_i x_i$ under the constraints (5.28) - (5.32). The previous discussion shows that the optimal value of (5.27) - (5.32) is equal to $\min(0, 1 - Z)$. This in turn implies that the lower bounds $LB_{LR}(\lambda)$, computed from (5.25), (5.20) - (5.24), is equal to $\sum_{i=1}^{N} \lambda_i + N \cdot \min(0, 1 - Z)$. As we already know, this bound is weaker than LB_{Farley} for all λ such that $Z > 1$ (see Theorem 5.4), and coincides with the optimal value of (5.1) - (5.3) when $Z \leq 1$. Thus, the Lagrangian relaxation approach described here does not yield better bounds than the column generation procedure. Observe that a "best possible" choice of the multipliers $\lambda_1, \ldots, \lambda_N$, i.e. one leading to the maximum value of $LB_{LR}(\lambda)$, could be searched for by a subgradient optimization procedure (Fisher, 1981) or by a multiplier adjustment procedure (Fisher, Jaikumar and Van Wassenhove, 1986). The column generation procedure can also be seen as using an LP-solver to adjust the values of the multipliers. The Lagrangian relaxation approach will not be considered any further in this work.

5.2.6   Other lower bounds

We discuss in this subsection some more lower bounds for the job grouping problem. By duality, the optimal value of the problem (5.8) - (5.10) is equal to the optimal value of (5.1) - (5.3), i.e. (up to rounding) LB_{CG}. Thus, the optimal value of (5.8) - (5.10) under the additional restriction

$$\lambda_i \in \{0,1\} \qquad i = 1, \ldots, N, \tag{5.33}$$

is a lower bound on LB_{CG}; we denote it by LB_{SP}. This lower bound can be interpreted as follows. Call two jobs compatible if they form a feasible group and incompatible otherwise. Then, LB_{SP} is nothing but the maximum number of pairwise incompatible jobs. The problem (5.8) - (5.10), (5.33) is a so-called set packing problem. Conversely, a construction similar to the one used for Theorem 5.1 shows that any instance of the set packing problem can arise in that way. It follows from this observation that computing LB_{SP} is $\mathcal{N}P$-hard (see e.g. Nemhauser and Wolsey (1988) p. 117).

Tang and Denardo (1988b) propose a lower bound which is also based on the concept of compatibility of jobs. In their so-called sweeping procedure, they sequentially create a number of groups as follows. In each step of the procedure, they first select a job (seed) which is compatible with the fewest number of other (not yet selected) jobs (in case of a tie, the job for which the set of compatible jobs requires the smallest number of tools is selected). Next, the seed, along with all jobs which are compatible with it, are selected to form one group. The procedure is repeated until all jobs have been selected. The number of groups so created, say L (i.e., the number of steps of the sweeping procedure) is a valid lower bound for the job grouping problem. In fact, L can best be seen as a lower bound on LB_{SP}, since the seeds are mutually incompatible, and hence define a feasible solution of the set packing problem (5.8) -(5.10), (5.33). From this viewpoint, the sweeping procedure is a greedy heuristic applied to (5.8) -(5.10), (5.33).

Tang and Denardo (1988b) also point to the lower bound $\lceil M/C \rceil$. Combining this bound with L yields the lower bound $LB_{SW} = \max \{\lceil M/C \rceil, L\}$ (Tang and Denardo, 1988b).

The lower bound LB_{SW} can be further improved by "incorporating" the lower bound $\lceil M/C \rceil$, in the sweeping procedure. More precisely, a lower bound for the job grouping problem can be calculated in each step of the sweeping procedure by summing the number of already created groups by the sweeping procedure and the lower bound $\lceil |\cup_{i \in I} T_i|/C \rceil$, where I is the set of "not yet selected" jobs, and T_i is the set of tools needed by job i. This procedure generates a sequence of valid lower bounds, the first of which is equal to $\lceil M/C \rceil$, and the last of which is equal to L. We refer to this procedure as the "modified sweeping procedure". It yields a new lower bound, equal to the maximum of the bounds in the sequence, which we denote by LB_{MSW}.

We have considered a number of lower bounds for the job grouping problem. Summarizing we have:

- $LB_{Farley} \leq LB_{CG}$ (see Section 5.2.4)

- $LB_{LR} \leq LB_{Farley}$ (see Section 5.2.5)

- $LB_{SP} \leq LB_{CG}$ (Duality)

- $LB_{SW} \leq LB_{MSW}$ (see this section)

In our implementation we use the bound LB_{MSW} for its computational simplicity and the lower bounds LB_{Farley} and LB_{CG} if LB_{MSW} is not strong enough.

5.3   Upper bounds

In this section a number of heuristic methods will be described to compute good solutions for the job grouping problem and hence upper bounds on its optimal value. First, we will describe a number of procedures that sequentially build groups. The second part will discuss procedures based on solving the set covering formulation.

5.3.1   Sequential heuristics for grouping

Sequential heuristic procedures use a two-step approach for building each group. In the first step, a job is picked to be used as a seed. Unless explained otherwise, we always pick a job that requires the highest number of tools. Then a selection rule is used to add jobs to the group until the tool magazine capacity constraint prohibits the addition of any other job to this group. The two-step procedure is repeated until all jobs are assigned to some group. For selecting the next job to be assigned to a group (in step 2) a number of different rules have been considered. We now describe them. For a group S and a job $i \notin S$, let

t_i = number of tools required by job i;

b_i = number of tools required both by job i and by some job already in S.

1. *MIMU rule*

   Tang and Denardo (1988b) select the job that has the largest number of tools in common with the jobs already in the group. In case of a tie, the job which requires the smallest number of additional tools is selected. The procedure is called Maximal Intersection Minimal Union. (Maximize b_i ; in case of a tie minimize t_i)

2. *MI rule*

   This is the rule obtained if only the first part of the MIMU rule is used, and ties are arbitrarily broken. (Maximize b_i)

3. *MU rule*

   It is also possible to select jobs according only to the Minimal Union criterion: select the job that requires a minimum number of additional tools. (Minimize $(t_i - b_i)$)

4. *Whitney and Gaul rule*

   Whitney and Gaul (1985) favour jobs that bring with them a large number of versatile tools. This idea is operationalized by selecting a job for which the ratio $(b_i + 1)/(t_i + 1)$ is maximal. (Maximize $(b_i + 1)/(t_i + 1)$)

5. *Rajagopalan rule*

   Rajagopalan (1985) proposes a number of procedures based on the First Fit Decreasing rule for bin-packing. Among these, we consider one that first assigns weights to the tools and then selects the job that requires the most 'expensive' tools. More precisely, each tool k receives a weight a_k equal to the number of jobs that require tool k among the jobs that still have to be assigned to a group. Then, the priority of job i is calculated by summing the weights a_k of the tools that must be added to the tool magazine in case job i is assigned to the group. The job with the largest priority is selected first. For this rule, the first job in each group (seed) is also selected according to the same criterion.

6. *Modified Rajagopalan rule*

   The procedure of Rajagopalan (1985) can be changed in the following way: the weight a_k for each tool k is defined as the number of jobs that require tool k among the jobs already selected in the group. The priority of a job is the sum of the weights of the tools that are needed for that job. The job with the highest priority is selected.

7. *Marginal gain rule*

   The addition of job i to a group usually requires that extra tools be loaded in the tool magazine. This new tool configuration may in turn allow the execution of other, not yet selected, jobs; denote by p_i the number of such jobs. This rule selects a job i that maximizes p_i (a similar idea is used by Dietrich et al. (1991)).

5.3.2   Set covering heuristics

In the course of the column generation procedure, several set covering subproblems of type (5.5) - (5.7) are formulated. Each such subproblem can be viewed as an approximation of the complete formulation (5.1) - (5.4). In particular, each feasible solution of the system (5.6) - (5.7) is a feasible solution of (5.2) - (5.3), and hence each 0-1 solution of (5.6) - (5.7) defines a heuristic solution to the job grouping problem. We have used this observation in various ways. First, the solution of (5.5) - (5.7) found by LINDO during the column generation procedure sometimes happens to be a 0-1 solution which improves upon the current best solution. Such solutions can be detected with very little additional computational effort and may avoid the use of other upper bounding procedures.

It is also possible to systematically generate "good" 0-1 solutions of the subproblem (5.5) - (5.7). This can be done using either a heuristic procedure or an exact algorithm. We have considered both possibilities. As a heuristic, we used the well-known greedy procedure (Nemhauser and Wolsey, 1988 p. 466); this constructive heuristic recursively selects as next group (column) one which contains a maximum number of jobs, until all jobs are included in some group (i.e. are covered by some column). Alternatively, subproblem (5.5) - (5.7) could also be solved to optimality in 0-1 variables, by relying on the capability of LINDO to handle integer programming problems. In view of the computational burden involved in this approach, we chose to turn it into a heuristic by requiring only a small number of variables to be integer. We only used this heuristic when the column generation procedure ended without an optimal solution. We will explain in Section 5.4 the implementational details of this approach.

5.4   Implementation

In Sections 5.2 and 5.3, an overview has been given of the methods that can be used for obtaining lower bounds and upper bounds for the job grouping problem. Also, the general principle of the column generation procedure and the difficulty of solving the generation problem have been discussed. Now, we focus on implementational issues. The procedure that we implemented consists of four main steps. We first briefly sketch the whole procedure before commenting on each individual step.

Step I: Use the heuristics of Section 5.3.1. to produce a first upper bound. Compute the simple lower bounds LB_{SW} and LB_{MSW}. If optimality is achieved then STOP. Otherwise construct an initial set covering formulation using the groups that have been generated using the heuristic procedures.

Step II: Use the greedy heuristic to solve the initial set covering formulation. If optimality is achieved then STOP. Otherwise use a heuristic to add a number of columns to the initial formulation. Solve again the resulting set covering formulation using the greedy procedure. If optimality is achieved then STOP.

Step III: Solve the LP-relaxation of the current formulation. Check whether the primal solution is integral and whether its value improves the current upper bound. Use the dual variables to formulate the generation subproblem and generate new columns with negative reduced cost. Calculate LB_{Farley}. If optimality is achieved then STOP. If no columns with negative reduced cost have been found, then continue with Step IV. Otherwise, update the set covering formulation and repeat Step III.

Step IV: Use the last set covering formulation for finding an improved heuristic solution.

In Step I an upper bound is obtained by using the 7 heuristics of Section 5.3.1 and retaining the best solution. A lower bound is obtained by calculating the bounds LB_{SW} and LB_{MSW} of Section 5.2.6. If the lower bound equals the upper bound, the procedure stops and steps II-IV are not necessary. Otherwise the groups generated by the heuristics are used to generate an initial set covering formulation of the problem.

Step II aims at improving the initial formulation and the current upper bound before starting the column generation procedure. The first set covering formulation is solved using the greedy heuristic (Section 5.3.2.). If optimality is not established yet, then a heuristic based on the work of Dietrich et al. (1991) is used for generating additional columns as follows. Each job is considered as a seed, around which a group is built by iteratively adding that job i for which the ratio $p_i/(t_i - b_i)$ is maximal, where $(t_i - b_i)$ is the number of additional tools needed for job i and p_i is the number of additional jobs that may be executed with the new set of tools in the tool magazine (see Section 5.3.1). In this way N (number of jobs) new groups (i.e. columns) are constructed and used to extend the set covering formulation. This new formulation is solved again using the greedy heuristic. Notice that the second part of step II is time consuming (see Section 5.5.2); this is the main reason why we first apply the greedy heuristic to the initial formulation rather than directly extending this formulation.

The third step is critical to the procedure. First, the LP-relaxation of the current set covering formulation is solved using the linear programming package LINDO. The primal and dual solutions are stored, and the primal solution is checked for integrality. If it is integral and involves fewer groups than the current best solution, then its value is stored as a new upper bound. The dual variables are then used in the generation subproblem. This problem is solved using the enumeration strategy described in Section 5.2.3. In the first steps of the column generation procedure only a limited enumeration takes place because of (the self-imposed) maximum of 100 columns that may be generated by the enumeration procedure. When a complete enumeration is performed, the optimal value Z of the generation subproblem is used for computing the bound LB_{Farley}. If this lower bound is equal to the upper bound the procedure stops. If no new column has been generated (i.e. $Z = 1$ and $LB_{Farley} = LB_{CG}$), then the column generation subroutine terminates, and we continue with step IV. Otherwise, the new columns are added to the set covering formulation. Also, to limit the size of the formulation, all columns with a small reduced cost are eliminated. More precisely, columns for which $\sum_{i=1}^{N} q_{ij}\lambda_i < 1 - \alpha$ are removed from the formulation, where α is an arbitrary chosen parameter ($\alpha = 0.25$ in our implementation). This may cause the procedure to cycle, as columns are removed from the formulation, then enter it again, etc. In our tests (with $\alpha = 0.25$) cycling occurred for 4 instances out of 550, but could be avoided when the procedure was run anew with α set to a larger value.

When there is still a gap between the upper and lower bound generated in Steps I-III, more work has to be done. A branch-and- bound procedure could be used to establish optimality. However, it is also possible to use the last set covering formulation to improve the upper bound, as we explained in Section 5.3.2. In our implementation, we first solve this formulation by the greedy heuristic. If this is not effective, we solve a slightly modified set covering formulation with LINDO, requiring only a limited number of variables to take 0-1 values. More precisely, the T variables which assume the largest value in the continuous solution of the set covering formulation (where columns for which $\sum_{i=1}^{N} q_{ij}\lambda_i < 1 - \beta$ are removed to limit the size of the formulation, with $\beta = 0.10$), extended by the additional constraint $\sum_{j=1}^{P} y_j \geq LB_{CG}$, are forced to be integer. The parameter T is taken equal to $LB_{CG} + 5$ if the number of columns is smaller than 50 (resp. $LB_{CG} + 15$ if the number of columns is between 50 and 150, and $LB_{CG} + 25$ otherwise). Because of the small number of integer variables, the resulting mixed 0-1 problem is easily solved by branch-and-bound.

Notice that the choices made for the various parameters of the procedure (maximum number of columns generated in each iteration, α, T, β) influence the sequence of LP subproblems generated, and hence also the heuristic solutions produced in Steps III and IV. These choices may sometimes determine whether an optimal solution is found or not by the procedure.

At the end of the procedure, a lower bound and an upper bound have been obtained. In the next section, we discuss our computational experiments with this procedure, and we show that both bounds often coincide (and hence, are optimal).

5.5 Computational experiments

5.5.1 Generation of problem instances

We generated three sets of random instances. The first set contains 120 instances, the second set 400 instances and the third set 30 instances. Each instance falls into an instance type, characterized by the size (M, N) of the tool-job matrix and the value C of the capacity. Accordingly, we denote the type of an instance by a triple (M, N, C). The first set of instances contains 12 instance types obtained by combining each of the matrix sizes (20,15), (40,30) or (60,40) with four different capacity values C_1, C_2, C_3, C_4, as indicated in Table 5.1. For each size (M, N), we also define a pair (Min,Max) of parameters with the following interpretation:

- Min = lower bound on the number of tools per job,
- Max = upper bound on the number of tools per job.

The second set of instances was created according to rules suggested by Tang and Denardo (1988b) in order to allow some comparison with the results of these authors. It involves four instance types, defined by the values of the parameters displayed in Table 5.2.

Problem size M × N	C_1	C_2	C_3	C_4	Min	Max
20 × 15	6	8	10	12	2	6
40 × 30	15	17	20	25	5	15
60 × 40	20	22	25	30	7	20

Table 5.1 Parameters first set of instances.

Problem size M × N	C_1	Min	Max
10 × 10	4	1	3
15 × 20	8	1	7
20 × 30	10	1	9
25 × 30	10	1	9

Table 5.2 Parameters second set of instances.

For each problem size (M, N) in the first (resp. second) set, 10 (resp. 100) random matrices A were generated. For each $j = 1, \ldots, N$, the j-th column of A was generated as follows. First, an integer t_j was drawn from the uniform distribution over [Min,Max]: this number denotes the number of tools needed for job j, i.e. the number of 1's in the j-th column of A. Next, a set T_j of t_j distinct integers were drawn from the uniform distribution over $[1, M]$: these integers denote the tools required by job j, i.e. $a_{kj} = 1$ if and only if $k \in T_j$. Finally, we checked whether $T_j \subseteq T_i$ or $T_i \subseteq T_j$ held for any $i < j$. If any of these inclusions was found to hold, then the previous choice of T_j was cancelled, and a new set T_j was generated (as observed by Tang and Denardo (1988b) the job grouping problem trivially simplifies by removal of the columns included in other columns of the tool-job matrix). A problem instance of type (M, N, C) is now obtained by combining an $M \times N$ tool-job matrix A with one of the corresponding capacities displayed in Tables 5.1 and 5.2. The random instances described above are similar to those generated e.g. by Rajagopalan (1985), Tang and Denardo (1988b), Hwang and Shogan (1989) and Kuhn (1990). It turns out that, for these instances, the feasible groups of jobs are usually rather small (typically, 2 to 5 jobs). This can be explained by the fact that the tool requirements of the jobs are completely independent of each other, and that large subsets of jobs are therefore unlikely to be compatible. This lack of interdependence between jobs is, however, unlikely to reflect the structure of "realistic" tool-job matrices. Indeed, real-world instances are more likely to exhibit subsets of "similar" jobs, characterized by "similar" tool requirements. Our third set of random instances results from an attempt to capture this type of features. The parameters for this set are displayed in Table 5.3.

Problem size M × N	C	Min	Max	Minjob	Maxjob
40 × 40	20	7	10	5	8
50 × 50	25	8	12	6	10
60 × 60	30	10	15	8	12

Table 5.3 Parameters third set of instances.

Ten instances of each type (M, N, C) were generated as follows. First, a number N_1 is drawn uniformly between Minjob and Maxjob, and a subset of tools M_1 of size exactly C is randomly chosen. Then, we create N_1 "similar" jobs, by making sure that these jobs use only the tools in M_1

(and hence, form a feasible group). These jobs are generated as explained before for the first and the second sets of instances (except that they are restricted to the tools in M_1). When N_1 jobs have been defined, then the procedure is iterated to produce $N_2, N_3, \ldots$ additional jobs. This process stops after k iterations, when almost all columns of the incidence matrix have been generated (specifically, when $\sum_{i=1}^{k} N_i \geq N-\text{Maxjob}$). Then, the last columns are filled independently of each other, as for the first two sets of instances.

This completes the description of our problem instances. It will be observed in the next section that the degree of difficulty of these instances is somewhat related to the relative size of the capacity with respect to the maximum number of tools used by the jobs (viz. the parameter Max). We call sparse those problem instances for which Max/C is small, and dense those for which the ratio is close to 1. Notice, in particular, that all instances of type (M, N, C_1) are dense, and that the instances of type (M, N, C_4), as well as the instances in the third set, are rather sparse.

5.5.2 Computational results

The column generation procedure has been implemented as described in Section 5.4, using Turbo Pascal, and tested on the instances described in Section 5.5.1. The experiments were run on an AT personal computer with 16 MHz 80386sx processor and 80387 mathematical coprocessor. No systematic attempts have been made to optimize the running times of the codes, because our primary goal was to establish the quality of the bounds computed.

Before going into detailed comments, we mention what we see as our two most interesting results. First, for all instances tested, the gap between the LP-relaxation of the set covering formulation and the value of the optimal solution was smaller than 1. In other words the column generation procedure always provided a lower bound LB_{CG} equal to the optimal value of the job grouping problem (note, however, that this empirical observation is definitely not a theorem: indeed, it follows from Theorem 5.1 that LB_{CG} can, for some possibly contrived examples, be arbitrarily far from the optimal value). Second, using the column generation procedure described in Section 5.4.1 we were able to solve 541 of our 550 instances to optimality. Moreover, all instances have been solved to optimality by variants of the same procedure, characterized by different choices of the parameters (number of new columns generated in each iteration, value of the reduced costs under which columns are deleted, etc.).

Table 5.4 Quality of lower and upper bounds.

Instance type M x N	C	OPT	Lower bounds						Upper bounds				
			LB_SW	LB_MSW	LB_CC	MIMU	MI	MU	Whitney and Gaul	Rajago-palan	Modified Rajago-palan	Marginal gain	Best
		1	2	3	4	5	6	7	8	9	10	11	12
20 x 15	6	9.3	-0.5 (5)	-0.4 (6)	0 (10)	0.3 (10)	0.3 (10)	0.4 (9)	0.3 (10)	1.1 (3)	0.3 (10)	0.5 (8)	0.3 (7)
	8	5.7	-1.2 (1)	-1.2 (1)	0 (10)	0.4 (7)	0.2 (9)	0.7 (4)	0.5 (6)	0.8 (4)	0.1 (10)	0.6 (5)	0.1 (9)
	10	3.9	-1.9 (0)	-1.8 (0)	0 (10)	0.4 (7)	0.4 (7)	0.6 (5)	0.4 (7)	1.0 (2)	0.4 (7)	0.6 (5)	0.1 (9)
	12	2.9	-0.9 (1)	-0.9 (1)	0 (10)	0.2 (9)	0.3 (8)	0.6 (5)	0.3 (8)	0.9 (3)	0.3 (8)	0.5 (6)	0.1 (9)
40 x 30	15	19.0	-0.7 (5)	-0.3 (7)	0 (10)	0.3 (7)	0.0 (10)	0.6 (5)	0.2 (8)	0.8 (3)	0.0 (10)	0.3 (7)	0.0 (10)
	17	15.5	-0.7 (5)	-0.7 (5)	0 (10)	0.3 (8)	0.2 (9)	0.6 (5)	0.2 (9)	1.1 (1)	0.1 (10)	0.6 (5)	0.1 (9)
	20	10.9	-2.1 (0)	-2.0 (1)	0 (10)	0.9 (7)	0.6 (10)	1.6 (2)	1.0 (6)	2.4 (0)	0.6 (10)	1.4 (3)	0.6 (4)
	25	6.7	-4.7 (0)	-4.3 (0)	0 (10)	0.9 (10)	0.9 (10)	1.9 (0)	1.0 (9)	3.0 (0)	0.9 (10)	2.0 (1)	0.9 (1)
60 x 40	20	25.9	-0.8 (5)	-0.6 (7)	0 (10)	0.5 (8)	0.3 (10)	0.6 (7)	0.4 (9)	0.9 (4)	0.3 (10)	0.6 (7)	0.3 (7)
	22	22.3	-8.6 (2)	-8.6 (2)	0 (10)	0.6 (5)	0.1 (10)	1.0 (3)	0.5 (6)	1.4 (0)	0.1 (10)	0.7 (5)	0.1 (9)
	25	17.0	-9.6 (0)	-9.6 (0)	0 (10)	1.5 (3)	0.8 (9)	2.5 (0)	1.6 (1)	2.3 (0)	0.7 (10)	1.9 (0)	0.7 (3)
	30	12.0	-7.0 (0)	-6.9 (0)	0 (10)	1.3 (6)	0.9 (10)	2.8 (0)	1.3 (6)	3.9 (0)	1.0 (9)	3.2 (0)	0.9 (1)
10 x 10	4	5.1	-0.7 (38)	-0.5 (54)	0 (100)	0.2 (95)	0.2 (95)	0.5 (62)	0.2 (95)	0.6 (58)	0.2 (95)	0.5 (65)	0.1 (87)
15 x 20	8	9.3	-0.7 (45)	-0.5 (57)	0 (100)	0.4 (88)	0.4 (90)	0.7 (65)	0.5 (83)	1.2 (31)	0.4 (89)	0.8 (59)	0.3 (68)
25 x 30	10	15.0	-0.7 (47)	-0.5 (62)	0 (100)	0.5 (79)	0.4 (90)	0.9 (43)	0.5 (73)	1.5 (11)	0.4 (90)	0.8 (50)	0.3 (75)
20 x 30	10	14.0	-0.8 (39)	-0.6 (45)	0 (100)	0.5 (81)	0.4 (92)	1.3 (26)	0.6 (73)	1.7 (15)	0.4 (91)	1.1 (33)	0.3 (66)
40 x 40	20	6.2	-4.2 (0)	-4.2 (0)	0 (10)	1.0 (6)	0.8 (8)	0.8 (8)	1.0 (6)	5.9 (0)	1.1 (6)	1.4 (3)	0.6 (4)
50 x 50	25	6.3	-4.3 (0)	-4.3 (0)	0 (10)	1.5 (2)	1.1 (6)	1.3 (6)	0.9 (6)	10.3 (0)	1.8 (4)	3.9 (1)	0.5 (5)
60 x 60	30	7.7	-5.7 (0)	-5.7 (0)	0 (10)	1.5 (6)	0.7 (9)	1.5 (4)	1.6 (4)	12.2 (0)	1.1 (6)	3.6 (3)	0.6 (5)

The quality of the lower bounds LB_{SW}, LB_{MSW}, LB_{CG} and of the solutions obtained by the sequential heuristics in step I of the procedure is compared in Table 5.4. The first column (labelled OPT) gives the average number of groups in the optimal solution, per instance type. The next three columns bear on the lower bounds; columns 5 to 11 correspond to the upper bounds delivered by the seven sequential heuristics, and the last column (labelled Best) reports on the upper bound obtained by retaining the smallest of the previous seven ones. Each entry in columns 2 to 12 has the format $\delta(\alpha)$. In a row labelled (M, N, C) and a column labelled X, δ is the average difference between the lower (or upper) bound X and the optimal value of the instance, over all instances of type (M, N, C); that is, $\delta = \overline{X} -$ OPT, where $\overline{X}$ is the average of the lower (or upper) bound X. In columns 5 to 11 (that is, for the sequential heuristics), the entry α denotes the number of instances of type (M, N, C) for which the upper bound X is best among the sequential heuristics. In the remaining columns 2, 3, 4 and 12, α is the number of instances for which X is equal to the optimal value of the instance.

As mentioned before, LB_{CG} is equal to the optimal value for all instances tested. The lower bounds LB_{SW} and LB_{MSW} are often not sufficiently sharp to prove optimality. For only 35 % of the instances (especially smaller, denser instances), LB_{SW} gives an optimal lower bound. For an additional 10 % of the instances, LB_{MSW} is optimal. But even LB_{MSW} is only optimal for 2 out of the 90 sparse instances of type (M, N, C_3) or (M, N, C_4). This bad behaviour of LB_{SW} and LB_{MSW} on sparse instances is intuitively easy to understand. Indeed, as capacity increases, each pair of jobs becomes more and more likely to be compatible; hence, the sweeping procedure tends to become useless, as only small sets of pairwise incompatible jobs can be produced (notice that the same conclusion applies for the set packing lower bound LB_{SP} - see Section 5.3.2). Tang and Denardo (1988b) recognized this weakness of the sweeping procedure, and proposed the lower bound M/C with the hope to partially palliate it. But the latter bound is usually weak too.

Table 5.5 Performance of different steps column generation procedure.

Instance type M x N	C	Step I	Step II	Step III CG	Step III IP	Step IV
20 x 15	6	6	+	2	2	
	8			9	1	
	10	1		9	1	
	12			8	1	
40 x 30	15	7		3		1
	17	5		4		4
	20			4	2	7 (1)
	25			1	1	1
60 x 40	20	7		7	2	3
	22	2		3	1	9
	25			1	4	
	30					
10 x 10	4	44	1	43	9 (2)	1
15 x 20	8	43	1 ++	27	19	7 (3)
25 x 30	10	46		29	20	4 (1)
20 x 30	10	27		38 (1)	29	5
40 x 40	20		++	4	4	2
50 x 50	25		+	6 (1)	3	
60 x 60	30			6	4	
All instances		188	2 (+6)	204 (2)	103 (2)	44 (5)

As far as the sequential heuristics go, it appears from columns 5 to 11 that the MIMU, MI, Whitney and Gaul and Modified Rajagopalan rules outperform the other rules. In particular, the MI rule performs extremely well for all instance types, whereas the Modified Rajagopalan rule is especially well suited for the first two sets of instances, but is slightly weaker for the third set. In some instances, the Whitney and Gaul or the MIMU rule provide an optimal solution where the other procedures leave a gap. The MU rule is not very effective for the first two sets of instances (which may help explain why MI performs better than MIMU), but is better for the third set (it is intuitively easy to understand that, for the instances in the latter set, the Minimal Union rule tends to preserve the feasible groups which have been artificially built into the instance). The performance of the Marginal gain and the Rajagopalan rule is very weak, especially for large, sparse instances.

The best upper bound (column 12) is optimal or within one unit of optimality for nearly all instances, which explains that the average deviation from the optimal value is smaller than 1 for all instance types. For large, sparse instances, a gap often remains. Notice however that the "structured" instances in the third set (though very sparse) behave better with this respect than other sparse instances of type (40,30,25) or (60,40,30). One may easily admit the idea that, for the latter instances, the built-in structure helps in finding an optimal solution (see also the comments on Table 5.5 hereunder).

Table 5.5 summarizes the results obtained by the complete procedure described in Section 5.4. We concentrate on the moments at which optimality is established; that is, Table 5.5 gives, for each instance type, the number of instances solved in each step of the procedure (the numbers in brackets refer to 4 instances for which LB_{CG} could not be computed exactly because cycling occurred in Step III, and to 5 instances for which no optimal solution had been found by the heuristics after completion of Step IV - see Section 5.4; all these instances were ultimately solved to optimality by a variant of the procedure using different parameter settings). Zero values are omitted from the table to improve readability.

Thus, for instance, the column labelled "Step I" displays the number of instances for which optimality is achieved in Step I of the procedure : these are the instances for which the lower bound LB_{MSW} is equal to Best, viz. the best sequential heuristic value. The instances for which LB_{MSW} is optimal and Step II produces an optimal solution are recorded in column "Step II" (a "+" in this column denotes an instance where LB_{MSW} is not optimal, but Step II produces an optimal solution). If optimality is not established in either Step I or Step II, the column generation process starts. Column "Step III-CG" records the number of instances for which the column generation procedure provides a lower bound (LB_{Farley} or LB_{CG}) equal to the best upper bound obtained in Steps I and II. Those instances for which an optimal 0-1 solution is found in the course of solving the set covering LP-relaxation are accounted for in column "Step III-IP". After Step III, instances remain for which the lower bound LB_{CG} is smaller than the best available upper bound. Column "Step IV" shows the number of instances for which solving the set covering formulation with a limited number of integer variables was enough to produce an optimal solution with value equal to LB_{CG}.

For 188 out of 550 instances (34 %), optimality is achieved in Step I. All these are dense instances (of type (M, N, C_1) or (M, N, C_2)), with the exception of one small $(20,15,12)$ instance. This comes as no surprise : as discussed before, both the lower bound LB_{MSW} and the best upper bound tend to deteriorate when sparsity increases (see Table 5.4).

The upper bound computed in Step II is used to prove optimality for 8 instances only. Thus, this step does not seem very useful as far as finding good solutions goes. One should however bear in mind that the additional columns produced in this step may improve the quality of the initial set covering model, and thus reduce the number of subsequent column generation steps. More on this topic below.

Optimality is achieved in Step III for 307 instances (56%). For 204 (37 %) of these, an optimal solution had already been found in either Step I or Step II, and only the lower bound is improved here; for the other 103 instances (19 %), both the optimal lower bound and the optimal solution are improved in Step III. These figures sustain our previous claims concerning the strength of the linear relaxation of the set covering formulation of the job grouping problem, and the usefulness of Step III in solving this problem to optimality (especially sparse instances).

Finally, for 44 instances (9%), Step IV has to be performed in order to find an optimal solution. This last step is mostly required for sparse instances, but is almost never needed for the "structured" instances in the third set. This confirms our earlier conjecture that most heuristics perform better on the latter instances than on completely unstructured ones.

Table 5.6 Computation times and size of problems.

| Instance type | | Computation times (in seconds) | | | | | |
M x N	C	Heuristics all instances 1	Steps I-IV all instances 2	Steps I-IV col. gen. instances 3	# iterations col. gen. instances 4	# columns col. gen. instances 5	# maximal feasible columns, all instances 6
20 x 15	6	2.6 (2.5,2.8)	12 (2.5,44)	26 (15,44)	4.0 (2,7)	23 (20,29)	33 (18,61)
	8	2.3 (2.3,2.4)	26 (10,40)	26 (10,40)	3.5 (1,6)	29 (23,41)	89 (51,138)
	10	2.2 (2.1,2.4)	27 (12,36)	27 (12,36)	3.0 (1,5)	41 (19,77)	189 (116,284)
	12	2.1 (2.0,2.3)	30 (2,51)	33 (14,51)	3.7 (1,8)	43 (23,74)	327 (238,514)
40 x 30	15	17 (16,18)	34 (16,79)	75 (66,79)	3.0 (2,4)	49 (47,52)	147 (57,283)
	17	16 (15,17)	56 (15,144)	96 (79,144)	3.2 (2,6)	71 (56,108)	310 (141,549)
	20	15 (14,15)	230 (134,349)	230 (134,349)	5.6 (3,7)	132 (67,180)	931 (342,1640)
	25	14 (13,14)	777 (422,1654)	777 (422,1654)	8.7 (7,11)	252 (175,344)	5909 (2032,8745)
60 x 40	20	42 (42,43)	102 (42,249)	242 (237,249)	5.7 (5,7)	85 (63,103)	215 (137,311)
	22	39 (37,42)	192 (41,318)	229 (183,318)	3.5 (1,6)	90 (62,125)	404 (247,694)
	25	37 (36,38)	449 (263,683)	449 (263,683)	5.5 (2,7)	178 (121,263)	1010 (597,1694)
	30	36 (35,36)	1168 (860,1512)	1168 (860,1512)	7.8 (7,10)	288 (224,364)	5036 (2871,9099)
10 x 10	4	1.1 (1.0,1.2)	7.1 (1.0,35)	12 (6,35)	2.1 (1,6)	13 (9,24)	18 (7,39)
15 x 20	8	3.8 (3.5,4.2)	24 (3.6,113)	39 (14,113)	4.0 (1,8)	32 (18,62)	76 (28,202)
25 x 30	10	12 (11,13)	54 (11,197)	90 (50,197)	4.3 (2,11)	67 (36,131)	263 (59,879)
20 x 30	10	10 (9.3,11)	62 (9.6,158)	81 (38,158)	4.7 (1,13)	58 (35,120)	230 (78,667)
40 x 40	20	25 (24,25)	1342 (494,2409)	1342 (494,2409)	14.5 (6,26)	184 (133,213)	5663 (4304,6950)
50 x 50	25	47 (46,47)	2202 (753,3887)	2202 (753,3887)	24.7 (6,42)	247 (186,325)	22562 (13823,32498)
60 x 60	30	79 (78,80)	4759 (1967,8626)	4759 (1967,8626)	29.9 (15,49)	284 (172,351)	31878 (20336,43827)

Table 5.6 contains information about the time required to solve the various instance types; comparison of these times provides additional information on the effectiveness of the procedure. Each entry has the format "average value (minimal value, maximal value)" (the four instances for which the column generation procedure cycles have not been taken into account when computing these average or extremal values). Column 1 gives the computation time for Step I of the procedure and column 2 records the total computation time for the whole procedure (Steps I to IV) (all times are in seconds). In columns 3, 4 and 5, averages and extremal values are restricted to those instances for which execution of the column generation step (Step III) was necessary. Column 3 reports the total computation time required by Steps I-IV for these instances. Column 4 gives the number of iterations of the column generation step, that is the number of calls on the linear programming package. Column 5 indicates the maximum number of columns occurring in the linear programming subproblems. The figures in this column are to be contrasted with those in Column 6, where the number of maximal feasible groups for each instance type is recorded. As mentioned in Section 5.2.1, this number indicates the size of the complete set covering formulation of the job grouping problem. Thus, it also gives a measure of the difficulty of the instances.

A look at column 6 immediately reveals that only the sparse instances are really big. For many of the dense instances (e.g., of type (M, N, C_1)), the complete column generation model could have been explicitly generated and solved by LINDO, rather than resorting to a column generation procedure. Let us remember, however, that the characteristics of the dense instances in the second set correspond to those of the instances solved by Tang and Denardo (1988b); therefore, considering such instances allows to put our computational results in perspective.

The time required by Step I of the procedure (column 1) remains very short in comparison with the total computing time. It exhibits a tendency to decrease as capacity increases; this may be explained by the fact that, as capacity grows larger, the number of groups built by the heuristics decreases (see Table 5.4).

As may be expected, the total computation time grows together with the problem dimension, and especially with the number of maximal feasible columns (column 6). The number of iterations of the column generation subroutine and the size of the LP subproblems grow simultaneously. For small or dense instances, the computation times remain very short. E.g., for the instances in the second set, the average computation times are between

7 and 62 seconds, and all these instances can be solved within 3+ minutes. The computation times grow by a factor of 3 when the dimension goes from (10,10,4) to (15,20,8), and by a factor of 2.5 from (15,20,8) to (20,30,10) or (25,30,10). Tang and Denardo (1988b) do not report computation times, but the number of nodes enumerated by their branch-and-bound procedure for the same instance types roughly grows by factors of 10 and 15, respectively.

For larger, sparser instances, computation times become more considerable. This can be explained in part by the larger number of iterations of the column generation step, and by the increasing size of the LP subproblems. Notice that these two factors may be influenced by the choice of some of the parameters defining the procedure; in particular, generating less columns in each step would result in a larger number of iterations, but would also decrease the time spent in each iteration. In fact, it is likely that the efficiency of the procedure could be boosted by using a heuristic to solve the generation subproblem, instead of the complete enumeration approach that we used. Complete enumeration would then only be required in the last iterations of the column generation step, to check that no more columns with negative reduced cost can be found. However, as explained in Section 5.2.3, such an approach could only be efficiently implemented if an LP solver more flexible than LINDO is available.

Finally, let us mention that the time needed to execute Step II also grows sharply with increasing capacity. This time is not singled-out in Table 5.6, but represents an important chunk of the total computation time: on average, 4 seconds (resp. 52, 146, 177, 505 and 1029 seconds) for the instances of size (20,15) (resp. (40,30), (60,40), (40,40), (50,50) and (60,60)). In order to assess the contribution of Step 2 to the efficiency of the whole procedure, we ran some experiments in which we disabled this step (more exactly, we disabled the demanding second half of this step, which extends the initial set covering formulation - see Section 5.4). It turned out that this modified procedure was slower, on the average, than the initial one - even though it was faster for some particular instances.

5.6 Summary and conclusions

In this chapter, various lower and upper bounds have been proposed for the job grouping problem. In particular, we showed how the optimal value of the LP-relaxation of the set covering formulation of the problem can be computed by a column generation procedure. Although the column generation subproblem is $\mathcal{N}P$-hard, the procedure that we implemented could solve to optimality 550 instances of the problem. Many of these instances are larger and sparser than the ones previously solved in the literature. This was only possible because of the tightness of the lower bound computed : for all 550 instances, the lower bound was equal to the optimal value of the instance.

An interesting area for further research may be the development of fast heuristics that would provide optimal results for large instances of the problem. It would also seem interesting to be able to compute good heuristic solutions and tight upper bounds for the column generation subproblem. In Chapter 6 we study extensions of the present setting to situations involving multiple machines, or where each tool requires several slots in the tool magazine.

Acknowledgments
We gratefully acknowledge useful discussions on the topic of this work with Antoon Kolen and F. Soumis.

Chapter 6

The job grouping problem for flexible manufacturing systems: some extensions

6.1 Introduction

In Chapter 5 the job grouping problem for flexible manufacturing systems
has been studied. This chapter concentrates on extensions of the previous
model. First, the extension where tools may require several slots in the tool
magazine is discussed. Next, we consider the case where several identical
machines are necessary for production. In both cases, the procedures used
in Chapter 5 are extended to derive strong lower and upper bounds on the
optimal value of the problem and results of computational experiments are
presented. In Section 6.4 we discuss the possibility to incorporate due dates
in the model. Section 6.5 summarizes and concludes the chapter.

6.2 Multiple slots

6.2.1 The job grouping problem

In Chapter 5 a job grouping model is considered in which each tool requires
exactly one slot in the tool magazine. However, tools often require several
slots in the magazine as observed by Stecke (1983; 1989), Kusiak (1985a),
Rajagopalan (1985; 1986) and Hwang (1986). Therefore, we relax the one-
slot assumption, by allowing the number of slots necessary for a tool to be
tool-dependent. We will perform computational experiments on problems for
which tools need 1 to 3 slots, as suggested by Rajagopalan (1985), Shanker
and Tzen (1985) and Mazzola, Neebe and Dunn (1989). First, we briefly
discuss the set covering formulation of the job grouping problem and the
column generation procedure used to solve it. The changes that are necessary
in case tools need several slots in the tool magazine are incorporated in this
explanation.

Assume there are N jobs and M tools. We denote by s_k the number
of slots that are necessary to place tool k in the tool magazine. The tool
requirements are represented by a so-called tool-job matrix A of dimension
$M \times N$, with:

$$a_{ki} = 1 \quad \text{if job } i \text{ requires tool } k$$
$$\phantom{a_{ki}} = 0 \quad \text{otherwise,}$$

for $k = 1, \ldots, M$ and $i = 1, \ldots, N$. A subset (group) S of jobs (or of columns
of A) is called feasible if the tools that are needed for these jobs together
require at most C slots, i.e. if $\sum_k \{s_k : a_{ki} = 1 \text{ for some } i \in S\} \leq C$. We do
not consider the possibility of tool overlap (where the total number of slots

needed by a set of tools is strictly less than the sum of the slot requirements of the separate tools (Stecke, 1983)). The job grouping problem consists in finding a minimum set of feasible groups such that each job is contained in (at least) one group. It can be formulated as a set covering problem, as shown in Chapter 5. Let us suppose that there exist P feasible groups, and let

$$q_{ij} = 1 \quad \text{if job } i \text{ is contained in the feasible group } j,$$
$$\quad\;\; = 0 \quad \text{otherwise,}$$

for $i = 1, \ldots, N$ and $j = 1, \ldots, P$. The job grouping problem is:

$$\text{minimize} \quad \sum_{j=1}^{P} y_j \tag{6.1}$$

$$\text{subject to} \quad \sum_{j=1}^{P} q_{ij} y_j \geq 1 \qquad i = 1, \ldots, N, \tag{6.2}$$

$$y_j \geq 0 \qquad j = 1, \ldots, P, \tag{6.3}$$

$$y_j \text{ integer} \qquad j = 1, \ldots, P, \tag{6.4}$$

where $y_j = 1$ if group j is part of the optimal covering. In comparison with the model described in Chapter 5 the introduction of tool-dependent slot requirements has influenced the set of feasible columns $\{q_j\}$ (where $q_j = (q_{1j}, \ldots, q_{Nj})^T$), but model (6.1) - (6.4) remains otherwise the same.

Notice that the job grouping problem with $s_k > 1$ for some k could also be transformed into an equivalent job grouping problem with $s'_k = 1$ for all k in a straightforward way. Namely, consider the tool-job matrix A and the values s_k for each tool k. Now, construct a new tool-job matrix A' where each row k in A is replaced by s_k similar rows in A'. The tool-job matrix A' has $\sum_{k=1}^{M} s_k$ rows and N columns. Solving the job grouping problem with tool-job matrix A', $s'_k = 1$ for all k and tool magazine capacity C is equivalent to solving the job grouping problem described by the parameters A, s_k and C. This transformation has the disadvantage that it expands the size of the problem, but clearly shows that the job grouping problem where tools need several slots is a special case of the single-slot problem. Thus, the lower and upper bounding procedures developed in Chapter 5 can be easily adjusted to this case. In fact, this section can be seen as restating the procedures described in Chapter 5 in such a way that they can be applied directly to the instance A, s_k, C. The result will be a general procedure for the "multiple slots" problem with no preprocessing of the data. The new formulation will be more compact. Notice that we may expect instances with $s_k > 1$ to have a different behaviour than the single-slot ones. This will be investigated by performing computational experiments.

6.2.2 Lower bounds via column generation

To find a lower bound for the set covering problem (6.1) - (6.4), we want to solve its LP-relaxation, i.e. the problem (6.1) - (6.3). A column generation procedure is used to calculate this bound, as in Chapter 5. At each iteration of the column generation procedure, we solve the LP obtained by restricting (6.1) - (6.3) to some subset T of columns, i.e. we solve a problem of the form:

$$\text{minimize} \quad \sum_{j \in T} y_j \tag{6.5}$$

$$\text{subject to} \quad \sum_{j \in T} q_{ij} y_j \geq 1 \qquad i = 1, \ldots, N, \tag{6.6}$$

$$y_j \geq 0 \qquad j \in T, \tag{6.7}$$

for some $T \subseteq \{1, \ldots, P\}$. Let y^* be an optimal solution to (6.5) - (6.7) and λ^* be an optimal solution to the dual of (6.5) - (6.7). In each iteration of the column generation procedure the generation subproblem has to be solved (see Section 5.2). The generation subproblem identifies columns that have negative reduced cost and may, when added to the set covering formulation, improve the optimal solution value. The generation subproblem is

given $\lambda_1^*, \ldots, \lambda_N^*$, is there a feasible group S such that $\sum_{i \in S} \lambda_i^* > 1$? $\tag{6.8}$

After introduction of different sizes for the tools the generation subproblem can be formulated as follows (see also Hirabayashi, Suzuki and Tsuchiya (1984)):

$$\text{maximize} \quad \sum_{i=1}^{N} \lambda_i^* x_i \tag{6.9}$$

$$\text{subject to} \quad a_{ki} x_i \leq z_k \qquad i = 1, \ldots, N; k = 1, \ldots, M, \tag{6.10}$$

$$\sum_{k=1}^{M} s_k z_k \leq C \tag{6.11}$$

$$x_i \in \{0, 1\} \qquad i = 1, \ldots, N, \tag{6.12}$$

$$z_k \in \{0, 1\} \qquad k = 1, \ldots, M, \tag{6.13}$$

where

$$x_i = 1 \quad \text{if job } i \text{ is in group } S$$
$$\quad = 0 \quad \text{otherwise,}$$

for $i = 1, \ldots, N$, and

$$z_k = 1 \quad \text{if tool } k \text{ is required by some job in } S,$$
$$\quad = 0 \quad \text{otherwise,}$$

for $k = 1, \ldots, M$. Only restriction (6.11) has changed in comparison with the generation subproblem in Section 5.2.3, so as to incorporate the number of tool slots needed for each tool. The problem (6.9) - (6.13) is $\mathcal{N}\mathcal{P}$-hard and we solve it using the same enumeration procedure as in Section 5.2.3. The column generation procedure that is used is basically the same as described in Section 5.2.4. When the column generation procedure stops we have an optimal solution y^* for the LP relaxation (6.1) - (6.3). Rounding up the solution value $\sum_{j \in T} y_j^*$ to the next integer gives a lower bound for the job grouping problem. We will refer to the bound $\lceil \sum_{j \in T} y_j^* \rceil$ as LB_{CG}. We will also consider the lower bound $LB_{Farley} = \lceil \sum_{i=1}^{N} \lambda_i^* / Z \rceil$, where Z is the optimal solution value of the generation subproblem (see also Farley (1990)).

6.2.3   Other lower bounds

The sweeping procedure (Tang and Denardo, 1988b) provides a lower bound for the job grouping problem when all tools need 1 slot. Tang and Denardo (1988b) did not consider the "multiple slots" problem. However, the sweeping procedure can be modified to be applicable to "multiple slots" instances. Call two jobs *compatible* if they form a feasible group. The sweeping procedure sequentially creates a number of groups as follows. In each step of the procedure, a job (seed) first is selected which is compatible with the fewest number of other (not yet selected) jobs (in case of a tie, the job for which the tools necessary for the set of compatible jobs require the smallest number of slots in the tool magazine is selected). Next, the seed along with all jobs which are compatible with it are selected to form one group. The procedure is repeated until all jobs have been selected. The number of groups so created, say L, is a valid lower bound for the job grouping problem. We also use the trivial lower bound $\lceil \sum_{k=1}^{M} s_k / C \rceil$. Combining this bound with L yields the lower bound $LB_{SW} = \max\{\lceil \sum_{k=1}^{M} s_k / C \rceil, L\}$.

A better lower bound can be obtained in each step of the sweeping procedure by summing the number of groups already created by the sweeping procedure and the lower bound $\lceil \sum_{k \in \cup_{i \in I} T_i} s_k / C \rceil$, where I is the set of "not yet selected" jobs, and T_i is the set of tools needed for job i. This procedure generates a sequence of valid lower bounds, the first of which is equal to $\lceil \sum_{k=1}^{M} s_k / C \rceil$ and the last of which is equal to L. We refer to this procedure as the "modified sweeping procedure". It yields a new lower bound LB_{MSW}, equal to the maximum of the bounds in the sequence.

6.2.4 Upper bounds

We apply sequential heuristic procedures that use a two-step approach for building groups. In the first step, a job is picked as a seed. Unless explained otherwise, we always pick a job for which the tools require the highest number of slots. Then a selection rule is used to add jobs to the group until the tool magazine capacity constraint prohibits the addition of any other job to this group. The two-step procedure is repeated until all jobs are assigned to some group. For selecting the next job to be assigned to a group (in step 2) a number of different rules have been considered.

For a group S and a job $i \notin S$, let

t_i =number of slots necessary for the tools required by job i;
b_i =number of slots necessary for the tools required both by job i and by some job already in S.

1. *MIMU rule:* select a job i for which b_i is maximal; in case of a tie select a job for which t_i is minimal (this is a straightforward generalization of the procedure by Tang and Denardo (1988b)).

2. *MI rule:* select a job i for which b_i is maximal.

3. *MU rule:* select a job i for which $(t_i - b_i)$ is minimal.

4. *Whitney and Gaul rule:* select job i for which $(b_i + 1)/(t_i + 1)$ is maximal (Whitney and Gaul (1985) did not consider the "multiple slots" problem, but this rule is a straightforward extension of the single-slot rule).

5. *Rajagopalan rule:* Each tool k receives a weight a_k equal to the number of jobs that require tool k among the jobs that still have to be assigned to a group. Then, the priority of job i is calculated by summing the weights $s_k \cdot a_k$ of the tools that must be added to the tool magazine in case job i is assigned to the group. The job with the largest priority is selected first. For this rule, the first job in each group (seed) is also selected according to the same criterion (see Rajagopalan (1985)).

6. *Modified Rajagopalan rule:* The Rajagopalan rule can be changed in the following way: the weight a_k for each tool k is defined as the number of jobs that require tool k among the jobs already selected in the group. The priority of a job is the sum of the weights $s_k \cdot a_k$ of the tools that are needed for that job. The job with the highest priority is selected.

7. *Marginal gain rule:* The addition of job i to a group usually requires that extra tools be loaded in the tool magazine. This new tool configuration may in turn allow the execution of other, not yet selected, jobs; denote by p_i the number of such jobs. This rule selects a job i that maximizes p_i.

Compared to what was done in Section 5.3.1, the MIMU, MI, MU and Whitney and Gaul rule have been adjusted by simply updating the definitions of parameters t_i and b_i. Rules 5 and 6 have been changed by incorporating the number of slots in the definition, as in Rajagopalan (1985). The Marginal gain rule uses the new definition of feasibility of a group. The set covering heuristics can also be used as described in Section 5.3.2.

6.2.5   Adjusting the column generation procedure

The column generation approach can be easily adapted to the multiple slots per tool-case. The procedure that is implemented consists of four main steps. We first briefly sketch the whole procedure before commenting on each individual step (see also Section 5.4).

Step I: Use the sequential heuristics to produce a first upper bound. Compute the simple lower bounds LB_{SW} and LB_{MSW}. If optimality is achieved then STOP. Otherwise construct an initial set covering formulation using the groups that have been generated using the heuristic procedures.

Step II: Use the greedy heuristic to solve the initial set covering formulation. If optimality is achieved then STOP.

Step III: Solve the LP-relaxation of the current formulation. Check whether the primal solution is integral and whether its value improves the current upper bound. Use the dual variables to formulate the generation subproblem and generate new columns with negative reduced cost. Calculate LB_{Farley}. If optimality is achieved then STOP. If no columns with negative reduced cost have been found, then continue with Step IV. Otherwise, update the set covering formulation and repeat Step III.

Step IV: Use the last set covering formulation for finding an improved heuristic solution.

The lower and upper bounding procedures of Step I have been described in Sections 6.2.2 - 6.2.4. In Step II no additional columns are generated (contrary to what was done in Section 5.4 for the single-slot case) for reasons of time-efficiency. The set covering formulation is solved using the well-known greedy heuristic (Nemhauser and Wolsey, 1988). The LP-relaxation is solved using the package LINDO. When the generation subproblem is solved to optimality (i.e. when a complete enumeration is performed), its optimal value Z is used for computing the bound LB_{Farley}. If this lower bound is equal to the upper bound the procedure stops. If no new column has been generated (i.e. $Z = 1$ and $LB_{Farley} = LB_{CG}$), then the column generation subroutine terminates, and we continue with step IV. Otherwise, at most 200 new columns are added to the set covering formulation. Also, to limit the size of the formulation all columns with a small reduced cost are eliminated. More precisely, columns for which $\sum_{i=1}^{N} q_{ij}\lambda_i < 1 - \alpha$ are removed from the formulation, where α is an arbitrary chosen parameter ($\alpha = 0.25$). Furthermore, columns with $\sum_{i=1}^{N} q_{ij}\lambda_i < 0.85$ are removed when the number of columns exceeds 700 (an arbitrary maximum). Step IV of the procedure is extended in the following way. We first solve the last set covering formulation by the greedy heuristic. If this is not effective, we solve a slightly modified set covering formulation with LINDO, requiring only a limited number of variables to take 0-1 values. More precisely, the T variables which assume the largest value in the continuous solution of the set covering formulation (columns for which $\sum_{i=1}^{N} q_{ij}\lambda_i < 0.9$ are removed to limit the size of the formulation), extended by the additional constraint $\sum_{j=1}^{P} y_j \geq LB_{CG}$, are forced to be integer. The parameter T is taken equal to $LB_{CG} + 5$ if the number of columns is smaller than 50 (resp. $LB_{CG} + 15$ if the number of columns is between 50 and 150, and $LB_{CG} + 25$ otherwise). Because of the small number of integer variables, the resulting mixed 0-1 problem can be solved by LINDO's branch-and-bound subroutine (see also Section 5.4). If the solution is still fractional after this step, additional variables (that still have positive fractional values) are forced to take 0-1 values and the formulation is solved again. This procedure is repeated until an integer solution is obtained.

6.2.6   Computational experiments

We generated two sets of random instances. Table 6.1 contains the parameter settings for the first set. This set of instances involves four instance sizes (M, N). The capacity of the tool magazine takes one of the values C_1, C_2, C_3. Min (resp. Max) represent the minimal (resp. maximal) number of tool slots needed by each job. For each instance type (M, N, C) two ranges of values for $s_k(k = 1, \ldots, M)$ are considered, as shown in column labelled "$s_k \in$". We assume that tools need a small number of tool slots ($s_k \in \{1, 2, 3\}$), as often seems to be the case in real-world systems. Rajagopalan (1985), Shanker and Tzen (1985) and Mazzola et al. (1989) perform computational experiments using these values. Stecke (1989) gives a detailed description of a system for which the tools take either 1 or 3 slots. For the first range of values, s_k only takes values in $\{1, 2, 3\}$, namely $s_k = 1$ for $k = 1, \ldots, \lfloor \frac{2}{3} M \rfloor$, $s_k = 2$ for $k = \lfloor \frac{2}{3} M \rfloor + 1, \ldots, \lfloor \frac{5}{6} M \rfloor$ and $s_k = 3$ for $k = \lfloor \frac{5}{6} M \rfloor + 1, \ldots, M$. For the second range, $s_k \in \{1, 3\}$ for all k, with $s_k = 1$ for $k = 1, \ldots, \lfloor \frac{2}{3} M \rfloor$ and $s_k = 3$ for $k = \lfloor \frac{2}{3} M \rfloor + 1, \ldots, M$.

Problem size M × N	C_1	C_2	C_3	$s_k \in$	Min	Max
10 × 10	7	10	13	$\{1,2,3\}$	1	6
10 × 10	7	10	13	$\{1,3\}$	1	6
15 × 20	13	15	18	$\{1,2,3\}$	1	12
15 × 20	13	15	18	$\{1,3\}$	1	12
25 × 30	15	20	25	$\{1,2,3\}$	1	14
25 × 30	17	21	25	$\{1,3\}$	1	16
60 × 40	30	40	45	$\{1,2,3\}$	1	29
60 × 40	33	40	45	$\{1,3\}$	1	32

Table 6.1 Parameters first set of instances.

For each problem size (M, N, C) 10 random matrices A were generated. For each $j = 1, \ldots, N$, the j-th column of A was generated as follows. First, an integer t_j was drawn from the uniform distribution over [Min,Max]: this number denotes the number of tool slots available for job j. Next, a set T_j of distinct integers were drawn from the uniform distribution over $[1, M]$ until at most t_j slots were used, i.e. until $\sum_{k \in T_j} s_k > t_j - 3$. These integers denote the tools required by job j, i.e. $a_{kj} = 1$ if and only if $k \in T_j$. Finally, we checked whether $T_j \subseteq T_i$ or $T_i \subseteq T_j$ held for any $i < j$. If any of these inclusions was found to hold, then the previous choice of T_j was cancelled, and a new set T_j was generated.

Problem size $M \times N$	C_1	$s_k \in$	Min	Max	Minjob	Maxjob
30×30	20	$\{1,2,3\}$	7	11	4	7
30×30	20	$\{1,3\}$	7	11	4	7
40×40	30	$\{1,2,3\}$	10	16	5	8
40×40	30	$\{1,3\}$	10	16	5	8

Table 6.2 Parameters second set of instances.

In Table 6.2 the parameter settings are described for the second set of instances (comparable to the third set in Section 5.5.1). For each instance class (M, N, C) 10 instances were generated. This second set explicitly takes into account the interdependence between jobs. First, a number N_1 is drawn uniformly between Minjob and Maxjob, and a subset M_1, containing tools that together require exactly C tool slots, is randomly chosen. Then, we create N_1 "similar" jobs, by making sure that these jobs use only the tools in M_1. These jobs are generated as explained before for the first set of instances (except that they are restricted to the tools in M_1). When N_1 jobs have been defined, then the procedure is iterated to produce $N_2, N_3, \ldots$ additional jobs. This process stops after k iterations, when almost all columns of the incidence matrix have been generated (specifically, when $\sum_{i=1}^{k} N_i \geq N$ - Maxjob). Then, the last columns are filled independently of each other, as for the first set of instances. Finally, a real-world instance described in Stecke (1989) was also tested. This instance involves 10 jobs and 141 tools, with 100 tools using 1 slot and 41 tools using 3 slots.

6.2.7 Computational results

The column generation procedure has been implemented using Turbo Pascal, and tested on the instances described in Section 6.2.6. The experiments were run on an AT personal computer with a 16MHz 80386sx processor and 80387 mathematical coprocessor. This section reports on the results of our experiments.

Using the procedure of Section 6.2.5. 271 of the 280 "multiple slots" instances were solved to optimality. The gap between the value of the LP-relaxation of the set covering formulation and the value of the optimal solution was smaller than 1 for all instances solved to optimality. In other words the lower bound LB_{CG} was optimal for these instances. For the remaining 9 instances the procedure finished with a lower and upper bound that differed by one unit. As a matter of fact, the gap between the optimal value of the LP-relaxation of the set covering formulation and the best known upper bound amounts to maximal 1.05 for these instances. For some of these instances, a branch- and-bound procedure was eventually used to show that the upper bound was optimal and there was indeed a gap between the lower bound LB_{CG} and the optimal solution value. Nevertheless, our experiments seem to show that the lower bound obtained by using the LP-relaxation of the set covering formulation is usually very good, even though it is not optimal for all instances.

The quality of the lower bounds LB_{SW}, LB_{MSW}, LB_{CG} and of the solutions obtained by the sequential heuristics in step I of the procedure is compared in Table 6.3. The first column (labelled OPT) gives the average number of groups in the optimal solution for the instances of each type that were solved to optimality using the procedure of Section 6.2.5. The next three columns bear on the lower bounds; columns 5 to 11 correspond to the upper bounds delivered by the seven sequential heuristics, and the last column (labelled Best) reports on the upper bound obtained by retaining the smallest of the previous seven ones. Each entry in columns 2 to 12 has the format $\delta\,(\alpha)$. In a row labelled (M, N, C) and a column labelled X, δ is the average difference over all instances of type (M, N, C) between the lower (or upper) bound X and the best lower (or upper) bound computed for this instance in the course of the procedure; that is, $\delta = \overline{X} - BOUND$, where $\overline{X}$ is the average of the lower (or upper) bound X and $BOUND$ is the average of the best lower (or upper) bound.

Table 6.3 Quality of lower and upper bounds.

Instance type M × N	C	($s_k \in$)	OPT (1)	LB$_{SW}$ (2)	LB$_{MSW}$ (3)	LB$_{CG}$ (4)	MIMU (5)	MI (6)	MU (7)	Whitney and Gaul (8)	Rajagopalan (9)	Modified Rajagopalan (10)	Marginal gain (11)	Best (12)
10 x 10	7		3.3	-0.3 (7)	-0.3 (7)	0 (10)	0.1 (9)	0.3 (7)	0.1 (9)	0.1 (9)	0.5 (5)	0.2 (8)	0.6 (4)	0.0 (10)
	10		2.0	0.0 (10)	0.0 (10)	0 (10)	0.2 (10)	0.2 (10)	0.4 (8)	0.4 (8)	0.5 (7)	0.2 (10)	0.4 (8)	0.2 (8)
	13	[1,2,3]	2.0	0.0 (10)	0.0 (10)	0 (10)	0.0 (10)	0.0 (10)	0.0 (10)	0.0 (10)	0.0 (10)	0.0 (10)	0.0 (10)	0.0 (10)
10 x 10	7		4.3	-0.4 (6)	-0.1 (9)	0 (10)	0.1 (10)	0.1 (10)	0.2 (9)	0.1 (10)	0.4 (7)	0.1 (10)	0.3 (8)	0.1 (9)
	10		2.8	-0.8 (2)	-0.8 (2)	0 (10)	0.0 (10)	0.0 (10)	0.1 (9)	0.0 (10)	0.2 (8)	0.0 (10)	0.0 (10)	0.0 (10)
	13	[1,3]	2.0	0.0 (10)	0.0 (10)	0 (10)	0.0 (10)	0.0 (10)	0.0 (10)	0.0 (10)	0.4 (6)	0.0 (10)	0.2 (8)	0.0 (10)
15 x 20	13		6.0	-1.2 (1)	-1.0 (2)	0 (10)	0.7 (6)	0.3 (10)	1.2 (1)	0.8 (5)	1.6 (1)	0.3 (10)	0.6 (7)	0.3 (7)
	15		4.2	-1.5 (1)	-1.3 (0)	0 (10)	0.5 (8)	0.3 (10)	0.8 (5)	0.5 (8)	1.6 (1)	0.4 (9)	0.8 (5)	0.3 (7)
	18	[1,2,3]	2.8	-0.8 (2)	-0.8 (2)	0 (10)	0.1 (9)	0.0 (10)	0.2 (8)	0.1 (9)	0.9 (2)	0.2 (8)	0.4 (6)	0.1 (7)
15 x 20	13		7.6	-1.0 (2)	-0.8 (3)	0 (10)	0.5 (8)	0.4 (9)	1.1 (3)	0.6 (7)	1.1 (4)	0.4 (8)	0.9 (4)	0.3 (7)
	15		5.1	-1.5 (1)	-1.4 (1)	0 (10)	0.6 (6)	0.4 (8)	1.0 (3)	0.5 (7)	2.1 (0)	0.4 (8)	1.0 (2)	0.2 (8)
	18	[1,3]	3.3	-1.3 (0)	-1.1 (0)	0 (10)	0.5 (6)	0.3 (8)	0.5 (7)	0.5 (7)	0.8 (5)	0.3 (8)	0.6 (5)	0.1 (7)
25 x 30	15		13.4	-1.2 (2)	-0.8 (6)	0 (10)	0.5 (8)	0.4 (8)	0.9 (5)	0.4 (9)	2.3 (0)	0.3 (10)	0.8 (5)	0.3 (7)
	20		7.2	-3.7 (0)	-3.3 (0)	0 (10)	0.9 (5)	0.5 (8)	1.3 (3)	0.8 (5)	3.2 (0)	0.9 (4)	1.5 (2)	0.3 (6)
	25	[1,2,3]	4.4	-2.4 (0)	-2.4 (0)	0 (10)	0.6 (9)	0.5 (10)	1.0 (5)	0.9 (6)	2.5 (0)	0.7 (8)	1.2 (4)	0.5 (4)
25 x 30	17		12.8	-0.9 (3)	-0.8 (4)	0 (10)	0.8 (3)	0.2 (9)	1.1 (2)	0.6 (5)	2.4 (0)	0.2 (9)	1.0 (1)	0.1 (9)
	21		7.9	-2.8 (0)	-2.7 (0)	0 (10)	1.3 (5)	0.8 (10)	1.7 (2)	1.2 (6)	3.3 (0)	0.9 (9)	2.0 (0)	0.8 (2)
	25	[1,3]	5.6	-3.2 (0)	-2.9 (0)	0 (10)	0.8 (6)	0.7 (7)	1.3 (1)	0.9 (5)	3.1 (0)	0.7 (7)	1.3 (2)	0.4 (5)
60 x 40	30		18.1	-11.3 (0)	-11.3 (0)	0 (10)	0.8 (5)	0.4 (9)	1.5 (1)	0.8 (5)	1.6 (1)	0.4 (9)	1.2 (4)	0.3 (7)
	40		10.7	-5.1 (0)	-4.8 (0)	0 (10)	1.6 (1)	0.6 (9)	2.2 (0)	1.4 (4)	2.9 (0)	0.7 (8)	2.0 (0)	0.5 (4)
	45	[1,2,3]	8.6	-6.0 (0)	-5.6 (0)	0 (10)	1.3 (4)	0.5 (10)	1.9 (1)	1.0 (5)	3.5 (0)	0.8 (7)	2.2 (0)	0.5 (5)
60 x 40	33		19.4	-11.8 (0)	-11.8 (0)	0 (10)	0.5 (9)	0.4 (10)	1.2 (3)	0.5 (9)	1.9 (1)	0.4 (10)	1.1 (4)	0.4 (6)
	40		13.7	-6.1 (0)	-6.1 (0)	0 (10)	1.6 (2)	0.6 (9)	2.1 (0)	1.5 (2)	2.9 (0)	0.7 (8)	1.9 (1)	0.5 (5)
	45	[1,3]	11.1	-5.6 (0)	-5.5 (0)	0 (10)	1.3 (5)	0.8 (10)	2.4 (0)	1.8 (1)	3.3 (0)	1.1 (7)	2.4 (0)	0.8 (2)
30x30 [1,2,3]	20		5.3	-2.3 (0)	-2.3 (0)	0 (10)	0.6 (7)	0.6 (7)	1.0 (5)	0.6 (7)	3.2 (0)	0.5 (8)	1.4 (1)	0.3 (6)
30x30 [1,3]	20		5.5	-2.5 (0)	-2.5 (0)	0 (10)	0.7 (8)	0.9 (6)	1.0 (6)	0.7 (8)	3.2 (0)	0.7 (8)	1.3 (3)	0.5 (5)
40x40 [1,2,3]	30		6.4	-3.4 (0)	-3.4 (0)	0 (10)	1.3 (2)	0.7 (7)	1.5 (3)	1.1 (3)	5.0 (0)	1.3 (2)	2.3 (1)	0.4 (5)
40x40 [1,3]	30		6.8	-3.7 (0)	-3.7 (0)	0 (10)	1.2 (7)	0.8 (9)	1.4 (5)	1.3 (5)	5.0 (0)	1.3 (5)	1.9 (2)	0.7 (3)

In columns 5 to 11 (that is, for the sequential heuristics), the entry α denotes the number of instances of type (M, N, C) for which the upper bound X is best among the sequential heuristics. In the remaining columns 2, 3, 4 and 12, α is the number of instances for which X is equal to the best lower (or upper) bound of the instance.

For 271 out of 280 instances the best lower bound (LB_{CG}) is equal to the optimal solution value. For the remaining 9 instances the best lower bound and the best upper bound differ by one group. The lower bounds LB_{SW} and LB_{MSW} are seldom sharp (only for small instances and instances of type (M, N, C_1)). Table 6.3 also shows that the MI and the Modified Rajagopalan rules (in that order) outperform the other rules. The performance of the MIMU and the Whitney and Gaul rule is quite good. The MU and the Marginal gain rules are much weaker. The Rajagopalan rule performs even worse (especially for the instances of the second set). Taking the best solution of the sequential heuristics, a solution is obtained which is optimal or close to optimality (gap of 1) for nearly all instances (for about half of the larger instances an optimal solution is obtained). Because of the poor quality of the lower bounds LB_{SW} and LB_{MSW} the column generation procedure is needed for a large majority of the instances.

Table 6.4 Performance of different steps of the column generation procedure.

Instance type M × N (s_k ∈)	C	Step I	Step II	Step III CG	Step III IP	Step IV A	Step IV B	Gap
10 × 10 [1,2,3]	7	7		3				
	10	8			2			
	13	10						
10 × 10 [1,3]	7	8		1	1			
	10	2		8				
	13	10						
15 × 20 [1,2,3]	13	1		6	1	2		2
	15			7	1	2		
	18	2		8				1
15 × 20 [1,3]	13	2		5	2	1		1
	15			8	2			
	18			7				
25 × 30 [1,2,3]	15	4		3	3	1		1
	20			6	1	2		
	25			4		2 (3)		
25 × 30 [1,3]	17	4	+	6	3	5		1
	21			2	1	3		
	25			5			2	
60 × 40 [1,2,3]	30			7	2	1		
	40			4	1	3 (1)		
	45			5		3		
60 × 40 [1,3]	33			6	3	4		
	40			5	2	1	1	
	45			2		4	2	
30 × 30 [1,2,3]	20			6	2	1	1	1
30 × 30 [1,3]	20			5	3	1		
40 × 40 [1,2,3]	30			5		4		1
40 × 40 [1,3]	30			3	2	4		1
All instances		58	0 (+1)	127	32	44 (4)	6	9

Table 6.4 summarizes the results obtained by the complete procedure described in Section 6.2.5. We concentrate on the moments at which optimality is established; that is, Table 6.4 gives, for each instance type, the number of instances solved in each step of the procedure (the numbers in brackets refer to 4 instances for which no optimal solution had been found after completion of Step IV; all these instances were ultimately solved to optimality by a variant of the procedure using different parameter settings). Zero values are omitted from the table to improve readability. Thus, for instance, the column labelled "Step I" displays the number of instances for which optimality is achieved in Step I of the procedure : these are the instances for which the lower bound LB_{MSW} is equal to Best, viz. the best sequential heuristic value. The instances for which LB_{MSW} is optimal and Step II produces an optimal solution are recorded in column "Step II" (a "+" in this column denotes an instance where LB_{MSW} is not optimal, but Step II produces an optimal solution). If optimality is not established in either Step I or Step II, the column generation process starts. Column "Step III-CG" records the number of instances for which the column generation procedure provides a lower bound (LB_{Farley} or LB_{CG}) equal to the best upper bound obtained in Steps I and II. Those instances for which an optimal 0-1 solution is found in the course of solving the set covering LP-relaxation are accounted for in column "Step III-IP". After Step III, instances remain for which the lower bound LB_{CG} is smaller than the best available upper bound. Column "Step IV - A" shows the number of instances for which solving the set covering formulation with a limited number of integer variables was enough to produce an optimal solution with value equal to LB_{CG}. Column "Step IV - B" shows the number of instances for which Step IV - A did not suffice, but for which an optimal solution was obtained after more variables were forced to take 0-1 values, as described in Section 6.2.5. Column "Gap" displays the number of instances for which the best lower bound (LB_{CG}) was strictly smaller than the best known upper bound at the end of the procedure.

Table 6.4 shows that for 21 % of the instances optimality is achieved in Step I (mainly smaller instances). For only one instance Step II offered a better upper bound. In Step III optimality is achieved for 159 instances (57 %). For 32 instances (11 %) the upper bound was improved in Step III. For 63 instances (23 %) Step IV had to be performed. Four of these instances were solved with different parameter settings. For another 6 instances the solution of the set covering formulation remained fractional after a number of variables were forced to take 0-1 values. Nine instances could not be solved. For these instances a gap remained between LB_{CG} and the best upper bound (the largest gap between the LP-relaxation value and the best upper bound amounts 1.05). A comparison with results of Section 5.6 shows that these instances seem to be harder than those considered in the previous study (see also column 6 in Table 6.5).

Table 6.5 contains information about the time required to solve the various instance types; comparison of these times provides additional information on the effectiveness of the procedure. Each entry has the format "average value (minimal value, maximal value)" (the four instances for which the column generation procedure cycles have not been taken into account when computing these average or extremal values). Column 1 gives the computation time for Step I of the procedure and column 2 records the total computation time for the whole procedure (Steps I to IV) (all times are in seconds). In columns 3, 4 and 5, averages and extremal values are restricted to those instances for which execution of the column generation step (Step III) was necessary. Column 3 reports the total computation time required by Steps I-IV for these instances. Column 4 gives the number of iterations of the column generation step, that is the number of calls on the linear programming package. Column 5 indicates the maximum number of columns occurring in the linear programming subproblems. The figures in this column are to be contrasted with those in Column 6, where the number of maximal feasible groups for each instance type is recorded. This number indicates the size of the complete set covering formulation of the job grouping problem (see Section 6.2.1). Thus, it also gives a measure of the difficulty of the instances.

The computation times in Table 6.5 show that the large instances (especially of type (M, N, C_3)) take a lot of time to reach optimality. This is due to the many calls to LINDO and the size of the set covering formulations that have to be solved in each step. For larger instances columns 2 and 3 are similar, because all instances need the execution of the column generation procedure. Column 4 shows that at most 26 calls to LINDO are necessary. The maximal average number of columns lies around 600 (which is close to the maximum of 700 columns). The last column shows that the size of the complete set covering formulation for the large instances is indeed very large.

The real-world instance of Stecke (1989) was solved to optimality by 6 out of 7 sequential heuristics (not recorded in Tables 6.3, 6.4 and 6.5). The lower bound LB_{CG} was optimal, in contrast with the other lower bounds.

Table 6.5 Computation times and size of problems.

Instance type M × N	C	(s_k ∈)	Computation times (in seconds)			# iterations col. gen. instances 4	# columns col. gen. instances 5	# maximal feasible columns, all instances 6
			Heuristics all instances 1	Steps I-IV all instances 2	Steps I-IV col. gen. instances 3			
10 x 10	7		1.1 (1.1,1.2)	6.8 (1.1,1.25)	20 (15,25)	4.0 (3,5)	13 (12,14)	26 (20,29)
	10		1.1 (1.0,1.1)	7.9 (1.0,0.45)	35 (25,45)	7.0 (5,9)	20 (17,23)	28 (21,37)
	13	[1,2,3]	1.1 (1.0,1.2)	1.1 (1.0,1.2)	n.a.	n.a.	n.a.	13 (7,21)
10 x 10	7		1.1 (1.0,1.2)	4.3 (1.0,0.19)	17 (15,19)	3.5 (3,4)	8 (7,9)	13 (6,23)
	10		1.1 (1.0,1.1)	26 (1.0,0.50)	32 (20,50)	6.4 (4,10)	15 (9,20)	29 (24,34)
	13	[1,3]	1.1 (1.0,1.1)	1.1 (1.0,1.1)	n.a.	n.a.	n.a.	25 (18,30)
15 x 20	13		3.5 (3.4,3.7)	43 (3.6,88)	47 (25,88)	5.6 (3,8)	43 (28,71)	122 (57,215)
	15		3.4 (3.2,3.6)	87 (42,173)	87 (42,173)	10.0 (5,16)	50 (36,79)	163 (98,250)
	18	[1,2,3]	3.2 (3.1,3.3)	86 (3.1,199)	107 (47,199)	11.6 (5,26)	54 (38,87)	148 (116,213)
15 x 20	13		3.6 (3.5,3.8)	35 (3.6,71)	43 (29,71)	6.0 (4,8)	30 (17,57)	70 (55,101)
	15		3.4 (3.2,3.6)	57 (41,86)	57 (41,86)	7.5 (5,12)	40 (27,54)	109 (77,149)
	18	[1,3]	3.2 (3.2,3.3)	111 (41,172)	111 (41,172)	10.8 (6,21)	49 (20,78)	146 (106,186)
25 x 30	15		11 (11,12)	49 (11,97)	73 (43,97)	5.8 (2,9)	82 (46,144)	230 (111,407)
	20		10 (9.8,10)	342 (120,862)	342 (120,862)	8.1 (5,10)	179 (146,226)	1432 (693,2581)
	25	[1,2,3]	9.7 (9.4,10)	1369 (632,2573)	1369 (632,2573)	13.4 (9,17)	255 (225,292)	5490 (3309,8669)
25 x 30	17		11 (11,12)	59 (11,136)	91 (41,136)	6.2 (3,8)	94 (51,126)	274 (135,425)
	21		10 (10,11)	219 (106,368)	219 (106,368)	7.2 (5,9)	155 (110,189)	968 (479,1649)
	25	[1,3]	9.9 (9.7,10)	554 (187,1230)	554 (187,1230)	9.2 (5,13)	202 (149,261)	2802 (1619,5053)
60 x 40	30		37 (36,38)	190 (49,478)	190 (49,478)	4.3 (1,10)	130 (49,276)	2851 (430,9604)
	40		35 (34,36)	3066 (573,13523)	3066 (573,13523)	8.6 (6,12)	444 (338,602)	27648 (3362,112876)
	45	[1,2,3]	34 (33,35)	5539 (1247,17333)	5539 (1247,17333)	13.0 (7,21)	600 (456,685)	82611 (9780,362517)
60 x 40	33		37 (37,38)	127 (58,305)	127 (58,305)	4.1 (2,10)	125 (53,232)	1312 (324,2642)
	40		36 (35,37)	506 (267,894)	506 (267,894)	6.8 (4,9)	253 (179,372)	5272 (1192,10676)
	45	[1,3]	35 (35,36)	1302 (492,2237)	1302 (492,2237)	8.2 (5,12)	381 (264,521)	13863 (3078,27955)
30 x 30 [1,2,3]	20		11 (11,11)	528 (257,1144)	528 (257,1144)	10.5 (7,14)	211 (125,281)	2286 (1727,2863)
30 x 30 [1,3]	20		11 (11,11)	440 (264,640)	440 (264,640)	10.0 (7,14)	195 (132,242)	1790 (1187,2967)
40 x 40 [1,2,3]	30		25 (24,26)	3530 (1629,8940)	3530 (1629,8940)	16.7 (12,21)	367 (230,439)	11855 (8537,16731)
40 x 40 [1,3]	30		25 (24,25)	2104 (1283,2894)	2104 (1283,2894)	15.3 (11,22)	316 (271,388)	7446 (4399,14903)

6.3 Multiple machines

6.3.1 The job grouping problem

In practice a flexible machine is likely to be part of a system of several machines. Rajagopalan (1985) and Tang and Denardo (1988b) developed models to describe "multiple machine" problems. In this section we consider the job grouping problem for a number of identical machines, where each job has to be processed by each machine. Early flexible manufacturing systems consisted of different types of machines. Nowadays many machines and tools have become so versatile that only one type of CNC machine can be used to produce a wide variety of part types (Hwang and Shogan, 1989). Many FMSs are configured with a group of these general-purpose CNC machines (Jaikumar, 1986; Jaikumar and Van Wassenhove, 1989) and a job entering such a system is routed to one of the available machines. If each job has to be processed by only one machine, the single machine job grouping model (see Chapter 5) can be used, extended by a final step in which the groups are assigned to the different machines. However, other criteria like workload balancing tend to become more important for these cases. This leads to a different type of problems which we did not consider in this research. Thus, we assume that each job has certain tool requirements on each machine. These requirements are described by the tool-job "matrix" (a_{kim}), where $a_{kim} = 1$ if tool k $(k = 1, \ldots, M)$ is used for job i $(i = 1, \ldots, N)$ on machine m $(m = 1, \ldots, V)$ and $a_{kim} = 0$ otherwise. We assume that each tool needs 1 slot in the tool magazine, and that all machines have the same capacity C (the latter assumption is mostly for ease of notation, and can be easily removed). The job grouping problem is to find a partition of the jobs into a minimum number of groups, such that the jobs in each group do not require more tools on each machine than can be stored in the tool magazine of the machine. A set covering formulation (6.1) - (6.4) of the problem is still valid. The columns in the formulation represent the groups that are feasible on all machines.

6.3.2 Lower bounds via column generation

A lower bound can again be computed by solving the linear relaxation of the formulation (6.1) - (6.4) using a column generation approach. However, a different generation subproblem must now be solved in order to find columns that can improve the solution value of (6.5) - (6.7). Indeed, the restrictions (6.10) and (6.11) must be included for each machine (with $s_k = 1$ for all k), thus leading to the following formulation of the generation subproblem:

$$\text{maximize} \quad \sum_{i=1}^{N} \lambda_i x_i \tag{6.14}$$

$$\text{subject to} \quad a_{kim} x_i \leq z_{km} \qquad i = 1, \ldots, N; k = 1, \ldots, M;$$
$$m = 1, \ldots, V, \tag{6.15}$$

$$\sum_{k=1}^{M} z_{km} \leq C \qquad m = 1, \ldots, V, \tag{6.16}$$

$$x_i \in \{0, 1\} \qquad i = 1, \ldots, N, \tag{6.17}$$

$$z_{km} \in \{0, 1\} \qquad k = 1, \ldots, M; m = 1, \ldots, V, \tag{6.18}$$

where

$$x_i = 1 \quad \text{if job } i \text{ is in group } S,$$
$$= 0 \quad \text{otherwise,}$$

for $i = 1, \ldots, N$, and

$$z_{km} = 1 \quad \text{if tool } k \text{ is required by some job in } S \text{ on machine } m,$$
$$= 0 \quad \text{otherwise,}$$

for $k = 1, \ldots, M; m = 1, \ldots, V$. As previously, we solve this subproblem by complete enumeration (see Section 5.2.3). The lower bounds LB_{Farley} and LB_{CG} are defined as in Section 5.2.4.

6.3.3   Other lower bounds

The sweeping procedure can be adjusted as described by Tang and Denardo (1988b). The concept of compatibility is changed for the "multiple machines" case. Two jobs are compatible if they form a feasible group on all machines. A number of groups are sequentially created as follows. In each step of the procedure, first a job (seed) is selected which is compatible with the smallest number of other (not yet selected) jobs (in case of a tie the job, for which the set of compatible jobs requires the smallest number of tools on all machines is selected). Next, the seed along with all jobs which are compatible with it, are selected to form one group. The procedure is repeated until all jobs have been selected. The number of groups so created, say L is a valid lower bound for the job grouping problem. We also have the trivial lower bound $\lceil M/C \rceil$. Combining this bound with L yields the lower bound $LB_{SW} = \max\{\lceil M/C \rceil, L\}$.

Another lower bound can be obtained in each step of the sweeping procedure by summing the number of groups already created by the procedure and the lower bound $\max_m\{\lceil|\cup_{i\in I}T_{im}|/C\rceil\}$, where I is the set of "not yet selected" jobs, and T_{im} is the set of tools needed for job i on machine m. This procedure generates a sequence of valid lower bounds, the first of which is equal to $\lceil M/C \rceil$ and the last of which is equal to L. We refer to this procedure as the "modified sweeping procedure". It yields a new lower bound, equal to the maximum of the bounds in the sequence, which we denote by LB_{MSW}.

6.3.4   Upper bounds

The MIMU, MI, MU and Whitney and Gaul rules are changed by simply adjusting the definitions of the parameters b_i and t_i introduced in Section 5.3.1. For a group S and a job $i \notin S$, let

$b_i =$ the sum over all machines of the number of tools required by job i

$t_i =$ the sum over all machines of the number of tools required both by job i and by some job already in S.

For the MIMU rule these changes have been described by Tang and Denardo (1988b). The Rajagopalan rule (resp. Modified Rajagopalan-rule) is changed similarly. For each machine m, each tool k receives a weight a_{km}, defined as a_k was for the one machine case. Next the priority of job i is calculated by summing the weights a_{km} over all tools that must be added to the tool magazine of machine m (resp. over all tools needed for job i on machine m) when job i is assigned to the current group, and over all machines. Rajagopalan (1985) also assigns weights to the different machines, based on the ratio of the total number of tool slots needed for the jobs executed on the machine to the capacity of the tool magazine. We decided to use equal weights for all machines. The Marginal gain rule is defined as in the single machine case. For all sequential heuristics the selection of the first job in each group is also based on the cumulative measures mentioned above. All set covering heuristics can also be used as described in Section 5.3.2.

6.3.5   Adjusting the column generation procedure

The generation subproblem has become more complicated. However, due to our enumerative approach for solving the generation subproblem (see Section 5.2.3), only straightforward adjustments to the procedure are needed. The column generation procedure is implemented as described in Section 6.2.5 (see also Section 5.4).

6.3.6   Computational experiments

We generated two sets of random instances. The first set was generated in the same way as the first set of Section 6.2.6. (and the first two sets of Section 5.5.1), except that all tools require just one slot in the tool magazine and each instance is described by V tool-job matrices. The values of M, N, C and V, describing each instance type, are given in Table 6.6.

Problem size M × N	C_1	C_2	C_3	V	Min	Max
10 × 10	4	5	7	3	1	3
10 × 10	4	5	7	5	1	3
15 × 20	8	10	12	3	1	7
15 × 20	8	10	12	5	1	7
25 × 30	10	12	15	3	1	9
25 × 30	10	12	15	5	1	9
60 × 40	20	25	30	3	1	19
60 × 40	20	25	30	5	1	19

Table 6.6 Parameters of the first set of instances.

The second set (see Table 6.7) consists of instances which have a block structure (that is, the tool requirements for subsets of jobs are interdependent) similar to the instances of the second dataset of Section 6.2.6. (or the third dataset of Section 5.5.1).

Problem size M × N	C_1	V	Min	Max	Minjob	Maxjob
30 × 30	15	3	5	8	4	7
30 × 30	15	5	5	8	4	7
40 × 40	20	3	7	10	5	8
40 × 40	20	5	7	10	5	8
50 × 50	25	3	8	12	6	10
50 × 50	25	5	8	12	6	10

Table 6.7 Parameters of the second set of instances.

For these instances, the jobs are divided from the start in a number of feasible subgroups. First, a number N_1 is drawn uniformly between Minjob and Maxjob, and for each machine a subset of C tools is drawn. Then, the tool requirements on the different machines for the first N_1 jobs are generated using the same procedure as in Section 5.5.1, that is, making sure that these jobs form a feasible group. When N_1 jobs have been defined, then the procedure is iterated to produce $N_2, N_3, \ldots$ additional jobs. The process stops when it is not possible to create a new group with Maxjob jobs. The last columns are filled independently of each other as for the first set of instances. We considered two cases, with resp. 3 and 5 machines (see Table 6.6 and Table 6.7). For each instance type 10 instances were created (i.e. 30 or 50 tool-job matrices had to be generated for each instance type) for a total of 300 instances.

6.3.7 Computational results

For a description of the software and hardware used we refer to Section 5.5.2. The results of the computational experiments are recorded in Tables 6.8, 6.9 and 6.10. The description of these tables is similar to that given in Section 6.2.7. (Table 6.8 (resp. 6.9 and 6.10) corresponds to Table 6.3 (resp. 6.4 and 6.5)).

With the procedure sketched in Section 6.3.5. 296 out of 300 instances were solved to optimality. Another 2 instances were solved to optimality by using different parameters while for 2 instances a gap of one unit remained between the best lower bound LB_{CG} and the best known upper bound on the solution value.

Table 6.8 shows that the lower bounds LB_{SW} and LB_{MSW} are only sufficient for instances of type (M, N, C_1). The number of jobs in a group for these instances is extremely small (1 or 2). The performance of the sequential heuristics gets worse for instances with larger capacities. The MI and the Modified Rajagopalan rules outperform the other rules, although the MIMU, Whitney and Gaul, MU and Marginal gain rules give reasonable results. For the instances of the second set the performance of the Rajagopalan and the Marginal gain rules is terrible; this is certainly due to the nature of these rules, which select jobs having few tools in common with the jobs already chosen in a group. The best heuristic solution is in general very good, but for instances of type (M, N, C_3) the gap between heuristic and optimal solution value is often equal to 2 (see Table 6.8, column 12).

Table 6.9 shows that nearly all instances of the first set (of type (M, N, C_1)) can be solved in Step I of the procedure. For the remaining instances optimality is reached in Step III in many cases (73 %). For 27 percent of the instances Step IV is necessary. Table 6.9 shows that for 3 instances additional variables of the last set covering formulation were forced to take 0-1 values to obtain an optimal solution, while 2 instances could not be solved to optimality. For these instances the maximal gap between the lower bound LB_{CG} and the best known upper bound amounts to 1.19.

In Table 6.10 the computation times are given. It appears that only the instances of type (M, N, C_3) of the first set and the instances of the second set require much computational effort. But of course, these are the only really large ones (see column 6). Column 6 also shows that the instances of the first set are usually small. The instances of the second set are probably more realistic. The number of calls to LINDO was considerable for some of these instances (on average 8 - 19, but with peaks of 53). The number of columns in the set covering formulation peaked at 453 for the instances of the second dataset. For the 3-machine instances of type (M, N, C_3) of the first set and the instances of the second set the column generation approach proved to be a helpful tool in decreasing the size of the set covering formulation. For the instances of the second set the number of maximal feasible columns increased by a factor 10 from instance type $(30, 30, 15)$ to $(50, 50, 25)$. The increases in computation time were similar, but the number of columns in the LP subproblems only grew by a factor of 3 to $4\frac{1}{2}$.

Table 6.8 Quality of lower and upper bounds.

Instance type M × N (V)	C	OPT		Lower bounds						Upper bounds				
				LB$_{SW}$	LB$_{MSW}$	LB$_{CG}$	MIMU	MI	MU	Whitney and Gaul	Rajagopalan	Modified Rajagopalan	Marginal gain	Best
		1		2	3	4	5	6	7	8	9	10	11	12
10 x 10 (3)	4	7.5		0.0 (10)	0.0 (10)	0 (10)	0.0 (10)	0.0 (10)	0.0 (10)	0.0 (10)	0.2 (8)	0.0 (10)	0.0 (10)	0.0 (10)
	5	4.8		-1.9 (0)	-1.3 (0)	0 (10)	0.3 (9)	0.3 (9)	0.4 (8)	0.3 (9)	0.6 (6)	0.3 (9)	0.3 (9)	0.2 (8)
	7	3.0		-1.0 (0)	-1.0 (0)	0 (10)	0.0 (10)	0.1 (9)	0.0 (10)	0.0 (10)	0.2 (8)	0.0 (10)	0.1 (9)	0.0 (10)
10 x 10 (5)	4	9.1		0.0 (10)	0.0 (10)	0 (10)	0.0 (10)	0.0 (10)	0.0 (10)	0.0 (10)	0.0 (10)	0.0 (10)	0.0 (10)	0.0 (10)
	5	5.0		-1.4 (0)	-1.1 (1)	0 (10)	0.4 (9)	0.5 (8)	0.3 (10)	0.4 (9)	0.6 (7)	0.5 (8)	0.4 (9)	0.3 (7)
	7	3.0		-1.0 (0)	-1.0 (0)	0 (10)	0.0 (10)	0.0 (10)	0.1 (9)	0.1 (9)	0.6 (4)	0.0 (10)	0.4 (6)	0.0 (10)
15 x 20 (3)	8	14.8		0.0 (10)	0.0 (10)	0 (10)	0.2 (10)	0.2 (10)	0.4 (8)	0.3 (9)	0.3 (9)	0.2 (10)	0.4 (8)	0.2 (8)
	10	7.6		-3.1 (0)	-3.0 (0)	0 (10)	0.8 (8)	0.6 (10)	1.1 (5)	0.7 (9)	1.9 (0)	0.6 (10)	1.6 (2)	0.6 (4)
	12	4.8		-2.7 (0)	-2.7 (0)	0 (10)	0.5 (9)	0.5 (9)	0.6 (8)	0.6 (8)	1.5 (2)	0.6 (8)	1.0 (4)	0.4 (5)
15 x 20 (5)	8	18.4		0.0 (10)	0.0 (10)	0 (10)	0.2 (8)	0.0 (10)	0.2 (8)	0.1 (9)	0.0 (10)	0.0 (10)	0.0 (10)	0.0 (10)
	10	9.3		-3.0 (0)	-2.8 (0)	0 (10)	0.8 (6)	0.5 (9)	1.2 (3)	0.7 (7)	1.1 (3)	0.5 (9)	1.1 (5)	0.4 (5)
	12	5.3		-3.2 (0)	-3.2 (0)	0 (10)	0.9 (6)	0.8 (7)	1.1 (4)	0.8 (7)	1.8 (0)	1.1 (4)	1.3 (3)	0.5 (5)
25 x 30 (3)	10	21.8		-0.3 (7)	-0.2 (8)	0 (10)	0.3 (8)	0.3 (8)	0.6 (5)	0.4 (7)	0.7 (6)	0.3 (8)	0.3 (8)	0.1 (9)
	12	13.6		-2.7 (0)	-2.6 (0)	0 (10)	1.8 (3)	1.2 (8)	2.0 (3)	1.6 (5)	1.6 (4)	1.2 (8)	1.8 (3)	1.0 (2)
	15	8.6		-6.2 (0)	-5.8 (0)	0 (10)	1.2 (7)	1.1 (8)	1.7 (3)	1.4 (5)	2.5 (0)	1.4 (5)	2.0 (0)	0.9 (1)
25 x 30 (5)	10	25.9		-0.1 (9)	0.0 (10)	0 (10)	0.1 (9)	0.0 (10)	0.1 (9)	0.0 (10)	0.8 (7)	0.5 (9)	0.1 (9)	0.0 (10)
	12	15.5		-2.2 (4)	-2.0 (4)	0 (10)	1.0 (4)	0.5 (9)	1.1 (3)	0.9 (5)	0.8 (7)	0.5 (9)	1.2 (3)	0.4 (6)
	15	9.5		-6.7 (0)	-6.3 (0)	0 (10)	1.6 (6)	1.5 (6)	1.9 (4)	1.5 (7)	3.0 (0)	1.5 (6)	2.4 (0)	1.1 (1)
60 x 40 (3)	20	29.2		-0.1 (0)	-0.1 (9)	0 (10)	0.5 (7)	0.3 (9)	0.6 (6)	0.3 (9)	0.4 (8)	0.3 (9)	0.4 (8)	0.2 (9)
	25	17.1		-11.2 (0)	-11.2 (0)	0 (10)	2.4 (3)	1.7 (8)	3.2 (1)	2.7 (3)	1.9 (7)	1.8 (7)	2.3 (3)	1.5 (0)
	30	12.2		-8.5 (0)	-8.3 (0)	0 (10)	2.3 (6)	1.8 (10)	2.9 (1)	2.2 (7)	2.9 (1)	1.9 (9)	2.8 (1)	1.8 (0)
60 x 40 (5)	20	35.5		-0.1 (9)	-0.0 (10)	0 (10)	0.2 (8)	0.1 (9)	0.2 (8)	0.2 (8)	0.1 (9)	0.1 (9)	0.1 (9)	0.0 (10)
	25	19.8		-10.7 (0)	-10.7 (0)	0 (10)	1.9 (1)	1.2 (6)	2.2 (1)	1.9 (9)	0.9 (9)	1.2 (6)	1.5 (4)	0.8 (3)
	30	13.8		-9.6 (0)	-9.4 (0)	0 (10)	2.5 (3)	1.9 (9)	2.8 (2)	2.5 (3)	2.7 (2)	1.8 (10)	2.8 (2)	1.8 (0)
30x30 (3)	15	7.1		-5.1 (0)	-5.0 (0)	0 (10)	0.5 (9)	0.5 (9)	0.7 (7)	0.5 (9)	5.4 (0)	0.4 (10)	3.4 (0)	0.4 (7)
40x40 (3)	20	7.9		-5.9 (0)	-5.9 (0)	0 (10)	0.4 (8)	0.4 (8)	0.4 (8)	0.5 (7)	7.9 (0)	0.4 (8)	4.9 (0)	0.2 (8)
50x50 (3)	25	8.3		-6.3 (0)	-6.3 (0)	0 (10)	1.4 (4)	1.1 (7)	1.4 (4)	1.2 (6)	9.5 (0)	0.9 (9)	5.9 (0)	0.8 (3)
30x30 (5)	15	7.4		-5.3 (0)	-5.1 (0)	0 (10)	0.7 (8)	0.6 (9)	0.7 (8)	0.5 (10)	6.8 (0)	0.6 (9)	4.0 (1)	0.5 (5)
40x40 (5)	20	7.9		-5.9 (0)	-5.9 (0)	0 (10)	0.7 (8)	0.6 (9)	0.7 (9)	0.7 (8)	9.5 (0)	0.6 (9)	4.6 (0)	0.5 (5)
50x50 (5)	25	8.5		-6.5 (0)	-6.5 (0)	0 (10)	1.0 (8)	0.8 (10)	1.0 (8)	0.8 (10)	10.3 (0)	0.8 (10)	5.9 (1)	0.8 (4)

Table 6.9 Performance of different steps of the column generation procedure.

Instance type M × N (V)	C	Step I	Step II	Step III CG	Step III IP	Step IV A	Step IV B	Gap
10 x 10 (3)	4	10						
	5			8	2			
	7			10				
10 x 10 (5)	4	10						
	5			7	2	1		
	7			10				
15 x 20 (3)	8	8			2			
	10			4	4	2		
	12			5		4		1
15 x 20 (5)	8	10						
	10			5	2	2		1
	12			5	2	2 (1)		
25 x 30 (3)	10	7		2	1			
	12			2	5	3		
	15			1	1	7 (1)		
25 x 30 (5)	10	10						
	12	2		4	3	1		
	15			1		9		
60 x 40 (3)	30	8		1	1			
	25				6	4		
	30				1	9		
60 x 40 (5)	20	10						
	25		+	3	7			
	30				1	6	3	
30 x 30 (3) 40 x 40 (3) 50 x 50 (3)	15			7	2	1		
	20			8	2			
	25			3	6			
30 x 30 (5) 40 x 40 (5) 50 x 50 (5)	15			5	5			
	20			5	5			
	25			5	4	1		
All instances		75	0 (+1)	101	64	53 (2)	3	2

Table 6.10 Computation times and size of problems.

Instance type M x N (V)	C	Computation times (in seconds) Heuristics all instances 1	Steps I-IV all instances 2	Steps I-IV col. gen. instances 3	# iterations col.gen. instances 4	# columns col. gen. instances 5	# maximal feasible columns, all instances 6
10 x 10 (3)	4	2.1 (2.0,2.3)	2.1 (2.0,2.3)	n.a.	n.a.	n.a.	9 (8,11)
	5	1.9 (1.8,2.0)	13 (6.3,20)	13 (6.3,20)	2.5 (1,4)	17 (14,21)	30 (25,34)
	7	1.8 (1.8,1.9)	26 (12,40)	26 (12,40)	4.4 (2,7)	30 (22,38)	64 (57,69)
10 x 10 (5)	4	3.3 (3.2,3.5)	3.3 (3.2,3.5)	n.a.	n.a.	n.a.	9 (8,10)
	5	3.0 (2.9,3.0)	14 (8.1,24)	14 (8.1,24)	2.2 (1,4)	15 (12,18)	26 (20,34)
	7	2.7 (2.7,2.8)	24 (14,40)	24 (14,40)	3.7 (2,7)	25 (19,29)	67 (59,77)
15 x 20 (3)	8	11 (10,11)	15 (10,37)	30 (23,37)	3.0 (2,4)	20 (19,20)	26 (19,36)
	10	9.7 (9.6,10)	52 (27,75)	52 (27,75)	4.6 (2,8)	52 (35,68)	124 (97,166)
	12	9.1 (9.0,9.2)	166 (106,309)	166 (106,309)	5.6 (4,9)	143 (117,173)	513 (388,693)
15 x 20 (5)	8	18 (17,18)	18 (17,18)	n.a.	n.a.	n.a.	19 (17,20)
	10	16 (15,16)	49 (26,85)	49 (26,85)	3.3 (1,7)	37 (29,43)	90 (76,100)
	12	14 (14,15)	160 (87,313)	160 (87,313)	4.7 (3,9)	132 (97,163)	384 (306,469)
25 x 30 (3)	10	37 (35,38)	43 (35, 60)	59 (59,60)	2.0 (2,2)	32 (27,39)	55 (32,79)
	12	34 (33,35)	111 (58,164)	111 (58,164)	4.3 (2,8)	80 (41,136)	192 (110,284)
	15	31 (30,31)	591 (213,1095)	591 (213,1095)	5.9 (3,8)	278 (209,419)	1308 (646,1997)
25 x 30 (5)	10	59 (57,61)	59 (57,61)	n.a.	n.a.	n.a.	31 (26,37)
	12	53 (52,56)	99 (54,170)	109 (72,170)	3.4 (1,5)	48 (34,73)	127 (69,176)
	15	50 (49,51)	504 (365,729)	504 (365,729)	5.9 (4,8)	259 (150,384)	806 (445,1187)
60 x 40 (3)	20	141 (139,143)	154 (140,227)	204 (182,227)	3.0 (2,4)	54 (47,60)	97 (70,164)
	25	120 (119,121)	431 (266,614)	431 (266,614)	5.1 (3,8)	173 (105,252)	515 (361,876)
	30	117 (116,118)	1681 (963,2626)	1681 (963,2626)	6.6 (4,8)	480 (356,626)	2898 (1852,4953)
60 x 40 (5)	20	230 (228,232)	230 (228,232)	n.a.	n.a.	n.a.	45 (37,56)
	25	197 (192,213)	422 (248,661)	422 (248,661)	4.0 (1,7)	99 (53,147)	240 (189,269)
	30	191 (190,193)	1343 (795,1744)	1343 (795,1744)	5.3 (3,7)	288 (221,413)	1223 (860,1444)
30 x 30 (3)	15	36 (35,37)	240 (149,398)	240 (149,398)	7.9 (5,13)	114 (63,254)	752 (497,1058)
40 x 40 (3)	20	81 (80,82)	653 (360,1730)	653 (360,1730)	10.7 (7,30)	158 (85,236)	2164 (1655,2654)
50 x 50 (3)	25	154 (152,156)	2895 (824,7867)	2895 (824,7867)	18.5 (7,41)	319 (205,453)	7823 (6230,10411)
30 x 30 (5)	15	58 (57,59)	213 (131,322)	213 (131,322)	8.0 (4,15)	63 (43,107)	455 (373,609)
40 x 40 (5)	20	132 (131,133)	710 (319,1793)	710 (319,1793)	11.8 (7,21)	94 (48,162)	1247 (944,1556)
50 x 50 (5)	25	249 (247,251)	3274 (794,10386)	3274 (794,10386)	16.0 (8,53)	271 (143,431)	5341 (4267,6568)

6.4   Other extensions

The extension of the job grouping problem to several non-identical machines
is similar to the one described in Section 6.3. It is also possible to combine
these changes for the case where jobs have to be processed on several non-
identical machines with tools that require one or multiple slots in the tool
magazines.

Rajagopalan (1985) and Hwang and Shogan (1989) discuss the introduction of due dates in the job grouping problem. Their models are sequential
by nature and concentrate on finding one batch (optimal with respect to
some "local" criterion) at a time. Due dates are incorporated by weighting
jobs: jobs which have tight due dates receive larger weights and thus higher
priority for being added to a next batch. By contrast the set covering formulation aims at finding a minimal number of groups, with no decisions taken
on the order in which the groups have to be executed. Therefore the introduction of due dates does not fit very well into this formulation. Similarly,
the introduction of order quantities or production times would change the
nature of the formulation. Because we should decide on the order in which
groups are executed, additional variables should be added to incorporate
this information. A possible change in this direction is the introduction of
separate weights for groups in different planning periods, where the weights
depend on the planning period (each group (column) should be available
in the formulation for each appropriate planning period). Additional constraints must then be added to the set covering formulation to prohibit that
more than one group be assigned to some planning period (or that a job
be executed more than once). The introduction of due dates also requires
the separate evaluation of small groups. Previously, we only had to consider
groups that were maximal (groups for which it is not possible to add jobs
without destroying feasibility). Now, we must explicitly consider all groups
that are not maximal, because different costs are attached to these smaller
groups (increases in setup time can be traded off against decreases in the
number of jobs that are overdue). As a result, the size of the formulation
grows sharply with the number of possible planning periods. This discussion shows that the set covering formulation is probably not the right tool
to incorporate the introduction of due dates, production times and order
quantities, and therefore we did not further investigate these extensions.

6.5 Summary and conclusions

In this study, the results of Chapter 5 have been extended to some special cases of the job grouping problem. First, the job grouping problem was considered in the case where tools need more than one slot in the tool magazine. Next, the job grouping problem for several identical machines was investigated. Lower and upper bounds were derived for these extensions. A column generation approach was used to compute a lower bound. It appears that the lower bound obtained by computing the LP-relaxation value of the set covering formulation of the job grouping problem is very strong, though not always optimal. This is the case for both extensions studied. For 2 percent of the instances tested, this lower bound was strictly smaller than the best upper bound (gap equal to 1). In our computational experiments, the "multiple slots" instances tend to be more difficult and the "multiple machines" instances tend to be easier than the instances studied in Chapter 5.

Acknowledgments
We gratefully acknowledge useful discussions on the topic of this work with Antoon Kolen. We thank Ron van der Wal for solving some problems using a branch-and-bound procedure.

Chapter 7

A local search approach to job grouping

7.1 Introduction

In Chapters 5 and 6, lower and upper bounding procedures were proposed for the *job grouping problem*. It appeared that, in many cases, sequential heuristic procedures were not sufficient to provide an optimal solution. *A column generation approach* was also developed to compute a strong lower bound, based on the linear relaxation of the *set covering formulation* of the job grouping problem. In the course of this procedure, it was sometimes possible to derive improved upper bounds. Notice, however, that solving the job grouping problem may be done faster if a better upper bound is known from the start. For instance, execution of the column generation procedure can be avoided if simple lower bounds like LB_{SW} and LB_{MSW} (see Chapters 5 and 6) are optimal and an optimal upper bound is also available. Alternatively, improved solutions provide additional columns to be included in the set covering formulation, which may speed up the column generation procedure.

Local search procedures may provide such improved solutions. Loosely speaking, a local search procedure tries to improve the current solution of a problem by searching the neighbourhood of that solution for improved solutions, until no better solution can be found, optimality is achieved or the procedure is stopped according to some other criterion. In this chapter, we investigate four possible ways for searching the neighbourhood, namely a *simple improvement approach*, a *tabu search approach*, a *simulated annealing approach* and a *variable-depth approach*, based on ideas of Kernighan and Lin (1970). For each of these methods three different objective functions and two different neighbourhood structures are considered for two different types of starting solutions. The environment in which these methods are applied is discussed in the next section. Section 7.3 contains the description of the methods. The results of our computational experiments are reported in Section 7.4. In this study, we consider instances where tools require several slots and instances with several machines. Some conclusions are drawn in Section 7.5.

7.2 Local search environment

Our objective is to partition the set of jobs into a minimal number of *feasible* groups, where a group is called feasible if the tools needed for the jobs in the group fit in the tool magazine of the machine(s). Our local search heuristics are designed to solve this problem indirectly, by answering a sequence of questions of the form: "Given a number g, is there a partition of the jobs into at most g feasible groups?". This approach is motivated by the observation, made in Chapters 5 and 6, that simple sequential heuristics provide good estimates for the optimal number of groups. For most instances tested the sequential heuristics provided a solution within 2 groups of the optimal solution. Therefore, the local search procedure can be applied to find a solution which uses a number of groups equal to best known upper bound minus one. If a feasible solution is found the procedure is repeated for a smaller number of groups. If a solution is found with a number of groups equal to the lower bound the procedure ends. If we are not able to find a feasible solution for the given number of groups, the procedure is started again with a different starting solution. Other stopping criteria can be added to avoid endless runs. In this section we will discuss the setting of different parameters that are important for the execution of the local search procedures. All procedures rely on the choice of a *starting solution*, an *objective function* $f(G)$ which evaluates the 'quality' of each solution G (consisting of g groups of jobs), a *neighbourhood structure* defining what solutions are considered as *neighbours* or *perturbations* of a given solution, and a *stopping criterion*. Before discussing all these concepts in detail, we first present, for illustration, the structure of an unsophisticated local search procedure to which we will refer as the simple improvement approach. The other local search procedures can be seen as variants of this basic strategy.

Simple improvement approach (for finding a partition into g feasible groups).

(Initialization) find a starting solution, i.e. a partition $G = \{G_1, G_2, ..., G_g\}$

(Improve) **while** G is not feasible and the stopping criterion is not satisfied
    do
    begin
                select a neighbour of G, say G', which minimizes $f(G')$ among
                all neighbours;
                if $f(G') \geq f(G)$ and G' is not feasible
                then return FAIL (G is an infeasible local optimum)
                else let $G := G'$
    end

(Termination) **if** G is feasible
                then return G
                else return FAIL (stopping criterion satisfied)

7.2.1   Starting solution

A local search procedure starts from a given partition of the jobs into g groups. This partition does not have to be feasible (if it is, we can stop the local search procedure for this number of groups). In our implementation we used two types of starting solutions, viz. the *Maximal Intersection* solution and a *random* starting solution. The Maximal Intersection (MI) starting solution is created using the *Maximal Intersection rule* for job grouping (see Sections 5.3.1, 6.2.4 and 6.3.4). Remember that this rule sequentially creates a number of groups. Here, we run the procedure until g feasible groups are formed. Then, the remaining jobs (that are not (yet) assigned to some group) are distributed to the already created groups. This is done in a greedy way. The jobs are assigned to one of the g groups in an arbitrary order, so that the sum of the violations of the tool magazine capacity constraint of the groups is minimized in each step (see next section). A random starting solution is created by assigning jobs randomly to g different groups. Some experiments were carried out using another structured starting solution (based on the *Modified Rajagopalan rule*, see Sections 5.3.1, 6.2.4 and 6.3.4), but these experiments offered no improvement over the MI starting solution. The MI starting solution was eventually preferred because the overall performance of the MI rule was better for the job grouping problem (see Chapters 5 and 6).

7.2.2 Objective function

We used one of several measures to judge the quality of a partition of the jobs in a given number of groups.

- *Minimize violations*

  The violation $v(G)$ of a group G of jobs is defined as the difference between the number of slots needed for the jobs in G and the capacity of the tool magazine, if this difference is positive. The violation is zero if the tools fit in the tool magazine. The value of our first objective function is the sum of the violations of the groups. In case of several machines, we consider the sum of the violations over all machines. More precisely, define

  C = capacity of the tool magazine,

  V = number of machines,

  T_{im} = collection of tools necessary for job i on machine m,

  s_k = number of slots necessary for tool k,

  G = collection of groups ($G = \{G_1, G_2, \ldots, G_g\}$),

  $v(G_j)$ = violation of group G_j. Then the violation of group $G_j (\in G)$ is $v(G_j) = \sum_{m=1}^{V} \max \{0, \sum_{k \in \{\cup_{i \in G_j} T_{im}\}} s_k - C\}$. The objective function to be minimized is $f_1(G) = \sum_{G_j \in G} v(G_j)$. A feasible solution is found if the objective function is equal to 0. This approach is derived from the approach of Chams, Hertz and de Werra (1987) for graph coloring.

- *Minimize violations & maximize slack*

  Instead of only considering the violations, this objective function also takes into account the slack-capacity (i.e. the number of unused tool slots) in a group. It can be improved by increasing the slackcapacity in a group. If S_j is the slack ($S_j = \sum_{m=1}^{V} \max \{0, C - \sum_{k \in \{\cup_{i \in G_j} T_{im}\}} s_k\}$ in a group $G_j \in G$, then the objective function to be minimized is $f_2(G) = \sum_{G_j \in G} (C \cdot v(G_j) - S_j)$.

- *Maximize groupsize & minimize violations* This objective function is inspired from the objective function of Johnson, Aragon, McGeoch and Schevon (1991) for graph coloring. The objective function is $f_3(G) = -\sum_{G_j \in G} |G_j|^2 + 2 \sum_{G_j \in G} |G_j| \cdot v(G_j)$. When minimizing this function, the first term tends to favour large groups, whereas the second term favours feasible groups.

7.2.3   Neighbourhood structure

The neighbourhood structure defines the set of feasible moves from a certain solution. We studied two different neighbourhood structures:

- *Move and exchange* Given a solution, a neighbour solution is created by moving some job to another group or by exchanging two jobs. All possible moves and exchanges are considered in each iteration. To find a best move or exchange we visit all jobs consecutively. First, all possible moves for a job are considered. Then, all pairwise exchanges of the job with jobs in other groups are investigated. The best of these moves and exchanges is selected.

- *Move* Given a solution, a neighbour solution is created by moving some job to another group. We consider all moves for all jobs and select the best one. Compared to the first neighbourhood structure, the pairwise exchanges are not considered.

It is clear that the first neighbourhood structure uses more computation time per iteration than the other neighbourhood structure. On the other hand, the number of iterations to reach optimality will be decisive for the actual computational effort. In some procedures, the neighbourhood structure will be restricted by disallowing some moves or exchanges (see Section 7.3 on tabu-lists).

7.2.4   Stopping criteria

The local search procedure stops if feasibility is achieved or the computation time limit is reached. Use of a computation time limit is necessary to prevent some local search procedures from running endlessly. At the end of each step the solution is checked for feasibility since the values of the second and the third objective function give no conclusive evidence of feasibility of the solution. For some local search approaches (viz. the simple improvement and the variable-depth approaches, see Section 7.3) the procedure is stopped when no improvements are possible any more (the tabu search always has the possibility to leave a local optimum, while the simulated annealing approach only stops if repeatedly no suitable neighbour solution can be found after a large number of trials; see Section 7.3.3). For randomly generated starting solutions an additional stopping criterion is added to allow testing of several starting solutions within a fixed amount of computation time. Namely, only a maximal number of steps can be performed from each starting solution, after which the procedure is restarted with a new random starting solution (here, a step is defined as a transition from one solution to another). In our implementation the procedure was restarted after $3N$ steps, where N is the number of jobs. This type of restart is not used with the MI starting solution, which thus can use the full amount of computation time.

7.3   Local search approaches

Four different approaches have been considered. The simple improvement approach only considers those moves which improve the solution at hand. The second approach (tabu search) also accepts moves that give a deterioration of the objective function. The third approach (simulated annealing) introduces a stochastic element in accepting moves that worsen the objective function value. In the fourth approach, ideas of Kernighan and Lin (1970) are implemented.

7.3.1   Simple improvement approach

This approach has been formally described in Section 7.2. Given the neighbourhood structure and the objective function, a move is accepted only if it improves the objective function. If it is not possible to find an improvement after all possible moves and/or exchanges have been considered the procedure stops.

7.3.2   Tabu search approach

The simple improvement approach follows a so-called hill climbing (or better valley seeking) approach for finding an optimum. The chances that the procedure gets stuck in a local optimum using the simple improvement approach are considerable. To overcome this difficulty, the tabu search approach allows moves that worsen the solution value. The idea is that accepting a number of 'bad' moves may open up possibilities to move to another (better) local optimum. The approach has achieved impressive practical successes for other combinatorial problems; for a thorough discussion we refer to Glover (1989; 1990). When it is not possible to find an improved solution among the neighbours of the current one, a move is chosen that is the best among the 'bad' moves, that is a move that has the least impact on the value of the objective function. To avoid returning to a recent local optimum a *tabu-list* is used. More precisely, in our implementation, the tabu-list contains a list of jobs that are not allowed to be transferred to another group. The tabu-list may also contain a list of specified moves (in which explicitly the job, the old and the new group are recorded) that are not allowed, but preliminary tests showed no improvement over the current choice. We use a tabu-list of length 7, which means that the last seven jobs that have been moved (in steps where the objective function deteriorated) may not be moved again (preliminary tests with a tabu-list of variable length - equal to $\frac{1}{2}N$, where N is the total number of jobs - led to a significant deterioration of the performance of the procedure). A move remains tabu only during a certain number of iterations, so that we have a cyclical list where the oldest forbidden move (or job) is removed whenever a new forbidden move (or job) is added. The procedure stops when a feasible solution is obtained or the computation time limit is reached. To improve the performance of the procedure the concept of *aspiration levels* is introduced (see Glover (1989)). This offers the possibility of overriding the tabu status of a job (or move) on the tabu-list if the solution value which can be obtained by accepting this particular move is strictly smaller than the best known solution value.

7.3.3 Simulated annealing approach

Simulated annealing extends the simple improvement approach by allowing uphill moves during the minimization process, as in the tabu search approach (for a discussion on simulated annealing we refer to Van Laarhoven and Aarts (1987) and Johnson, Aragon, McGeoch and Schevon (1989; 1991)). However, the procedure of accepting uphill moves is randomized. If a move or exchange is selected in an iteration and this move offers an improvement of the objective function, the move is accepted. If it offers an increase of the objective function by Δ, then the move is accepted with a probability of $e^{-\Delta/T}$. The parameter T is referred to as *temperature* and is an important factor in the decision to accept uphill moves. If the temperature T is large, the possibility of accepting 'bad' moves is large. Therefore, the temperature is gradually decreased in the course of the procedure (*'annealing'*). The behaviour of a simulated annealing implementation may be largely influenced by the setting of certain parameters, like the initial temperature and the *cooling schedule*. We used some suggestions of Johnson et al. (1989; 1991) in our choices for these parameters; these are now as follows. At the start of the simulated annealing procedure T is fixed to some value $T_{start} = 4$. A number of iterations is carried out using this temperature. After maxiter iterations have been performed at a certain temperature, the temperature is decreased. The parameter maxiter is chosen proportional to the number of jobs (N), viz. maxiter $= 3N$. The temperature T is decreased using *geometric cooling* (the temperature in a next step is 95 % of the current temperature). To limit the time spent at high temperatures we introduce a parameter cutoff $(= 0.3)$. This parameter makes sure that the temperature T is decreased if too many moves are accepted. Thus, the temperature is decreased either after maxiter moves or after cutoff × maxiter accepted moves. Finally a parameter minpercent $(= 2$ %$)$ is used as follows to decide whether a simulated annealing run can be stopped. A counter is incremented after each temperature change, if less than minpercent of the selected moves have been accepted since the previous temperature change. The counter is reset to 0 whenever the current best solution is improved. If the counter reaches 5, the process is declared *frozen* and stopped (see Johnson et al. (1989)). The procedure also stops if the computation time limit is reached. Finally, we introduced a tabu-list to avoid the possibility of returning too fast to an already visited local optimum. This tabu-list was implemented as in the tabu search approach (see Section 7.3.2).

7.3.4   Variable-depth approach

Kernighan and Lin (1970) proposed an effective heuristic algorithm for the graph partitioning problem. We use an idea similar to theirs. Each iteration of our procedure consists of a number of steps. In each step, a move or exchange is performed (the best one according to the given objective function and neighbourhood structure), and the jobs involved are placed on a tabu-list of length N. After a number of steps, when all N jobs have been moved once (and placed on the tabu-list), a sequence of solutions has been obtained. From this sequence the best solution is chosen and a next iteration is performed starting from this solution. At the start of each new iteration all jobs are removed from the tabu-list (the tabu-list is emptied). The procedure is repeated until no improved solution can be found in an iteration or the maximum amount of computation time is used.

7.4 Computational experiments

Considering all combinations of two starting solutions, three objective functions, two different neighbourhood structures and four local search approaches, we get 48 possible implementations for a local search procedure (if we do not vary the other parameters). In this section we first make a selection among these methods, and then discuss the results of our computational experiments with the 'best' ones.

7.4.1 The dataset

Computational experiments were performed on a set of problem instances which emerged from the research described in Chapters 5 and 6. In these chapters, computational experiments were performed on a large set of randomly generated data (see Sections 5.6, 6.2.7 and 6.3.7). From this set, we selected a subset of instances for which the upper bounds computed by the sequential heuristics were not optimal (it is clear that this is not a random selection from the whole set of problems since all relatively easy instances were left out). The smallest instances were also discarded and, for each instance type (M, N, C) (where M is the number of tools, N is the number of jobs and C is the capacity of the tool magazine), at most 5 problems were retained. We investigated three types of instances:

- single slot, single machine instances,

- multiple slot, single machine instances,

- single slot, multiple machine instances.

The dataset we used is described in Table 7.1. In each row the parameters for each instance type (M, N, C) are given: M, N, C, the number of instances tested, the number of machines and the size of the tools. The upper part of Table 7.1 contains 45 instances of the single slot, single machine type (dataset 1). Then, 46 instances are described where tool sizes are tool-dependent (dataset 2). The last 54 instances are of the single slot, multiple machine type (dataset 3A and 3B). The sequential heuristics provided solutions close to optimality for all these instances (gap between upper bound and optimal solution is 1 or 2). Therefore, we tested all our local search heuristics by asking the question: "Is there a feasible solution involving exactly OPT groups?", where OPT was the optimal value of the instance at hand.

Dataset	Problem size M × N	C	Number of instances	Number of machines	Number of slots per tool
single	10 × 10	4	5	1	1
slot	15 × 20	8	5	1	1
single	20 × 30	10	5	1	1
machine	25 × 30	10	5	1	1
dataset 1	40 × 30	25	5	1	1
	60 × 40	30	5	1	1
	40 × 40	20	5	1	1
	50 × 50	25	5	1	1
	60 × 60	30	5	1	1
multiple	15 × 20	13,15	5	1	1,2,3
slots	15 × 20	13,15	5	1	1,3
single	25 × 30	20	5	1	1,2,3
machine	25 × 30	25	4	1	1,3
dataset 2	60 × 40	40	5	1	1,2,3
	60 × 40	45	5	1	1,3
	30 × 30	20	3	1	1,2,3
	30 × 30	20	5	1	1,3
	40 × 40	30	4	1	1,2,3
	40 × 40	30	5	1	1,3
single slot	15 × 20	12	4	3	1
3 machines	25 × 30	15	5	3	1
dataset 3A	60 × 40	30	5	3	1
	30 × 30	15	3	3	1
	40 × 40	20	2	3	1
	50 × 50	25	5	3	1
single slot	15 × 20	12	5	5	1
5 machines	25 × 30	15	5	5	1
dataset 3B	60 × 40	30	5	5	1
	30 × 30	15	5	5	1
	40 × 40	20	5	5	1
	50 × 50	25	5	5	1

Table 7.1 Dataset local search.

7.4.2 Computational results

The local search procedures were implemented in Turbo Pascal and run on an AT personal computer with 16 MHz 80386sx processor and 80387 mathematical coprocessor (except for the results of Table 7.4; see below for details).

The computational experiments were performed as follows. First, extensive computational experiments were performed on the first dataset for a wide variety of implementations. The results of a number of approaches that performed relatively well are presented in Table 7.2. For this selection of approaches, additional experiments were performed on the instances of the second and the third datasets (for the "multiple slots" and the "multiple machines" instances).

The experiments on the first dataset were carried out with a 600 seconds limit on the computation time. Each instance was tested for a given starting solution, objective function, neighbourhood structure and local search approach. When a random starting solution was used a number of restarts was allowed within the given time period of 600 seconds (see Section 7.2.4).

Early tests showed that the simple improvement approach was dominated strongly by the other local search approaches, and therefore we did not consider this approach any further. The lack of good results for this strategy is probably due to the fact that the objective functions are such that the possibility of getting stuck in local optima (minima) is indeed large if no uphill moves are allowed.

The results for the other three local search approaches (i.e. tabu search, simulated annealing, variable-depth) did not diverge too much for a given starting solution, objective function and neighbourhood structure. Table 7.2 gives the results of the computational experiments for the tabu search approach using the objective functions $f_1(G), f_2(G), f_3(G)$ defined in Section 7.2.2 and the neighbourhood structures "move and exchange" and "move" described in Section 7.2.3. The second column of Table 7.2 indicates the number of instances tested for each instance type (M, N) (5 for all instance types). Each entry of the table consists in a pair "A - B", where A describes the number of instances for which an optimal solution was found using the MI starting solution and B describes the number of instances that was solved using a random starting solution (possibly with multiple starts). The bottom line of the table gives the cumulative results.

Problem size	#	Move and exchange			Move		
M × N		obj.1	obj.2	obj.3	obj.1	obj.2	obj.3
10 × 10	5	5-5	5-5	5-5	5-5	5-5	5-5
15 × 20	5	5-5	5-5	4-5	5-5	5-5	4-4
20 × 30	5	4-2	4-3	4-2	2-3	3-2	4-2
25 × 30	5	1-1	2-1	1-0	0-1	1-3	1-1
40 × 30	5	5-4	4-5	5-3	3-3	3-4	2-2
60 × 40	5	2-1	3-3	2-0	1-0	1-2	1-0
40 × 40	5	2-1	3-3	3-4	0-1	2-3	3-2
50 × 50	5	4-0	5-0	3-0	5-1	5-2	4-4
60 × 60	5	2-0	5-0	3-0	3-0	4-0	4-4
Total	45	30-19	36-25	30-19	24-19	29-26	28-24

Table 7.2 Results dataset 1: tabu search.

The first two rows show that nearly all smaller instances can be solved by the tabu search approach, independently of the neighbourhood structure or the objective function. However, the results diverge for larger instances. It appears that the use of a MI starting solution gives better results than the implementation using a random starting solution. We come back to this issue in the discussion of Table 7.4. The second objective function, including the slacks, usually leads to the best results (an impression also confirmed by our other experiments). The "move" neighbourhood provides slightly better results than the "move and exchange" neighbourhood. This may be due to the fact that the latter neighbourhood is computationally more expensive to explore and can perform fewer steps within a fixed time period. The results show that even large instances can be solved to optimality using a tabu search approach.

The trends discussed above for the tabu search approach have also been observed for the simulated annealing and the variable-depth approach. We do not give complete results for these two approaches, but limit ourselves to some brief comments. The results of the simulated annealing approach, though sometimes different for individual instances, are on average comparable to the tabu search results. The performance of the variable-depth approach is somewhat weaker (especially for objective functions $f_1(G)$ and $f_3(G)$), which may be due to the absolute stopping criterion used (see Sections 7.2.4 and 7.3.4). As an illustration of these comparisons, Table 7.3 reports on the results obtained by the three approaches on the first dataset, when the objective function $f_2(G)$ is used.

Problem size M × N	#	Tabu search	Simulated Annealing	Variable-depth
10 × 10	5	5-5	5-5	5-5
15 × 20	5	5-5	5-5	3-5
20 × 30	5	4-3	4-1	5-3
25 × 30	5	2-1	2-1	2-1
40 × 30	5	4-5	4-5	3-5
60 × 40	5	3-3	3-2	3-3
40 × 40	5	3-3	3-3	4-2
50 × 50	5	5-0	5-0	5-0
60 × 60	5	5-0	5-0	5-0
Total	45	36-25	36-22	35-24

Table 7.3 Selected results dataset 1.

From these preliminary experiments, it appears that the objective function $f_2(G)$ combined with the "move" neighbourhood provides the best results. For the variable-depth approach the more elaborate "move and exchange" neighbourhood provides better results, which may again be related to the influence of the stopping criterion (the time limit criterion is not often the reason to cut off the variable-depth search). In the remainder of this section we limit ourselves to the discussion of the objective function $f_2(G)$ combined with the "move and exchange" or the "move" neighbourhood.

Table 7.4 displays the influence of computation time when using a random starting solution within the tabu search framework, with the "move" neighbourhood structure. Of course, we expect the tabu search approach to give better results if the time limit is increased, but the extent of improvement is not clear. These experiments were run on a faster computer (with 25 Mhz 80386 processor), approximately twice as fast as the previous one. For each instance type (M, N), 5 instances were tested, and for each instance 25 random starting solutions were considered. Each column of Table 7.4 records the number of times (maximal 125) that an optimal solution was obtained within the given time limit (resp. 1, 5, 15, 30, 60, 150, 300, 450 and 600 seconds).

The instances are roughly arranged by increasing size and the zeros in the lower diagonal part of Table 7.4 speak for themselves. Table 7.4 shows that the largest instances are indeed hard to solve using a random starting solution, especially if this performance is compared to the results using a

MI starting solution (see Table 7.2 for the occurrence of optimality within 600 seconds on the slower computer). One may consider these computation times as very high, compared to the time it takes to solve similar instances to optimality (see Table 5.6, Chapter 5). These experiments were also carried out for the simulated annealing approach, with comparable results.

Problem size	#	Cumulative # of instances solved to optimalty after						
M × N		15 s	30 s	60 s	150 s	300 s	450 s	600 s
10 × 10	5	125	125	125	125	125	125	125
15 × 20	5	41	83	97	104	107	109	110
20 × 30	5	0	0	16	59	73	75	78
25 × 30	5	1	1	8	34	48	50	55
40 × 30	5	0	2	43	107	118	122	122
60 × 40	5	0	0	0	2	64	77	84
40 × 40	5	0	0	0	22	79	85	93
50 × 50	5	0	0	0	0	8	54	97
60 × 60	5	0	0	0	0	0	0	1

Table 7.4 Results tabu search with random starting solution.

In Tables 7.5 and 7.6, a further comparison is made between the three local search approaches for the "multiple slots" and the "multiple machines" instances. As mentioned before, we choose to present the results of implementations using the superior objective function $f_2(G)$. Tests with the other objective functions yield results that are in general worse than the results obtained for this objective function, as previously illustrated in Table 7.2.

Table 7.5 displays the results for the "multiple slots" case (dataset 2). In the third column of Table 7.5 the size of the tools is given. Because the "multiple slots" instances are expected to be harder (see Chapter 6), the time limit is increased from 600 to 900 seconds (on the 'slower' computer). Objective function $f_2(G)$ combined with the "move" neighbourhood structure form the best parameter set for the "multiple slots" instances. The results obtained with a random starting solution are similar to those using the MI starting solution if the tabu search or simulated annealing approach is used. However, if the time limit stopping criterion is decreased from 900 to 600 seconds, the results for the random starting solution deterio- rate much faster than for the MI starting solution. The total scores for the "move and exchange" neighbourhood change from 33 - 29, 33 - 35 and 22 -27 (see last line of Table 7.5) to 33 - 24, 32 - 25, 22 - 25 if the time limit is set to 600 seconds. The influence of a time limit reduction is also present (though less significantly) in case of the "move" neighbourhood. Thus, it seems that the relatively good results for the random starting solution are related to the large time limit.

Problem size M × N	#	$s_k \in$	Tabu search	Simulated Annealing	Variable-depth
15 × 20	5	1,2,3	4-5	4-5	2-5
15 × 20	5	1,3	4-5	4-5	3-5
25 × 30	5	1,2,3	2-2	2-4	3-3
25 × 30	4	1,3	4-3	4-2	1-3
60 × 40	5	1,2,3	3-2	3-3	3-2
60 × 40	5	1,3	4-5	4-5	3-4
30 × 30	3	1,2,3	2-2	2-2	1-2
30 × 30	5	1,3	3-4	3-4	2-2
40 × 40	4	1,2,3	4-1	4-3	3-1
40 × 40	5	1,3	3-0	3-2	1-0
Total	46		33-29	33-35	22-27

Table 7.5 Results dataset 2.

Table 7.5 also shows that the time limit of 900 seconds is probably not enough for the largest instances in case of a random starting solution. The performance of the variable-depth approach is systematically worse than that of the other approaches if a MI starting solution is used. This may be partly explained by the stronger stopping criterion adopted (12 out of 24 (resp. 28 out of 29) unsolved instances for the variable-depth approach using a "move and exchange" (resp. "move") neighbourhood structure were stopped before the computation time limit was reached). The influence of the stopping criterion is largely decreased in case multiple random starts are used. The results for the variable-depth approach are comparable to the other results if a random starting solution is employed.

Table 7.6 records the results for the "multiple machines" instances (datasets 3 A & B). The computations were performed using a 900 seconds time limit (in Chapter 6 it is shown that these instances are probably easier than those of the second dataset; however, in each step of the local search approach more function evaluations have to be made). The upper (resp. lower) part of Table 7.6 presents results on "3 machines" (resp. "5 machines") instances. The tabu search and simulated annealing approaches give similar results, with the variable-depth approach trailing behind. The tests using a MI starting solution were more successful than those using a random starting solution, which may indicate that the time limit was too low for randomly generated starting solutions (compare with the results presented in Table 7.4). Nearly all structured instances (of sizes (30, 30), (40, 40) and (50, 50)) were solved to optimality when a MI starting solution was used. The results were better for the "move and exchange" neighbourhood structure than for the "move" neighbourhood structure in case a MI starting solution was used. For random starting solutions the more time-efficient "move" neighbourhood structure was more appropriate.

Problem size M × N	#	V	Tabu search	Simulated Annealing	Variable-depth
15 × 20	4	3	4-4	4-4	4-4
25 × 30	5	3	3-4	3-4	3-3
60 × 40	5	3	2-1	2-0	1-1
30 × 30	3	3	3-3	3-3	2-3
40 × 40	2	3	2-0	2-1	2-0
50 × 50	5	3	5-0	5-0	5-0
15 × 20	5	5	5-5	5-4	3-3
25 × 30	5	5	4-4	4-4	1-2
60 × 40	5	5	0-0	0-0	0-0
30 × 30	5	5	5-5	5-5	5-5
40 × 40	5	5	5-0	5-0	5-0
50 × 50	5	5	4-0	4-0	4-0
Total	54		42-26	42-25	35-21

Table 7.6 Selected results dataset 3A and 3B.

7.5 Summary and conclusions

In this chapter, we investigated the use of local search approaches to improve the solution for the job grouping problem. Four local search approaches were considered, namely simple improvement, tabu search, simulated annealing and the variable-depth approach; for each of these methods, several starting solutions, objective functions, neighbourhood structures and stopping criteria were tested. Computational experiments using three sets of data seem to indicate that the latter choices considerably influence the performance of the different approaches, while the influence of the specific local search approach seems less serious as long as some kind of local optimum evading procedure is used. The opportunity to leave local optima is particularly important given the rigidity of some objective functions.

The differences in performance of the tabu search, simulated annealing and variable-depth approach are relatively small for the job grouping problem. In some cases the results for the variable-depth approach are a bit disappointing, but this may be partly related to the stopping criteria used (that is, the variable-depth approach does not always benefit from additional computation time as the other two approaches do). Local search approaches are well known for their extensive use of computation time and, in this study, they live up to this expectation. However, initial solutions are sometimes improved in a limited amount of time, especially for smaller instances. The MI starting solution outperforms the random starting solutions in most cases. Since the MI starting solution can be quickly obtained, we find it advisable to use it as a starting point. The objective function $f_2(G)$, which combines minimizing the number of violations with increasing the slack in groups that have spare capacity, seems to be the most adequate objective function. Combined with either of the neighbourhood structures "move and exchange" or "move", it provided good results for all three datasets considered. In conclusion, the experiments with local search approaches show that these approaches can be helpful in finding improved solutions for the job grouping problem. One important application could be the use of these methods for improving the initial set covering formulation of the job grouping problem by a column generation approach, as described in Chapters 5 and 6.

Chapter 8

Minimizing the number of tool switches on a flexible machine

8.1 Introduction

The importance of tool management for the efficient use of automated manufacturing systems has been recently stressed by several authors; we refer for instance to Gray, Seidmann and Stecke (1988) or Kiran and Krason (1988) for a thorough discussion of this issue. In particular, a central problem of tool management for flexible machines is to decide how to sequence the parts to be produced, and what tools to allocate to the machine, in order to minimize the number of tool setups. The problem becomes especially crucial when the time needed to change a tool is significant with respect to the processing times of the parts, or when many small batches of different parts must be processed in succession. These phenomena have been observed in the metal-working industry by Hirabayashi, Suzuki and Tsuchiya (1984), Finke and Kusiak (1987), Bard (1988), Tang and Denardo (1988a), Bard and Feo (1989), etc. Blazewicz, Finke, Haupt and Schmidt (1988) describe for instance an NC-forging machine equipped with two tool magazines, each of which can handle eight tools. The tools are very heavy, and exchanging them requires a sizeable fraction of the actual forging time. Another situation where minimizing the number of tool setups may be important is described by Förster and Hirt (1989, p. 109). These authors mention that, when the tool transportation system is used by several machines, there is a distinct possibility that this system becomes overloaded. Then, minimizing the number of tool setups can be viewed as a way to reduce the strain on the tool transportation system. Bard (1988) mentions yet another occurrence of the same problem in the electronics industry. Suppose several types of printed circuit boards (PCBs) are produced by an automated placement machine (or a line of such machines). For each type of PCB, a certain collection of component feeders must be placed on the machine before boards of that type can be produced. As the machine can only hold a limited number of feeders, it is usually necessary to replace some feeders when switching from the production of one type of boards to that of another type. Exchanging feeders is a time-comsuming operation and it is therefore important to determine a production sequence for the board types which minimizes the number of "feeder-setups". Identifying the feeders with tools, we see that this constitutes again an instance of the "job-sequencing and tool loading" problem evoked above.

This chapter deals with a particular formulation of this problem, due to Bard (1988) and Tang and Denardo (1988a). Suppose that a batch of N jobs have to be successively processed, one at a time, on a single flexible machine. Each job requires a subset of tools, which have to be placed in the tool magazine of the machine before the job can be processed. The number of tools needed to produce all the jobs in the batch is denoted by M. We represent these data by an $M \times N$ *tool-job* matrix A, with:

$$a_{ij} = 1 \quad \text{if job } j \text{ requires tool } i,$$
$$\quad\quad = 0 \quad \text{otherwise,}$$

for $i = 1, 2, \ldots, M$ and $j = 1, 2, \ldots, N$. Without loss of generality, A has no zero row. The tool magazine has a limited *capacity*: it can accommodate at most C tools, each of which fits in one slot of the magazine. To ensure feasibility of the problem, we assume that no job requires more than C tools. We also assume that, while the jobs are in process, the tool magazine is always loaded at full capacity (as will explained below, this is in fact a non-restrictive assumption for our problem). We thus call any subset of C tools a *loading* of the magazine.

A *job sequence* is a permutation of $\{1, 2, \ldots, N\}$, or, equivalently, of the columns of A. As the number of tools needed to produce all jobs is generally larger than the capacity of the tool magazine (i.e., $M > C$), it is sometimes necessary to change tools between two jobs in a sequence. When this occurs, one or more tools are removed from the tool magazine and are replaced by a same number of tools retrieved from a storage area. We call *setup* the insertion of a tool in the magazine. A *switch* is the combination of a tool setup and a tool removal. Since each tool has to be set up at least once in order to process the whole batch of jobs, we will also pay attention to the *extra setups* of a tool, that is, to all setups of the tool other than the first one.

The *tool switching problem* is now defined as follows: determine a job sequence and an associated sequence of loadings for the tool magazine, such that all tools required by the j-th job are present in the j-th loading, and the total number of tool switches is minimized. In matrix terms, the tool switching problem translates as follows: determine an $M \times N$ $0 - 1$ matrix $P = (p_{kj})$, obtained by permuting the columns of A according to a given job sequence, and an $M \times N$ $0 - 1$ matrix $T = (t_{kj})$ containing C ones per column (each column of T represents a tool loading), such that $t_{kj} = 1$ if $p_{kj} = 1$ (i.e., tool k is placed in the j-th loading if it is needed for the j-th job in the sequence; $k = 1, \ldots M$; $j = 1, \ldots, N$), and the following quantity is minimized:

$$\sum_{j=2}^{N} \sum_{k=1}^{M} (1 - t_{k,j-1}) \cdot t_{kj}$$

(this quantity is exactly the number of switches required for the loading sequence represented by T). Observe that minimizing the number of tool switches is equivalent to minimizing the number of setups or of extra setups, since the following relations hold:

$$\text{number of setups} = \text{number of switches} + C$$
$$= \text{number of extra setups} + M.$$

Let us now briefly discuss some of the (explicit and implicit) assumptions of the tool switching model.

(1) As mentioned before, the assumption that the tool magazine is always fully loaded does not affect the generality of the model. Indeed, since no cost is incurred for tools staying in the magazine, one may consider that the first C tools to be used are all incorporated in the very first loading; thereafter, a tool only needs to be removed when it is replaced by another one.

(2) Each tool is assumed to fit in one slot of the magazine. Removing this assumption would create considerable difficulties. For instance the physical location of the tools in the magazine would then become relevant, since adjacent slots would need to be freed in order to introduce a tool requiring more than one slot.

(3) The time needed to remove or insert each tool is constant, and is the same for all tools. This assumption is in particular crucial for the correctness of the KTNS procedure (see Subsection 8.2.2) which determines the optimal tool loadings for a given job sequence. Many of our heuristic procedures, however, can easily be adapted in the case where switching times are tool dependent.

(4) Tools cannot be changed simultaneously. This is a realistic assumption in many situations, e.g. for the forging or for the PCB assembly applications mentioned above.

(5) The subset of tools required to carry out each job is fixed in advance. This assumption could be relaxed by assuming instead that, for each job, a list of subsets of tools is given, and that the job can be executed by any subset in the list; (i.e., several process plans are given for each job; see e.g. Finke and Kusiak (1987)). Choosing the right subset would then add a new dimension (and quite a lot of complexity) to the problem.

(6) Tools do not break down and do not wear not. This assumption is justified if the tool life is long enough with respect to the planning horizon. Otherwise, one may want to lift the assumption "deterministically", e.g. by assuming that tool k is worn out after the execution of w_k jobs, for a given value of w_k. Alternatively, breakdowns and wear may also be modelled probabilistically. This would obviously result in a completely new model.

(7) The list of jobs is completely known. This assumption is realistic if the planning horizon is relatively short.

This chapter deals with various aspects of the tool switching problem. Section 8.2 contains some basic results concerning the computational complexity of this problem; in particular, we establish that the problem is already $\mathcal{N}P$-hard for $C = 2$, and we present a new proof of the fact that, for each fixed job sequence, an optimal sequence of tool loadings can be found in polynomial time. In Section 8.3, we describe several heuristics for the tool switching problem, and the performance of these heuristics on randomly generated problems is compared in Section 8.4. Section 8.5 discusses, in general terms, the difficult problem of computing good lower bounds for the optimal value of the tool switching problem. The Appendix contains some graph-theoretic definitions.

8.2 Basic results

We present in this section some results concerning the computational complexity of the tool switching problem. We assume that the reader is familiar with the basic concepts of complexity theory (see e.g. Nemhauser and Wolsey (1988)). Let us simply recall here that, loosely speaking, a problem is $\mathcal{N}P$-hard if it is at least as hard as the traveling salesman problem (see the Appendix).

8.2.1 $\mathcal{N}P$-hardness results

Tang and Denardo (1988a) claim that the tool switching problem is $\mathcal{N}P$-hard. They do not present a formal proof of this assertion, but rather infer it from the observation that the problem can be modelled as a traveling salesman problem with variable edge lengths. Our immediate goal will be to establish the validity of two slightly stronger claims.

Consider first the following restricted version of the tool switching problem:

Input   : an $M \times N$ matrix A and a capacity C.
Problem P1 : is there a job sequence for A requiring exactly M setups
             (i.e., no extra setups)?

Theorem 8.1 *Problem P1 is NP-hard.*

Proof:
It is straightforward to check that $P1$ is precisely the decision version of
the so-called *matrix permutation problem*, which has been extensively investigated in the VLSI design literature (see Möhring (1990) and references
therein). Several equivalent versions of the matrix permutation problem
have been shown to be NP-hard (see Kashiwabara and Fujisawa (1979),
Möhring (1990)), and hence $P1$ is NP-hard.   □

In the description of problem $P1$, both A and C are regarded as problem
data. But, from the viewpoint of our application, it may also be interesting
to consider the situation where a specific machine, with fixed capacity, has to
process different batches of jobs. The matrix A can then be regarded as the
sole data of the tool switching problem. This observation leads us to define
the following problem, where C is now considered as a fixed parameter :

Input   : an $M \times N$ matrix A.
Problem P2 : find a job sequence for A minimizing the number of setups
             required on a machine with capacity C.

Theorem 8.2 *Problem P2 is NP-hard for any fixed $C \geq 2$.*

Proof:
Let $G = (V, E, d)$ be a graph and $H = (E, I, \delta)$ be its edge-graph (see
the Appendix). We consider the problem of finding a minimal length TS
path in H (problem $P3$ in the Appendix). We are now going to prove
Theorem 8.2 by showing that this NP-hard problem can be formulated as
a special case of problem $P2$, for any fixed $C \geq 2$. For simplicity, we first
concentrate on a proof of Theorem 8.2 for $C = 2$. Let $V = \{1, 2, \ldots, M\}$
and $E = \{e_1, e_2, \ldots, e_N\}$. Define an $M \times N$ matrix A, with rows associated
to the nodes of G, columns associated to the edges of G, and such that:

$$a_{ij} = 1 \quad \text{if edge } e_j \text{ contains node } i,$$
$$= 0 \quad \text{otherwise.}$$

Consider now A as an instance of the tool switching problem, with capacity $C = 2$. A job sequence for this problem corresponds to a permutation of E, and hence to a TS path in the edge-graph of G. Also, it is easy to see that the number of tool switches between two jobs j and k, corresponding to the edges e_j and e_k of G, is:

- equal to 1 if e_j and e_k share a common node, that is, if $\delta(e_j, e_k) = 1$ in H;

- equal to 2 if e_j and e_k do not share a common node, that is, if $\delta(e_j, e_k) = +\infty$ in H.

This discussion immediately implies that an optimal job sequence for A (with capacity 2) always corresponds to a minimal length TS path in H. Hence, we can solve $P3$ by solving $P2$, and this entails that $P2$ is $\mathcal{N}P$-hard. To see that Theorem 8.2 is also valid for $C > 2$, it suffices to adapt the definition of A in the previous argument, by adding $C - 2$ rows of 1's to it; that is, A now has $(M + C - 2)$ rows, and $a_{ij} = 1$ if $i \geq M + 1$. The reasoning goes through with this modification.   □

8.2.2   Finding the minimum number of setups for a fixed job sequence

The tool switching problem naturally decomposes into two interdependent issues, namely:

(1) *sequencing* : compute an (optimal) job sequence, and
(2) *tooling*   : for the given sequence, determine what tools should be
                  loaded in the tool magazine at each moment, in order
                  to minimize the total number of setups
                  required.

In their paper, Tang and Denardo (1988a) proved that the sequencing subproblem actually is the hard nut to crack, since the tooling problem can be solved in $O(MN)$ operations by applying a so-called Keep Tool Needed Soonest (KTNS) policy. A KTNS policy prescribes that, whenever a situation occurs where some tools should be removed from the magazine, so as to make room for tools needed for the next job, then those tools which are needed the soonest for a future job should be removed last (we refer to Tang and Denardo (1988a) or Bard (1988) for a more precise description).

Tang and Denardo's proof of the correctness of KTNS relies on ad-hoc interchange arguments and is rather involved (as observed by Finke and

Roger - see Roger (1990) - the correctness of KTNS was already established by Mattson, Gecsei, Slutz and Traiger (1970) in the context of storage techniques for computer memory, in the case where each job requires exactly one tool; their proof is similar to Tang and Denardo's).

We now look at the tooling subproblem from a different angle, and show that the problem can be modelled as a specially structured 0-1 linear programming problem, which can be solved by a greedy algorithm due to Hoffman, Kolen and Sakarovitch (1985) (see also Nemhauser and Wolsey (1988), pp. 562–573; Daskin, Jones and Lowe (1990) present another application of the same greedy algorithm in a flexible manufacturing context). When translated in the terminology of the tool switching problem, this algorithm precisely yields KTNS. Thus, this argument provides a new proof of correctness for KTNS.

The bulk of the work in our derivation of the KTNS procedure will simply consist in reformulating the tooling problem in an appropriate form. With this goal in mind, we first introduce some new notations and terminology. For the remainder of this section, assume that the job sequence σ is fixed. Let the $M \times N(0,1)$-matrix P be defined by:

$$p_{ij} = 1 \quad \text{if tool } i \text{ is required for the j-th job in } \sigma,$$
$$= 0 \quad \text{otherwise}$$

(that is, P is obtained by permuting the columns of A according to the job sequence at hand). A tooling policy can now be described by flipping some entries of P from 0 to 1, until each column of P contains exactly C ones. If we denote by c_j the *remaining capacity* of column j, that is the quantity:

$$c_j = C - \sum_{i=1}^{M} p_{ij}$$

then a tooling policy must flip c_j entries from 0 to 1 in the j-th column of P.

Let us next define a *0-block* of P as a maximal subset of consecutive zeroes in a row of P. More formally, a 0-block is a set of the form $\{(i,j),(i,j+1),\ldots,(i,j+k)\}$, for which the following conditions hold:

(1) $1 < j \leq j + k < N$,

(2) $p_{ij} = p_{i,j+1} = \ldots = p_{i,j+k} = 0$,

(3) $p_{i,j-1} = p_{i,j+k+1} = 1$.

Intuitively, a 0-block is a maximal time interval before and after which tool i is needed, but during which it is not needed. It is easy to see that each

0-block of P is associated with an extra setup of tool i. Thus, flipping an element of P from 0 to 1 can only reduce the number of extra setups if this element belongs to a 0-block, and if all other elements of this 0-block are also flipped. In other words, only flipping *whole* 0-blocks can help reducing the number of setups.

Example 8.1 The matrix

$$P = \begin{bmatrix} 0 & 1 & 0 & 0 & 1 & 1 \\ 1 & 1 & 0 & 0 & 0 & 0 \\ 1 & 0 & 1 & 1 & 0 & 1 \end{bmatrix}$$

contains three 0-blocks, namely $\{(1,3),(1,4)\}$, $\{(3,2)\}$ and $\{(3,5)\}$. They correspond to an extra setup of tool 1 in period 5, and two extra setups of tool 3, in periods 3 and 6. Assume that the capacity is $C = 2$. Then, the number of extra setups can be minimized by flipping the first and the third 0-blocks to 1, thus resulting in the matrix:

$$T = \begin{bmatrix} 0 & 1 & 1 & 1 & 1 & 1 \\ 1 & 1 & 0 & 0 & 0 & 0 \\ 1 & 0 & 1 & 1 & 1 & 1 \end{bmatrix}$$

□

From the previous discussion, it should now be clear that the tooling problem can be rephrased as follows : flip to 1 as many 0-blocks of P as possible, while flipping at most c_j entries in column j $(j = 1, 2, \ldots, N)$.

Denote by B the number of 0-blocks in P, and, for $k = 1, 2, \ldots, B$, introduce the decision variables:

$x_k = 1$ if the k-th 0-block is flipped to 1,
$\quad = 0$ otherwise.

For $j = 1, 2, \ldots, N$ and $k = 1, 2, \ldots, B$, let also:

$m_{jk} = 1$ if the k-th 0-block "meets" column j in P,
$\quad = 0$ otherwise

(formally, a 0-block meets column j if it contains an element of the form (i, j), for some i; for instance, in Example 8.1, the first 0-block meets columns 3 and 4).

Now, the tooling problem admits the following 0-1 linear programming formulation:

$$(TP) \quad \text{maximize} \quad \sum_{k=1}^{B} x_k$$

$$\text{subject to} \quad \sum_{k=1}^{B} m_{jk} x_k \leq c_j, \qquad j = 1, 2, \ldots, N$$

$$x_k \in \{0, 1\},$$

Assume now that the 0-blocks of P have been ordered in non-decreasing order of their "endpoints": that is, the 0-blocks of P have been numbered from 1 to B in such a way that the index of the last column met by the k-th 0-block is smaller than or equal to the index of the last column met by the $(k+1)$-st 0-block, for $k = 1, \ldots, B-1$. Then, the matrix (m_{jk}) is a so-called *greedy matrix*, i.e. it does not contain the matrix $\begin{bmatrix} 1 & 1 \\ 1 & 0 \end{bmatrix}$ as a submatrix.

Hoffman et al. (1985) considered the following, more general problem on an $N \times B$ greedy matrix:

$$(GP) \quad \text{maximize} \quad \sum_{k=1}^{B} b_k x_k$$

$$\text{subject to} \quad \sum_{k=1}^{B} m_{jk} x_k \leq c_j, \qquad j = 1, 2, \ldots N,$$

$$0 \leq x_k \leq d_k, x_k \text{ integer}, \quad k = 1, 2, \ldots, B,$$

where b_k, d_k $(k = 1, 2, \ldots, B)$ and c_j $(j = 1, 2, \ldots, N)$ are integers with $b_1 \geq b_2 \geq \ldots \geq b_B$. They proved that, when the matrix (m_{jk}) is greedy, problem (GP) can be solved by a greedy algorithm, in which each x_k $(k = 1, 2, \ldots, B)$ is successively taken as large as possible while respecting the feasibility constraints. Reformulating this algorithm for (TP), we see that we should successively flip 0-blocks to 1, in order of nondecreasing endpoints, as long as the remaining capacity of all columns met by the 0-block is at least one. We leave it to the reader to check that this procedure is precisely equivalent to a KTNS policy.

Remark. In a more general situation where the setup times are not identical for all tools, the tooling subproblem can still be formulated as a problem of the form (GP), where b_k is now the time required to set up the tool associated with the k-th 0-block. Since the condition $b_1 \geq b_2 \geq \ldots \geq b_B$ does not generally hold for these setup times, the greedy algorithm of Hoffman et al. (1985) and KTNS are no longer valid. However, the matrix (m_{jk}), being an interval matrix, is totally unimodular (see Subsection 8.3.4 and Nemhauser and Wolsey (1988) for definitions). It follows that the tooling subproblem can still be solved in polynomial time in that case, by simply solving the linear programming relaxation of the formulation (GP).

8.3   Heuristics

The tool switching problem being NP-hard, and hence probably difficult to solve to optimality, we concentrate in the sequel on heuristic techniques for its solution. We propose hereunder six basic approaches, falling into two main categories (we adopt the terminology used by Golden and Stewart (1985) for the traveling salesman problem) :

- *construction strategies*, which exploit the special structure of the tool switching problem in order to construct a single (hopefully good) job sequence (Subsections 8.3.1 to 8.3.4 below);

- *improvement strategies*, which iteratively improve a starting job sequence (Subsections 8.3.5 and 8.3.6 below).

Composite strategies will be obtained by combining construction and improvement procedures. A computational comparison of the resulting procedures will be presented in Section 8.4.

As explained in Section 8.1, the data of our problem consist of an $M \times N$ tool-job matrix A and a capacity C. We focus on the solution of the sequencing subproblem (see Subsection 8.2.2), since we already know that the tooling subproblem is easy to solve. Whenever we speak of the *cost* of a (partial) job sequence, we mean the minimal number of tool switches required by the sequence, as computed using KTNS.

8.3.1   Traveling salesman heuristics

These heuristics are based on an idea suggested by Tang and Denardo (1988a). They consider a graph $G = (V, E, lb)$ (see the Appendix for definitions), where V is the set of jobs, E is the set of all pairs of jobs, and the length $lb(i, j)$ of edge $\{i, j\}$ is an underestimate of the number of tool switches needed between jobs i and j when these jobs are consecutively processed in a sequence. More precisely:

$$lb(i,j) = \max(|T_i \cup T_j| - C, 0),$$

where T_k is the set of tools required by job k ($k = 1, 2, \ldots, N$). Notice that, if each job requires exactly C tools (i.e. $|T_k| = C$ for all k), then $lb(i,j)$ is equal to the number of tool switches required between jobs i and j in any schedule.

Each traveling salesman (TS) path of G corresponds to a job sequence for the tool switching problem. So, as suggested by Tang and Denardo (1988a), computing a short TS path in G constitutes a reasonable heuristic for the generation of a good sequence. As a matter of fact, when all jobs use full capacity, then the tool switching problem is precisely equivalent to the TS problem on G.

In our computational experiments, we have considered the following procedures for constructing a short TS path in G:

(1) *Shortest Edge* heuristic: this is the heuristic used by Tang and Denardo (1988a), and called "greedy feasible" in Nemhauser and Wolsey (1988); complexity: $O(N^2 \log N)$;

(2) *Nearest Neighbor* heuristic with all possible starting nodes: see Golden and Stewart (1985), Johnson and Papadimitriou (1985); complexity: $O(N^3)$;

(3) *Farthest Insertion* heuristic with all possible starting nodes: see Golden and Stewart (1985), Johnson and Papadimitriou (1985); complexity: $O(N^4)$;

(4) *B & B* algorithm: this is a state-of-the-art branch and bound code, which solves TS problems to optimality: see Volgenant and Jonker (1982); complexity: exponential in the worst-case.

Procedures (1), (2) and (3) are well-known heuristics for the traveling salesman problem. In addition to the complexity mentioned for each procedure, an overhead of $O(MN^2)$ operations has to be incurred for the computation of the edge lengths $lb(i,j)$.

8.3.2 Block minimization heuristics

We describe now another way of associating a traveling salesman instance to any given instance of the tool switching problem. We first introduce a directed graph $D = (V^*, U, ub)$. Here, V^* is the set of all jobs, plus an additional node denoted by 0. Each ordered pair of nodes is an arc in U. The length $ub(i,j)$ of arc (i,j) is given by:

$$ub(i,j) = |T_i \backslash T_j|,$$

where T_k is the set of tools required by job k ($k = 1, 2, \ldots, N$), and T_0 is the empty set. In other words, $ub(i,j)$ is the number of tools used by job i but not by job j; hence, $ub(i,j)$ is an upper-bound on the number of tool switches between jobs i and j, for any sequence in which i and j must be consecutively processed. If every job requires exactly C tools, then $ub(i,j) = ub(j,i) = lb(i,j)$ is equal to the number of switches between i and j. But in general, $ub(i,j)$ differs from $ub(j,i)$.

Each TS path of D finishing at node 0 defines a sequence of jobs, and the length of the path is an upper-bound on the total number of switches entailed by the sequence. For reasons explained below, we refer to heuristics which attempt to construct a short TS path in D as *block minimization* heuristics. We have implemented two such heuristics:

(1) *NN Block Minimization*, based on a nearest neighbor heuristic with all possible starting nodes; complexity: $O(N^3)$;

(2) *FI Block Minimization*, based on a farthest insertion heuristic with all possible starting nodes; complexity: $O(N^4)$.

Let us mention another interesting interpretation of the block minimization approach. As in Subsection 8.2.2, consider the matrix P obtained after permuting the columns of A according to a job sequence σ. We define a *1-block* of P as a set of entries, of the form $\{(i,j), (i,j+1), \ldots, (i,j+k)\}$, for which the following conditions hold:

(1) $1 \leq j \leq j + k \leq N$,

(2) $p_{ij} = p_{i,j+1} = \ldots = p_{i,j+k} = 1$,

(3) either $j = 1$ or $p_{i,j-1} = 0$,

(4) either $j + k = N$ or $p_{i,j+k+1} = 0$

(this definition does not exactly mimic the definition of 0-blocks, but the difference is irrelevant here). Notice that, were it not for the possibility to carry out KTNS on P, then each 1-block of P would induce a tool setup in the job sequence σ. Thus, the number of 1-blocks of P is an overestimate of the number of setups required by σ.

We leave it to the reader to check that the number of 1-blocks in P is also equal to the length of the TS path associated with σ in D (and finishing at node 0). So, finding a shortest TS path in D is equivalent to determining a permutation of the columns of A which minimizes the number of 1-blocks in the permuted matrix. This observation is essentially due to Kou (1977). Kou (1977) also proved that finding a permutation which minimizes the number of 1-blocks is $\mathcal{NP}$-hard (our proof of Theorem 8.2 establishes the same result). This justifies the use of heuristics in our block minimization approach.

8.3.3 Greedy heuristics

One of the obvious drawbacks of the heuristics described in Subsections 8.3.1 and 8.3.2 is that they do not take a whole job sequence into account when estimating the number of tool switches required between pairs of jobs. For instance, $lb(i,j)$ is in general only a lower-bound on the actual number of switches between jobs i and j, and this lower-bound can sometimes be a quite poor estimate of the actual value. An extreme case would arise when no job requires more than $C/2$ tools; then, $lb(i,j) = 0$ for each pair (i,j), and any traveling salesman heuristic based on these edge-lengths picks a random job sequence! Similarly, $ub(i,j)$ can also be a rough upper-bound on the number of switches required. In order to alleviate this difficulty, we propose now the following *(Simple) Greedy* heuristic:

Step 1 start with the partial job sequence $\sigma = (1)$; let $Q = \{2, 3, \ldots, N\}$.

Step 2 for each job j in Q, let $c(j)$ be the cost of the partial sequence (σ, j) (i.e., the number of tool switches entailed by this partial sequence, disregarding the remaining jobs).

Step 3 let i be a job in Q for which $c(i) = \min_{j \in Q} c(j)$; let $\sigma := (\sigma, i)$ and $Q := Q \backslash \{i\}$.

Step 4 if Q is not empty, then repeat Step 2; else, stop with the complete sequence σ.

Greedy runs in time $O(MN^3)$, since it requires $O(N^2)$ applications of the KTNS procedure (in Step 2). Its empirical performance can be slightly improved by taking advantage of the fact that all the partial sequences considered in Step 2 share the same initial segment.

Of course, there is no mandatory reason to select job 1 first in Step 1 of Greedy, rather than any other job. This observation suggests to consider the following, more elaborate *Multiple-Start Greedy* heuristic: run N times Greedy, once for each initial sequence $\sigma = (j)$ $(j = 1, 2, \ldots, N)$, and retain the best complete sequence found. This heuristic clearly dominates Greedy, in terms of the quality of the job sequence that it produces. Its worst-case complexity is $O(MN^4)$.

As a final note on this approach, it may be interesting to observe that, if each job requires exactly C tools, then Multiple-Start Greedy is identical to the TS Nearest Neighbor heuristic (Subsection 8.3.1) or to the NN block minimization heuristic (Subsection 8.3.2).

8.3.4   Interval heuristic

In order to motivate our next heuristic, let us first consider a special situation: assume that the matrix P arising by permuting the columns of A according to some sequence σ has precisely one 1-block in each row. In other words, the ones in each row of P occur consecutively. When this is the case we say that A is an *interval matrix* (or that A has the *consecutive ones property*; see e.g. Fulkerson and Gross (1965), Booth and Lueker (1976), Nemhauser and Wolsey (1988)). Then, the job sequence σ requires only one setup per tool, and is obviously optimal.

Thus, every $M \times N$ interval matrix admits an optimal sequence with M setups. Moreover, given an arbitrary matrix A, one can decide in time $O(MN)$ whether A is an interval matrix, and, in the affirmative, one can find within the same time bound a sequence entailing M setups for A (Booth and Lueker (1976)) (notice that this does not contradict Theorem 8.1: by applying KTNS, a sequence with M setups can sometimes be found for non-interval matrices). On the other hand, it is by no means clear that any of the heuristics described in Subsections 8.3.1, 8.3.2 or 8.3.3 would find an optimal job sequence for an interval matrix.

These observations suggest the implementation of the following *Interval heuristic*. The heuristic simultaneously builds a "large" interval submatrix of A, and computes an optimal job sequence for the submatrix. This sequence is the solution returned by the heuristic. More precisely:

Step 1   initialize $I = \{\}, i = 1$.

Step 2   determine whether the submatrix of A consisting of the rows with index in $I \cup \{i\}$ is an interval matrix; if so, then let $I := I \cup \{i\}$ and let σ be an optimal job sequence for the submatrix; else, continue.

Step 3 if $i < M$, then let $i := i + 1$ and go to Step 2; else, continue.

Step 4 return the last job sequence found; stop.

The Interval heuristic has the attractive property that it produces an optimal job sequence for every interval matrix. The complexity of the heuristic is $O(MN)$ if the algorithm by Booth and Lueker (1976) is used. In our implementation, we have used a slower, but simpler recognition algorithm for interval matrices, due to Fulkerson and Gross (1965).

In the following subsections, we concentrate on improvement strategies. The input for each procedure is some initial job sequence σ, that we subsequently attempt to improve in an iterative way.

8.3.5 2-Opt strategies

This class of strategies is based on an idea that has been widely used for other combinatorial optimization problems: given a sequence σ, try to produce a better sequence by exchanging two jobs in σ (if i is the k-th job and j is the p-th job in σ, then *exchanging* i and j means putting i in p-th position and j in k-th position). We have considered two versions of this basic approach. The first one, called *Global 2-Opt*, can be described as follows:

Step 1 find two jobs i and j whose exchange results in an improved sequence; if there are no such jobs, then return σ and stop; else, continue.

Step 2 exchange i and j; call σ the resulting sequence; repeat Step 1.

Global 2-Opt has been proposed by Bard (1988) for the tool switching problem. Notice that each execution of Step 1 requires $O(N^2)$ applications of KTNS, i.e. $O(MN^3)$ operations. But the number of potential executions of this step does not appear to be trivially bounded by a polynomial in N and M (contrary to what is claimed by Bard (1988)). In order to reduce the computational effort by iteration of Global 2-Opt, the following *Restricted 2-Opt* procedure can also be considered:

Step 1 find two *consecutive* jobs in σ, say the k-th and $(k + 1)$-st ones, whose exchange results in an improved sequence; if there are no such jobs, then return σ and stop.

Step 2 exchange the jobs found in Step 1; call σ the resulting sequence; repeat Step 1.

The complexity of Step 1 in Restricted 2-Opt is $O(MN^2)$. This exchange strategy has also been proposed by Finke and Roger (see Roger (1990)).

8.3.6   Load-and-Optimize strategy

Consider again a job sequence σ and the matrix P obtained by permuting the columns of A according to σ. Applying KTNS to P results in a new matrix T, each column of which contains exactly C ones (the j-th column of T describes the loading of the tool magazine while the j-th job in σ is being processed). Suppose now that we look at T as defining a new instance of the tool switching problem (with capacity C). If we can find for T a better sequence than σ, then this sequence will obviously be a better sequence than σ for the original matrix A as well. On the other hand, the problem instance (T, C) is a little bit easier to handle than the instance (A, C). Indeed, since each column of T contains C ones, the tool switching problem (T, C) can be reformulated as a TS problem, as explained in Subsections 8.3.1, 8.3.2, 8.3.3. These observations motivate our *Load-and-Optimize* strategy:

Step 1   permute the columns of A according to σ and apply KTNS; call T the resulting matrix.

Step 2   compute an optimal sequence σ' for the tool switching instance (T, C).

Step 3   if σ' is a better sequence than σ for A, then replace σ by σ' and repeat Step 1; else return σ and stop.

From a practical viewpoint, we have found it easier to slightly alter this basic strategy, in the following way. In Step 2, rather than computing an optimal sequence for T (which is computationally demanding), we simply use the farthest insertion heuristic to produce a good sequence σ' (as in Subsection 8.3.1). On the other hand, in Step 3, we accept the new sequence σ' even if it entails the same number of setups as σ. We only stop when 10 iterations of the procedure have been executed without producing a strictly improved sequence. In the sequel, we also refer to this variant as "Load-and-Optimize".

8.4 Computational experiments

8.4.1 Generation of problem instances

We tested our heuristics on 160 random instances of the tool switching problem. Of course, tool-job matrices occurring in practice may have characteristics not present in the ones we generated. For instance, as pointed out by an anonymous referee, realistic matrices are likely to display inter-row and inter-column correlations, as well as "tool clusters". However, in the absence of real-world data or even of detailed statistical information about these, we decided to follow a procedure similar to the one proposed by Tang and Denardo (1988a) in generating our test problems.

Each random instance falls into one of 16 *instance types*, characterized by the size (M, N) of the tool-job matrix and by the value C of the capacity. Accordingly, we denote the type of an instance by a triple (M, N, C). There are 10 instances of each type. The tool-job matrices are $M \times N$ matrices, where (M, N) is either (10,10), (20,15), (40,30) or (60,40). For each size (M, N), we also define a pair (Min, Max) of parameters with the following interpretation:

- Min = lower-bound on the number of tools per job,

- Max = upper-bound on the number of tools per job.

The specific values of these parameters are displayed in Table 8.1.

Problem size	Min	Max
(10,10)	2	4
(20,15)	2	6
(40,30)	5	15
(60,40)	7	20

Table 8.1

For each problem size (M, N), 10 random matrices A were generated. For each $j = 1, 2, \ldots, N$, the j-th column of A was generated as follows. First, an integer t_j was drawn from the uniform distribution over [min, max]: this number denotes the number of tools needed for job j, i.e. the number of 1's in the j-th column of A. Next, a set T_j of t_j distinct integers were drawn from the uniform distribution over $[1, M]$: these integers denote the tools required by job j, i.e. $a_{kj} = 1$ if and only if k is in T_j. Finally, we checked whether $T_j \subseteq T_i$ or $T_i \subseteq T_j$ held for any $i < j$. If any of these inclusions was found to hold, then the previous choice of T_j was cancelled, and a new set T_j was generated (Tang and Denardo (1988a) and Bard (1988) have observed that any column of A contained in another column can be deleted without affecting the optimal solution of the problem; thus, we want to make sure that our problem instances actually involve N columns, and cannot be reduced by this simple trick). Notice that this generation procedure does not a priori prevent the occurrence of null rows in the matrix. In practice, only two of the 40 matrices that we generated contained null rows (these were two (20,15) matrices, containing respectively one and three null rows).

A problem instance of type (M, N, C) is now obtained by combining an $M \times N$ tool-job matrix A with one of the four capacities C_1, C_2, C_3 and C_4 displayed in Table 8.2.

Problem size	C_1	C_2	C_3	C_4
(10,10)	4	5	6	7
(20,15)	6	8	10	12
(40,30)	15	17	20	25
(60,40)	20	22	25	30

Table 8.2

We will see that the performance of some heuristics strongly depends on the value of the ratio $\max /C$. We call *sparse* those problem instances for which $\max /C$ is small, and *dense* those for which the ratio is close to 1. Notice, in particular, that all instances of type (M, N, C_1) have $\max /C_1 = 1$. Varying the capacity as indicated in Table 8.2 will allow us to examine the behavior of our heuristics under different sparsity conditions. Let us mention here that, according to the empirical observation of many real-world systems described by Förster and Hirt (1989), sparse instances are probably more "realistic" than dense ones. But of course, this conclusion is very much system-dependent.

8.4.2 Computational results

All heuristics described in Section 8.3 have been implemented in Turbo Pascal and tested on the problem instances described above. The experiments were run on an AT personal computer equipped with an 80286 microprocessor and an additional 80287 coprocessor. Since our primary goal was to compare the quality of the solutions produced by the heuristics, no systematic attempts were made to optimize the running time of the codes. Accordingly, we will not report here on precise computing times, but simply give some rough indication of the relation between the times required by the various methods.

The performance of heuristic H on problem instance I is measured in terms of "percentage above the best solution found", namely, by the quantity:

$$\delta_H(I) = \left(\frac{H(I) - \text{Best } (I)}{\text{Best } (I)} \right) \cdot 100,$$

where $H(I)$ is the number of tool setups required by the job sequence produced by heuristic H, and Best (I) is the number of setups required by the best sequence found by *any* of our heuristics.

For information, Table 8.3 indicates the evolution of Best (I) as a function of the problem type (average of Best (I) over all ten instances of each type). All subsequent tables (Tables 8.4, 8.5, 8.6 report averages and (in brackets) standard deviations of $\delta_H(I)$ over all instances I of a given type.

	Tool magazine capacity			
Problem size	C_1	C_2	C_3	C_4
(10,10)	13.2	11.2	10.3	10.1
(20,15)	26.5	21.6	20.0	19.6
(40,30)	113.6	95.9	76.8	56.8
(60,40)	211.6	189.7	160.5	127.4

Table 8.3

Heuristic	(10,10, $C = 4$)	(20,15, $C = 6$)	(40,30, $C = 15$)	(60,40, $C = 20$)
Shortest edge	12.4 (6.8)	23.9 (9.8)	20.3 (3.1)	18.8 (3.4)
Farthest Insertion	12.1 (9.8)	15.5 (8.6)	9.6 (5.3)	6.9 (2.7)
Nearest Neighbor	13.7 (7.8)	19.8 (7.7)	21.0 (6.0)	18.9 (3.5)
Branch-and-Bound	12.6 (4.6)	16.2 (5.8)	12.4 (4.3)	10.9 (2.9)

Table 8.4

Table 8.4 compares the behavior of the four traveling salesman heuristics described in Subsection 8.3.1. We will see later that TS heuristics perform best on dense instances, and tend to behave very badly on sparse instances. Therefore, we limit ourselves here to a comparison of these heuristics on the densest instances, that is, those instances where $C = C_1 = \max$.

From Table 8.4, it appears that on average, and mostly for large instances, Farthest Insertion yields better solutions than the other TS heuristics. Farthest Insertion is also a very fast heuristic, which produces solutions in a matter of seconds (about 30 seconds for the largest instances). The Shortest Edge and Nearest Neighbor heuristics are even faster, but Farthest Insertion presents in our view the best quality *vs.* efficiency trade-off. Thus, we will select Farthest Insertion as our "winner" among TS heuristics, and no longer report on the other TS heuristics in the sequel.

A similar comparison between the two block minimization heuristics presented in Subsection 8.3.2 would lead to similar conclusions. Here again, FI is slightly better and slightly slower than NN. In the remainder of this section, we only report on the performance of FI, and no longer of NN.

Tables 8.5 displays the performance of "constructive" and "improvement" heuristics over our complete sample of problem instances. The results (averages and standard deviations) for each heuristic are given in different columns.

The results presented under the labels "2-Opt" or "Load-and-Optimize" have been obtained by first picking a random job sequence, and then applying the corresponding improvement strategies to it. The columns labelled "Random" provide, for the sake of comparison, the number of tool setups entailed by the initial random job sequence.

(M,N,C)	Farthest Insertion	FI Block Minimization	Simple Greedy	Multiple-Start Greedy
(10,10,4)	12.1 (9.8)	14.3 (7.7)	12.3 (6.3)	4.6 (3.8)
(10,10,5)	19.0 (7.8)	13.6 (7.6)	8.1 (6.0)	3.7 (4.6)
(10,10,6)	17.8 (10.8)	9.7 (6.4)	5.7 (4.7)	2.9 (4.4)
(10,10,7)	11.7 (10.3)	3.9 (4.8)	1.0 (3.0)	0.0 (0.0)
(20,15,6)	15.5 (8.6)	12.0 (4.2)	13.7 (7.0)	4.6 (3.5)
(20,15,8)	37.3 (10.8)	13.9 (8.4)	11.0 (7.3)	4.6 (3.0)
(20,15,10)	30.5 (5.8)	8.3 (6.2)	5.6 (4.3)	1.5 (2.3)
(20,15,12)	15.3 (5.5)	2.1 (3.5)	1.0 (2.1)	0.0 (0.0)
(40,30,15)	9.4 (5.3)	8.8 (4.4)	11.4 (4.8)	6.2 (3.1)
(40,30,17)	16.3 (7.5)	9.4 (3.8)	9.8 (3.5)	5.5 (2.2)
(40,30,20)	33.8 (9.1)	12.1 (3.6)	9.8 (4.2)	3.2 (2.0)
(40,30,25)	39.4 (6.6)	15.0 (2.7)	8.3 (4.9)	2.6 (2.3)
(60,40,20)	6.9 (2.7)	9.7 (2.4)	10.2 (2.6)	5.8 (1.5)
(60,40,22)	9.9 (2.7)	8.7 (2.6)	7.9 (3.1)	3.3 (1.7)
(60,40,25)	21.8 (5.7)	10.5 (3.1)	8.2 (2.8)	2.8 (2.0)
(60,40,30)	36.7 (4.0)	13.1 (3.7)	6.5 (2.4)	1.7 (1.4)

(M,N,C)	Interval	Restricted 2-opt	Global 2-opt	Load-and-Optimize	Random
(10,10,4)	22.6 (12.2)	26.0 (7.7)	8.7 (4.7)	5.8 (5.3)	41.2 (18.9)
(10,10,5)	14.1 (14.1)	24.3 (10.1)	7.4 (7.1)	10.1 (7.2)	33.8 16.2)
(10,10,6)	9.7 (11.8)	18.3 (7.7)	3.0 (4.6)	6.7 (4.4)	26.3 (9.1)
(10,10,7)	3.0 (6.4)	9.8 (7.5)	0.0 (0.0)	3.0 (6.4)	13.8 (7.9)
(20,15,6)	25.7 (9.7)	33.6 (7.2)	10.0 (4.3)	12.3 (6.8)	45.9 (8.8)
(20,15,8)	20.4 (9.2)	35.7 (10.8)	9.7 (4.1)	23.8 (8.5)	42.2 (11.8)
(20,15,10)	10.4 (8.2)	24.3 (9.2)	6.4 (7.3)	25.6 (11.7)	30.1 12.3)
(20,15,12)	3.5 (5.0)	13.6 (8.3)	1.0 (2.0)	16.6 (9.6)	18.1 (11.3)
(40,30,15)	30.5 (4.3)	30.3 (5.0)	6.0 (4.0)	16.6 (5.3)	42.9 (6.1)
(40,30,17)	31.2 (5.4)	31.0 (4.6)	4.5 (3.3)	27.5 (4.3)	44.6 (6.4)
(40,30,20)	30.4 (6.0)	33.0 (6.6)	6.0 (2.9)	35.1 (6.4)	45.5 (8.9)
(40,30,25)	27.8 (6.6)	34.5 (7.4)	6.1 (3.7)	37.8 (7.0)	40.5 (7.1)
(60,40,20)	30.6 (2.7)	25.8 (3.8)	4.8 (2.4)	20.0 (3.8)	37.1 (3.6)
(60,40,22)	29.3 (4.1)	25.4 (2.9)	3.7 (2.6)	25.4 (4.1)	36.5 (3.5)
(60,40,25)	30.2 (3.6)	29.7 (3.0)	2.1 (1.9)	35.5 (4.3)	38.0 (3.6)
(60,40,30)	28.8 (3.4)	30.1 (3.3)	4.5 (2.7)	36.7 (4.4)	37.6 (3.8)

Table 8.5 Average (and standard deviation) of $\delta_H(I)$.

Let us now try to sketch some of the conclusions that emerge from this table. Consider first the case of dense instances, that is, the instances of type $(10, 10, 4), (20, 15, 6), (40, 30, 15)$ and $(60, 40, 20)$. As the size of these instances increases, the ranking of the solutions delivered by the various heuristics seems to become more or less stable. Namely, Multiple-Start Greedy and Global 2-Opt produce (on the average) the best results. Next comes a group made up of Farthest Insertion, Simple Greedy and FI Block Minimization, which usually yield solutions of slightly lower quality. Finally, the worst solutions are produced by Load-and-Optimize, Restricted 2-Opt and Interval (and, as expected, the random procedure).

We get a somewhat different ranking of the heuristics when we look at sparse instances. Consider e.g. the instances of type $(10, 10, 7), (20, 15, 12)$, $(40, 30, 25), (60, 40, 30)$. Multiple-Start Greedy, Global 2-Opt, Simple Greedy and FI Block Minimization remain, in that order, the best heuristics. But Farthest Insertion performs now almost as badly as the random procedure! As a matter of fact, for larger instances, it appears that the performance of Farthest Insertion deteriorates very systematically as sparsity increases. This behavior is matched by all other TS heuristics (Shortest Edge, Nearest Neighbor, and B& B). It can be explained by observing that, for sparse instances, the bounds $lb(i, j)$ tend to be poor estimates of the number of switches required between jobs i and j (see Subsections 8.3.1 and 8.3.3).

Our conclusion at this point would be that, if we are only concerned with the quality of the solution produced by each heuristic, then Multiple-Start Greedy and Global 2-Opt come out the winners, while Simple Greedy and FI Block Minimization are good contenders. For dense problems, Farthest Insertion also is a very good technique.

This first picture becomes more nuanced when we also take computing times into account. Indeed, the various heuristics run at very different speeds. For instance, solving an instance of type $(10, 10, 4)$ takes about 0.30 seconds by Farthest Insertion, FI Block Minimization or by Simple Greedy, 2 seconds by Global 2-opt and 3 seconds by Multiple-Start Greedy. More strikingly, the instances of type $(60, 40, 20)$ require about 30 seconds by Farthest Insertion or by FI Block Minimization, 1.5 minutes by Simple Greedy, 30 minutes by Global 2-Opt, and 1 hour by Multiple-Start Greedy (these times are rather stable, for a given method, over all instances of the same type). Even though some of these procedures could certainly be accelerated by implementing them more carefully, it is probably safe to say that the first three heuristics are fast, while the latter two are computationally more demanding. Therefore, for those applications where a solution of high quality has to be found quickly, FI Block Minimization and Simple Greedy seem to be perfectly adequate procedures (as well as Farthest Insertion, for dense instances). On the other hand, when computing time does not matter too much, and the thrust is instead on the quality of the solution, Multiple Start Greedy and Global 2-Opt could be considered.

Table 8.6 contains the results of our experiments with composite heuristics. The idea is here to quickly compute a good job sequence using one of the constructive heuristics, and to subsequently improve it by relying on some improvement strategy. In view of our previous experiments, we consider five ways to produce an initial solution (namely, by Farthest Insertion, FI Block Minimization, Simple Greedy, Interval and by a random procedure), and we choose Global 2-Opt as improvement strategy.

(M,N,C)	Farthest Insertion	FI Block Minimization	Simple Greedy	Interval	Global 2-opt
(10,10,4)	5.0 (5.5)	8.7 (6.9)	5.4 (3.6)	6.9 (4.5)	8.7 (4.7)
(10,10,5)	8.3 (5.3)	7.3 (7.1)	5.3 (5.5)	3.6 (4.4)	7.4 (7.1)
(10,10,6)	4.9 (4.9)	2.9 (4.4)	1.9 (3.8)	2.0 (4.0)	3.0 (4.6)
(10,10,7)	2.0 (4.0)	1.0 (3.0)	0.0 (0.0)	1.0 (3.0)	0.0 (0.0)
(20,15,6)	6.3 (5.1)	6.4 (3.8)	6.6 (3.8)	4.7 (2.9)	10.0 (4.3)
(20,15,8)	12.3 (6.4)	6.2 (4.9)	7.1 (3.4)	8.9 (5.5)	9.7 (4.1)
(20,15,10)	5.0 (5.5)	3.6 (4.0)	3.9 (3.0)	3.9 (5.2)	6.4 (7.3)
(20,15,12)	1.5 (3.2)	0.0 (0.0)	0.5 (1.5)	1.0 (3.0)	1.0 (2.0)
(40,30,15)	2.5 (3.1)	2.8 (2.0)	5.3 (4.3)	5.3 (3.1)	6.0 (4.0)
(40,30,17)	3.1 (1.3)	3.0 (2.5)	5.0 (2.4)	6.5 (2.6)	4.5 (3.3)
(40,30,20)	6.6 (4.1)	3.4 (2.1)	5.3 (2.7)	6.6 (2.9)	6.0 (2.9)
(40,30,25)	7.7 (3.0)	3.9 (2.2)	4.6 (3.4)	9.1 (5.1)	6.1 (3.7)
(60,40,20)	1.5 (1.6)	2.2 (1.8)	5.2 (1.5)	5.0 (1.5)	4.8 (2.4)
(60,40,22)	2.0 (2.4)	2.6 (2.1)	2.5 (2.3)	2.7 (2.0)	3.7 (2.6)
(60,40,25)	3.7 (1.7)	2.7 (2.0)	2.3 (2.5)	4.1 (3.4)	2.1 (1.9)
(60,40,30)	3.2 (2.7)	1.6 (2.0)	2.4 (2.0)	3.7 (1.5)	4.5 (2.7)

Table 8.6 Average (and standard deviation) of $\delta_H(I)$ for composite heuristics.

We see from Table 8.6 that, for dense instances, Farthest Insertion usually provides a very good initial solution, while FI Block Minimization always performs among the best for sparser instances. But in fact, surprisingly enough, all initialization procedures for Global 2-Opt (including the random one) come extremely close to each other, in terms of the quality of the solution produced. Also, their running times do not differ significantly.

8.5   Lower bounds

In order to judge of the quality of the heuristics described above, it would have been desirable to know tight and easily computed lower bounds on the cost of an optimal job sequence. The knowledge of such lower bounds would also be a prerequisite for the development of an exact optimization procedure (e.g. of the branch-and-bound type) for the tool switching problem. At this moment, unfortunately, we do not have very good lower-bounding procedures for our problem. We now briefly discuss some of the directions which may be worth exploring in this regard. In this discussion, we denote by $\text{cost}(A, C)$ the total number of setups required by an optimal sequence for the problem instance (A, C).

8.5.1   Traveling salesman paths

Since the quantity $lb(i, j)$ introduced in Subsection 8.3.1 is a lower bound on the number of tool switches incurred between job i and job j in *any* sequence, the length of a shortest TS path in the graph $G = (V, E, lb)$ certainly is a lower bound for the total number of switches in the optimal sequence (see Subsection 8.3.1). In other words, denoting by $L(A, C)$ the length of such an optimal path, we see that $L(A, C) + C$ is a lower bound on $\text{cost}(A, C)$ (Tang and Denardo (1988)). Our computational experiments indicate that this bound is generally extremely weak.

   The lower bound $L(A, C) + C$ can sometimes be improved by relying on the following observations. It is obvious that, if (A', C) is a new problem instance obtained by deleting some jobs from A (i.e., the columns of A' form a subset of the columns of A), then the number of setups required for (A', C) is never larger than the number of setups required for (A, C), i.e. $\text{cost}(A', C) \leq \text{cost}(A, C)$. Thus, in particular, $L(A', C) + C$ is a lower bound on $\text{cost}(A, C)$. But it may happen that $L(A, C) < L(A', C)$, in which case $L(A', C) + C$ is a sharper bound than $L(A, C) + C$.

Example 8.2 Consider the instance (A, C) described in Tang and Denardo (1988a). After some reductions, the instance involves 6 jobs, and the matrix $lb(i, j)$ is given by:

$$lb = \begin{bmatrix} - & 2 & 3 & 2 & 2 & 1 \\ 2 & - & 3 & 1 & 0 & 1 \\ 2 & 3 & - & 3 & 2 & 2 \\ 2 & 1 & 3 & - & 2 & 2 \\ 2 & 0 & 2 & 2 & - & 2 \\ 1 & 1 & 2 & 2 & 2 & - \end{bmatrix}$$

The path $(3, 6, 1, 4, 2, 5)$ is a shortest TS path with respect to lb. Its length is $L(A, C) = 6$. On the other hand, deleting the second job from this instance results in an instance (A', C) for which the shortest Hamiltonian path $(3, 6, 1, 4, 5)$ has length $L(A', C) = 7$. Since the sequence $(3, 6, 1, 2, 4, 5)$ requires precisely 7 switches (see Tang and Denardo (1988a)), we conclude that this sequence is optimal for the instance (A, C). □

An interesting question is how the partial instance (A', C) should be (heuristically) picked in order to raise as much as possible the lower bound $L(A', C) + C$. This question has not been investigated yet.

8.5.2   Structures implying extra setups

Another approach for obtaining lower bounds on $\text{cost}(A, C)$ is to identify subsets of tools for which extra setups are needed in any sequence. This can for instance be done as follows. Let K be a subset of rows (viz. tools), and J a subset of columns (viz. jobs) of A. Say that a job $j \in J$ is *heavy* (with respect to J and K) if, for every partition of J into $J_1 \cup \{j\} \cup J_2$ (J_1 and J_2 nonempty),

$$|\{k \in K : a_{kj} = 1\}| + |\{k \in K : a_{kj} = 0 \text{ and } a_{kr} = a_{ks} = 1$$
$$\text{for some } r \in J_1, s \in J_2\}| > C. \tag{8.1}$$

The idea behind this definition is easy to grasp: the left-hand side of (8.1) represents the number of tools required to process job j ($a_{kj} = 1$), plus the number of tools which are not required by j ($a_{kj} = 0$), but which are used before and after j in a sequence of the form (J_1, j, J_2) ($a_{kr} = a_{ks} = 1$). Now, we have:

Theorem 8.3 *If J contains three heavy jobs with respect to J and K, then, in any sequence, at least one tool of K incurs an extra setup.*

Proof:
Consider any sequence. We can always find a partition J into $J_1 \cup \{j\} \cup J_2$

such that j is heavy, J_1 and J_2 are nonempty, all the jobs in J_1 occur before j in the sequence, and all the jobs in J_2 occur after j. It follows directly from (1) that, among all the tools of K which are needed both in J_1 and in J_2, some will not be present in the magazine when job j is processed (since this would exceed the magazine capacity). Hence, an extra setup will be necessary for these tools. $\square$

The statement of Theorem 8.3 is probably too general to be of direct interest. But it can nevertheless be used to identify some substructures in the tool-job matrix A which imply extra setups in any sequence. Two illustrations of such structures are now given.

1) Assume there exist three jobs (say, without loss of generality, $j = 1, 2, 3$) and a subset K of tools such that:

   (i) each tool in K is used by exactly two of the jobs 1, 2, 3;

   (ii) each of the jobs 1, 2, 3 needs (strictly) more than $C - K$ tools among those not in K.

   Under these conditions, one verifies that the jobs 1, 2, 3 are heavy with respect to K; hence, the conclusion of Theorem 8.3 applies.

2) Suppose that J and K are subsets of jobs and tools respectively, such that:

   (i) $|J| = |K| \geq 3$;

   (ii) the submatrix of A with column-set J and row-set K is the adjacency matrix of a cycle (see Nemhauser and Wolsey (1988));

   (iii) at least three jobs in J require C tools.

   Then, the three tools mentioned under (iii) are heavy, and Theorem 8.3 applies again.

Consider now p subsets of tools $K_1, K_2, \ldots, K_p$ for which we know (e.g., using Theorem 8.3) that at least one tool in K_i incurs an extra setup in any sequence $(i = 1, 2, \ldots, p)$. Let $K = \cup_i K_i$. Then, a lower bound on the total number of extra setups is provided by the optimal value of the following set-covering problem:

$$Z = \quad \text{minimize} \quad \sum_{k \in K} t_k \tag{8.2}$$

$$\text{subject to} \quad \sum_{k \in K_i} t_k \geq 1 \qquad (i = 1, 2, \ldots, p) \tag{8.3}$$

$$t_k \in \{0, 1\} \qquad (k \in K). \tag{8.4}$$

Hence, $Z + M$ is a lower bound on $\text{cost}(A, C)$ (where M is, as always, the total number of tools).

8.5.3 Valid inequalities

Tang and Denardo (1988a) propose the following formulation of the tool switching problem (see also Bard (1988)). Let $x_{ij} = 1$ if job i is the j-th job in a sequence, and $x_{ij} = 0$ otherwise; let $t_{kj} = 1$ if tool k is on the machine when the j-th job is processed, and 0 otherwise; let $y_{kj} = 1$ if tool k is setup just before processing the j-th job of the sequence, and 0 otherwise $(k = 1, 2, \ldots, M; \; i, j = 1, 2, \ldots, N)$. Then,

$$\text{cost}(A, C) = \quad \text{minimize} \quad \sum_k \sum_j y_{kj}$$

$$\text{subject to} \quad \sum_i x_{ij} = 1 \qquad (j = 1, 2, \ldots, N) \tag{8.5}$$

$$\sum_j x_{ij} = 1 \qquad (i = 1, 2, \ldots, N) \tag{8.6}$$

$$\sum_i a_{ki} x_{ij} \leq t_{kj} \qquad (k = 1, 2, \ldots, M;$$

$$j = 1, 2, \ldots, N) \tag{8.7}$$

$$\sum_k t_{kj} = C \qquad (j = 1, 2, \ldots, N) \tag{8.8}$$

$$y_{kj} \geq t_{kj} - t_{k,j-1} \qquad (k = 1, 2, \ldots, M;$$

$$j = 2, \ldots, N) \tag{8.9}$$

$$y_{k1} \geq t_{k1} \qquad (k = 1, 2, \ldots, M) \tag{8.10}$$

$$x_{ij} \in \{0, 1\} \qquad (i, j = 1, 2, \ldots, N) \tag{8.11}$$

$$t_{kj}, y_{kj} \in \{0, 1\} \qquad (k = 1, 2, \ldots, M;$$

$$j = 1, 2, \ldots, N). \tag{8.12}$$

Call SW this 0-1 programming problem. The linear programming relaxation of SW provides a lower bound on $\text{cost}(A, C)$. But this bound is extremely weak (Tang and Denardo (1988a)). One way of improving it would be to add more valid constraints to the formulation of SW. For instance, the following inequalities are valid for the tool switching problem:

$$\sum_j y_{kj} \geq 1 \qquad\qquad (k = 1, 2, \ldots, M)$$

(notice that these trivial inequalities are not even satisfied, in general, by an optimal solution to the continuous relaxation of SW). Another family of valid inequalities can be derived as follows. Let K be a subset of tools for which we know that at least one extra setup is required in the optimal sequence (see Theorem 8.3). Then,

$$\sum_{k \in K} \sum_j y_{kj} \geq |K| + 1$$

is valid. More generally, if Z is the optimal value of (8.2)–(8.4), then a valid constraint is given by:

$$\sum_{k \in K} \sum_j y_{kj} \geq |K| + Z.$$

More work is needed on the strengthening of the formulation SW.

Still another possible approach would be to replace SW by a formulation of the tool switching problem using different variables. For instance, one may want to consider the "disaggregated" variables t_{kij}, with the interpretation that $t_{kij} = 1$ if tool k is set up just after finishing the i-th job and is removed just after finishing the j-th job. It is easy to write a formulation of our problem involving only the variables x_{ij}, t_{kij} and y_{kj}. It is also relatively easy to derive exponentially many valid inequalities using these variables, which can in principle be added to the initial formulation in order to strengthen it. But our preliminary computational experiments along these lines were quite disappointing, in that they did not allow us to noticeably improve our previous lower bounds on the optimal value of the problem.

8.5.4   Lagrangian relaxation

Lagrangian relaxation is a classical tool in deriving bounds on the optimal value of an integer programming problem (see Nemhauser and Wolsey (1988)). For problem SW, one may for instance try to relax the groups of constraints (8.7) and (8.8). Indeed, as observed by Bard (1988), the resulting subproblems are then easy to solve (Bard (1988) uses this relaxation scheme in order to produce a sequence of heuristic solutions for the tool switching problem). But it is easy to prove that the optimal value of the Lagrangian dual problem obtained in this way is equal to the optimal value of the linear relaxation of SW (this is because all extreme points of the system defined by (8.5), (8.6), (8.9), (8.10) and the relaxation of (8.11), (8.12) are integral; see Nemhauser and Wolsey (1988)).

The possibility of deriving good lower bounds on $cost(A, C)$ using Lagrangian relaxation is an avenue that should be further explored.

Appendix: Graph-theoretic definitions

In this chapter, a *graph* G is a triple of the form (V, E, d), where:

- V is a finite set; the elements of V are the *nodes* of G;

- E is a set of pairs of nodes, called *edges*;

- d is a function which assigns a nonnegative *length* to each pair of nodes; we assume that $d(u, v) = +\infty$ when $\{u, v\}$ is not an edge.

A *path* in a graph is a sequence of nodes, i.e. a permutation of a subset of V. A *traveling salesman path* (or *TS path*) is a permutation of V. The length of a path $(u_1, \ldots, u_k)$ is by definition:

$$d(u_1, u_2) + d(u_2, u_3) + \ldots + d(u_{k-1}, u_k).$$

Notice, in particular, that the length of such a path is infinite if some pair $\{u_i, u_{i+1}\}$ is not an edge of the graph. The *traveling salesman* problem on a graph G can be stated as follows: find a TS path of minimal length in G.

With a graph $G = (V, E, d)$, we can associate another graph $H = (E, I, \delta)$, called the *edge-graph* of G, and defined as follows:

- each node of H is an edge of G;

- a pair $\{e, f\}$, with $e, f \in E$, is an edge of H if and only if the edges e and f share a common node in G;

- $\delta(e, f) = 1$ if $\{e, f\}$ is an edge of H, and $\delta(e, f) = +\infty$ otherwise.

Observe that, in an edge-graph, every TS path has length either $|E| - 1$ or $+\infty$. Consider now the restriction of the traveling salesman problem to edge-graphs, that is:

Input   : a graph G.
Problem P3 : find a TS path of minimal length in the edge-graph of G.

Equivalently, $P3$ asks whether there exists a TS path of finite length in the edge-graph of G. Bertossi (1981) proved that this problem is $\mathcal{N}P$-hard.

We also deal in this chapter with *directed graphs*. A directed graph is a triple (V, U, d), where V is defined as for a graph, and:

- U is a set of ordered pairs of nodes, called *arcs*; i.e., $U \subset V \times V$;

- d is a (nonnegative) length function defined on $V \times V$, with the property that $d(u, v) = +\infty$ when (u, v) is not an arc.

So, in a directed graph, $d(u, v)$ may differ from $d(v, u)$. The definitions of a TS path and of the TS problem extend in a straightforward way for directed graphs.

References

Aanen, E. (1988), *Planning and scheduling in a flexible manufacturing system*, Ph.D. thesis, University of Twente, Enschede.

Aboudi, R. and G.L. Nemhauser (1990), *An assignment problem with side constraints: strong cutting planes and separation*, in: Economic Decision-Making: Games, Econometrics and Optimisation, J.J. Gabszewicz, J.-F. Richard and L.A. Wolsey (editors), Elsevier, Amsterdam, 457–471.

Aboudi, R. and G.L. Nemhauser (1991), *Some facets for an assignment problem with side constraints*, Operations Research 39, 244–250.

Ahmadi, J., R. Ahmadi, H. Matsuo and D. Tirupati (1990), *Component fixture positioning for printed circuit board assembly with concurrent operations*, Working Paper 90-03-01, ICC Institute, University of Texas, Austin, Texas.

Ahmadi, J., S. Grotzinger and D. Johnson (1988), *Component allocation and partitioning for a dual delivery placement machine*, Operations Research 36, 176–191.

Akella, R., Y. Choong and S.B. Gershwin (1984), *Performance of hierarchical production scheduling policy*, in: Proceedings of the first ORSA/TIMS Special Interest Conference on Flexible Manufacturing Systems, Ann Arbor, MI, 385–396.

Ammons, J.C., C.B. Lofgren and L.F. McGinnis (1985), *A large scale machine loading problem in flexible assembly*, Annals of Operations Research 3, 319–332.

Balas, E. and A. Ho (1980), *Set covering algorithms using cutting planes, heuristics and subgradient optimization: a computational study*, Discrete Applied Mathematics 23, 201–229.

Balas, E. and M.J. Saltzman (1989), *Facets of the three-index assignment polytope*, Discrete Applied Mathematics 23, 201–229.

Balas, E. and M.J. Saltzman (1991), *An algorithm for the three-index assignment problem*, Operations Research 39, 150–161.

Ball, M.O. and M.J. Magazine (1988), *Sequencing of insertions in printed circuit board assembly*, Operations Research 36, 192–201.

Bandelt, H.-J., Y. Crama and F.C.R. Spieksma (1991), *Approximation algorithms for multidimensional assignment problems with decomposable costs*, to appear in Discrete Applied Mathematics.

Bard, J.F. (1988), *A heuristic for minimizing the number of tool switches on a flexible machine*, IIE Transactions 20, 382–391.

Bard, J.F. and T.A. Feo (1989), *The cutting path and tool selection problem in computer aided process planning*, Journal of Manufacturing Systems 8, 17–26.

Bastos, J.M. (1988), *Batching and routing: two functions in the operational planning of flexible manufacturing systems*, European Journal of Operational Research 33, 230–244.

Berrada, M. and K.E. Stecke (1986), *A branch and bound approach for machine load balancing in flexible manufacturing systems*, Management Science 32, 1316–1335.

Bertossi, A.A. (1981), *The edge hamiltonian path problem is $\mathcal{N}P$-complete*, Information Processing Letters 13, 157–159.

Blazewicz, I., G. Finke, R. Haupt and G. Schmidt (1988), *New trends in machine scheduling*, European Journal of Operational Research 37, 303–317.

Booth, K.S. and G.S. Lueker (1976), *Testing for the consecutive ones property, interval graphs, and graph planarity using PQ-tree algorithms*, Journal of Computer and System Sciences 13, 335–379.

Browne, J., D. Dubois, K. Rathmill, S. Sethi and K.E. Stecke (1984), *Classification of flexible manufacturing systems*, The FMS Magazine 2, 114–117.

Burkard, R.E. (1984), *Quadratic assignment problems*, European Journal of Operational Research 15, 283–289.

Buzacott, J.A. and D.D. Yao (1986), *Flexible manufacturing systems: a review of analytical models*, Management Science 32, 890–905.

Chaillou, P., P. Hansen and Y. Mahieu (1989), *Best network flow bounds for the quadratic knapsack problem*, in: Combinatorial Optimization, B. Simeone (editor), Springer-Verlag, Berlin, 225–235.

Chakravarty, A.K. and A. Shtub (1984), *Selecting parts andloading flexible manufacturing systems*, in: Proceedings of the first ORSA/TIMS Special Interest Conference on Flexible Manufacturing Systems, Ann Arbor, MI, 284–289.

Chams, M., A. Hertz and D. de Werra (1987), *Some experiments with simulated annealing for coloring graphs*, European Journal of Operational Research 32, 260–266.

Chang, Y.-L., R.S. Sullivan, U. Bagchi and J.R. Wilson (1985), *Experimental investigation of real-time scheduling in flexible manufacturing systems*, Annals of Operations Research 3, 355–377.

Charles Stark Draper Laboratory (1984), *Flexible Manufacturing Systems Handbook*, Noyes Publications, Park Ridge, NJ.

Chung, C.H. (1991), *Planning tool requirements for flexible manufacturing systems*, Journal of Manufacturing Systems 10, 476–483.

Chvátal, V. (1983), *Linear Programming*, W.H. Freeman & Co, New York.

CQM (1988), Philips Center for Quantitative Methods, Eindhoven, The Netherlands.

Crama, Y., A.W.J. Kolen, A.G. Oerlemans and F.C.R. Spieksma (1989), *Throughput rate optimization in the automated assembly of printed circuit boards*, Research Memorandum RM 89.034, Faculty of Economics, University of Limburg, Maastricht, The Netherlands.

Dantzig, G.B. and P. Wolfe (1960), *Decomposition principle for linear programs*, Operations Research 8, 101–111.

Daskin, M., P.C. Jones and T.J. Lowe (1990), *Rationalizing tool selection in a flexible manufacturing system for sheet-metal products*, Operations Research 38, 1104–1115.

Desrosiers, J., F. Soumis and M. Desrochers (1984), *Routing with time windows by column generation*, Networks 14, 545–565.

Dietrich, B.L., J. Lee and Y.S. Lee (1991), *Order selection on a single machine with high set-up costs*, Working Paper OR 90-19, Yale University, New Haven.

Dupont-Gatelmand, C. (1982), *A survey of flexible manufacturing systems*, Journal of Manufacturing Systems 1, 1–16.

ElMaraghy, H.A. (1985), *Automated tooling management in flexible manufacturing*, Journal of Manufacturing Systems 4, 1–13.

Farley, A.A. (1990), *A note on bounding a class of linear programming problems, including cutting stock problems*, Operations Research 38, 922–923.

Finke, G. and A. Kusiak (1987), *Models for the process planning problem in a flexible manufacturing system*, International Journal of Advanced Manufacturing Technology 2, 3–12.

Fisher, M.L. (1981), *The lagrangean relaxation method for solving integer programming problems*, Management Science 27, 1–18.

Fisher, M.L., R. Jaikumar and L.N. van Wassenhove (1986), *A multiplier adjustment method for the generalized assignment problem*, Management Science 32, 1095–1103.

Fisk, J. and P.G. McKeown (1979), *The pure fixed charge transportation problem*, Naval Research Logistics Quarterly 26, 631–641.

Frieze, A.M. (1974), *A bilinear programming formulation of the 3-dimensional assignment problem*, Mathematical Programming 7, 376–379.

Frieze, A.M. and J. Yadegar (1981), *An algorithm for solving 3-dimensional assignment problems with application to scheduling a teaching practice*, Journal of the Operational Research Society 32, 989–995.

Förster, H.-U. and K. Hirt (1989), *Entwicklung einer Handlungsanleitung zur Gestaltung von Produktionsplanungs- und -Steuerungskonzepten beim Einsatz flexibler Fertigungssysteme, Schlussbericht zum Forschungvorhaben*, Nr. S 172, Forschungsinstitut für Rationalisierung, Rheinisch-Westfälischen Technischen Hochschule, Aachen.

Fulkerson, D.R. and D.A. Gross (1965), *Incidence matrices and interval graphs*, Pacific Journal of Mathematics 15, 835–855.

Gallo, G., P.L. Hammer, and B. Simeone (1980), *Quadratic knapsack problems*, Mathematical Programming Study 12, 132–149.

Gallo, G. and B. Simeone (1988), *On the supermodular knapsack problem*, Mathematical Programming 45, 295–309.

Garey, M.R. and D.S. Johnson (1979), *Computers and intractability: a guide to the theory of NP-completeness* , W.H. Freeman & Co, New York.

Garey, M.R., D.S. Johnson, B.B. Simons and R.E. Tarjan (1981), *Scheduling unit-time tasks with arbitrary release times and deadlines*, SIAM Journal on Computing 10, 256–269.

Gerwin, D. (1982), *Do's and don'ts of computerized manufacturing*, Harvard Business Review 60, 107–116.

Gilmore, P.C. and R.E. Gomory (1961), *A linear programming approach to the cutting-stock problem*, Operations Research 9, 849–859.

Glover, F. (1989), *Tabu search - part I*, ORSA Journal on Computing 1, 190–206.

Glover, F. (1990), *Tabu search - part II*, ORSA Journal on Computing 2, 4–32.

Golden, B.L. and W.R. Stewart (1985), *Empirical analysis of heuristics*, in: The Traveling Salesman Problem, E.L. Lawler, J.K. Lenstra, A.H.G. Rinnooy Kan and D.B. Shmoys (editors), John Wiley & Sons, Chichester, United Kingdom, 207–249.

Graver, T.W. and L.F. McGinnis (1989), *A tool provisioning problem in an FMS*, The International Journal of Flexible Manufacturing Systems 1, 239–254.

Gray, A.E., A. Seidmann and K.E. Stecke (1988), *Tool management in automated manufacturing: operational issues and decision problems*, Working Paper CMOM 88-03, Simon Graduate School of Business Administration, University of Rochester, New York.

Greene, T.J. and R.P. Sadowski (1986), *A mixed integer program for loading and scheduling multiple flexible manufacturing cells*, European Journal of Operational Research 24, 379–386.

Groover, M.P. (1980), *Automation, Production Systems and Computer-Aided Manufacturing*, Prentice-Hall, Englewood Cliffs, New Jersey.

Gruver, W.A. and M.T. Senninger (1990), *Tooling management in FMS*, Mechanical Engineering 112, 40–44.

Hansen, P. and L. Kaufman (1973), *A primal-dual algorithm for the three-dimensional assignment problem*, Cahiers du Centre d'Etudes de Recherche Opérationnelle 15, 327–336.

Hartley, J. (1984), *FMS at work*, IFS Publications, Bedford, United Kingdom.

Hirabayashi, R., H. Suzuki and N. Tsuchiya (1984), *Optimal tool module design problem for NC machine tools*, Journal of the Operations Research Society of Japan 27, 205–228.

Hoffman, A.J., A.W.J. Kolen and M. Sakarovitch (1985), *Totally balanced and greedy matrices*, SIAM Journal on Algebraic and Discrete Methods 6, 721–730.

Holstein, W.K. (1968), *Production planning and control integrated*, Harvard Business Review 46, 121–140.

Holyer, I. (1981), *The $\mathcal{NP}$-completeness of some edge-partition problems*, SIAM Journal on Computing 10, 713–717.

Huang, P.Y. and C. Chen (1986), *Flexible manufacturing systems: an overview and bibliography*, Production and Inventory Management, Third Quarter, 80–90.

Hwang, S. (1986), *A constraint-directed method to solve the part selection problem in flexible manufacturing systems planning stage*, in: FMS, Operations Research Models and Applications, K.E. Stecke and R. Suri (editors), Elsevier, Amsterdam, 297–309.

Hwang, S.S. and A.W. Shogan (1989), *Modelling and solving an FMS part selection problem*, International Journal of Production Research 27, 1349–1366.

Jaikumar, R. (1986), *Postindustrial manufacturing*, Harvard Business Review 64, 69–76.

Jaikumar, R. and L.N. van Wassenhove (1989), *A production planning framework for flexible manufacturing systems*, Journal of Manufacturing and Operations Management 2, 52–79.

Jain, A.K., G. Kasilingam and S.D. Bhole (1991), *Joint consideration of cell formation and tool provisioning problems in flexible manufacturing systems*, Computers and Industrial Engineering 20, 271–277.

Jaumard, B., P. Hansen and M. Poggi de Aragão (1991), *Column generation methods for probabilistic logic*, ORSA Journal on Computing 3, 135–148.

Johnson, D.S., C.R. Aragon, L.A. McGeoch and C. Schevon (1989), *Optimization by simulated annealing: an experimental evaluation; part I, graph partioning*, Operations Research 37, 865–892.

Johnson, D.S., C.R. Aragon, L.A. McGeoch and C. Schevon (1991), *Optimization by simulated annealing: an experimental evaluation; part II, graph coloring and number partioning*, Operations Research 39, 378–406.

Johnson, D.S. and C.H. Papadimitriou (1985), *Computational complexity*, in: The Traveling Salesman Problem, E.L. Lawler, J.K. Lenstra, A.H.G. Rinnooy Kan and D.B. Shmoys (editors), John Wiley & Sons, Chichester, United Kingdom, 37–85.

Kashiwabara, T. and T. Fujisawa (1979), *$\mathcal{N}\mathcal{P}$-completeness of the problem of finding a minimum-clique-number interval graph containing a given graph as a subgraph*, Proceedings of the 1979 International Symposium on Circuits and Systems, 657–660.

Kavvadias, D. and C.H. Papadimitriou (1989), *A linear programming approach to reasoning about probabilities*, Annals of Mathematics and Artificial Intelligence 1, 189–205.

Kernighan, B.W. and S. Lin (1970), *An efficient heuristic procedure for partioning graphs*, The Bell System Technical Journal 49, 291–307.

Kim, Y.D. and C.A. Yano (1992), *An iterative approach to system setup problems in flexible manufacturing systems*, The International Journal of Flexible Manufacturing Systems 4, 183–209.

Kiran, A.S. and R.J. Krason (1988), *Automating tooling in a flexible manufacturing system*, Industrial Engineering, April, 52–57.

Kiran, A.S. and B.C. Tansel (1986), *The system set-up in FMS: concepts and formulation*, in: FMS, Operations Research Models and Applications, K.E. Stecke and R. Suri (editors), Elsevier, Amsterdam, 321–332.

Korte, B. (1989), *Applications of combinatorial optimization*, in: Mathematical Programming, Recent Developments and Applications, M. Iri and K. Tanabe (editors), KTK Scientific Publishers, Tokyo, 1–55.

Kou, L.T. (1977), *Polynomial complete consecutive information retrieval problems*, SIAM Journal on Computing 6, 67–75.

Kuhn, H. (1990), *Einlastungsplanung von flexiblen Fertigungssystemen*, Physica-Verlag, Heidelberg.

Kumar, K.R., A. Kusiak and A. Vanelli (1986), *Grouping parts and components in flexible manufacturing systems*, European Journal of Operational Research 24, 387–397.

Kusiak, A. (1985a), *Flexible manufacturing systems: a structural approach*, International Journal of Production Research 23, 1057–1073.

Kusiak, A. (1985b), *Integer programming approaches to process planning*, International Journal of Advanced Manufacturing Technology 1, 73–83.

Kusiak, A. (1985c), *The part families problem in flexible manufacturing systems*, Annals of Operations Research 3, 279–300.

Kusiak, A. (1986), *Application of operational research models and techniques in flexible manufacturing systems*, European Journal of Operational Research 24, 336–345.

Laarhoven, P.J.M. van, and E.H.L. Aarts (1987), *Simulated Annealing: Theory and Applications*, D. Reidel Publishing Company, Dordrecht.

Laarhoven, P.J.M. van, and W.H.M. Zijm (1993), *Production preparation and numerical control in PCB assembly*, The International Journal of Flexible Manufacturing Systems 5, 187–207.

Lawler, E.L., J.K. Lenstra, A.H.G. Rinnooy Kan and D.B. Shmoys (editors) (1985), *The traveling salesman problem*, John Wiley & Sons, New York.

Leipälä, T. and O. Nevalainen (1989), *Optimization of the movements of a component placement machine*, European Journal of Operational Research 38, 167–177.

Looveren, A.J. van, L.F. Gelders and L.N. van Wassenhove (1986), *A review of FMS planning models*, in: Modelling and design of flexible manufacturing systems, A. Kusiak (editor), Elsevier, Amsterdam, 3–31.

Mamer, J.W. and A.W. Shogan (1987), *A constrained capital budgeting problem with applications to repair kit selection*, Management Science 27, 800–806.

Mattson, R., J. Gecsei, D.R. Slutz and I.L. Traiger (1970), *Evaluation techniques for storage hierarchies*, IBM Systems Journal 9, 78–117.

Mazzola, J.B., A.W. Neebe and C.V.R. Dunn (1989), *Production planning of a flexible manufacturing system in a material requirements planning environment*, The International Journal of Flexible Manufacturing Systems 1, 115–142.

Minoux, M. (1987), *A class of combinatorial problems with polynomially solvable large scale set covering/partioning relaxations*, RAIRO 21, 105–136.

Möhring, R.H. (1990), *Graph problems related to gate matrix layout and PLA folding*, in: Computational Graph Theory, G. Tinhofer et al. (editors), Springer-Verlag, Wien, 17–51.

Montazeri, M. and L.N. van Wassenhove (1990), *Analysis of scheduling rules for an FMS*, International Journal of Production Research 28, 785–802.

Mullins, P. (1990), *PCB assembly: a total package*, Production 102, 60–61.

Nemhauser, G.L. and L.A. Wolsey (1988), *Integer and combinatorial optimization*, John Wiley & Sons, New York.

Oerlemans, A.G. (1992), *Production planning for flexible manufacturing systems*, Ph.D. thesis, University of Limburg, Maastricht.

Panwalker, S.S. and W. Iskander (1977), *A survey of scheduling rules*, Operations Research 25, 45–61.

Papadimitriou, C.H. and K. Steiglitz (1982), *Combinatorial optimization: algorithms and complexity*, Prentice Hall, Englewood Cliffs, New Jersey.

Rajagopalan, S. (1985), *Scheduling problems in flexible manufacturing systems*, Working Paper, Graduate School of Industrial Administration, Carnegie-Mellon University, Pittsburgh, PA.

Rajagopalan, S. (1986), *Formulation and heuristic solutions for parts grouping and tool loading in flexible manufacturing systems*, in: FMS, Operations Research Models and Applications, K.E. Stecke and R. Suri (editors), Elsevier, Amsterdam, 311– 320.

Ránky, P.G. (1983), *The Design and Operation of an FMS*, IFS/North-Holland, Amsterdam.

Ribeiro, C.C., M. Minoux, and M.C. Penna (1989), *An optimal column-generation-with-ranking algorithm for very large scale set partioning problems in traffic assignment*, European Journal of Operational Research 41, 232–239.

Roger, C. (1990), *La gestion des outils sur machines à commande numérique*, Mémoire DEA de Recherche Opérationnelle, Université Joseph Fourier, Grenoble, France.

Shanker, K. and Y.J. Tzen (1985), *A loading and dispatching problem in a random flexible manufacturing system*, International Journal of Production Research 23, 579–595.

Singhal, K., C.H. Fine, J.R. Meredith and R. Suri (1987), *Research and models for automated manufacturing*, Interfaces 17, 5–14

Sousa, J.P. and L.A. Wolsey (1992), *A time indexed formulation of non-preemptive single-machine scheduling problems*, Mathematical Programming 54, 353–367.

Spieksma, F.C.R. (1992), *Assignment and scheduling algorithms in automated manufacturing*, Ph.D. thesis, University of Limburg, Maastricht.

Spieksma, F.C.R., K. Vrieze and A.G. Oerlemans (1990), *On the system setup and the scheduling problem in a flexible manufacturing system (FMS)*, Statistica Neerlandica 44, 125–138.

Stecke, K.E. (1983), *Formulation and solution of nonlinear integer production planning problems for flexible manufacturing systems*, Management Science 29, 273–288.

Stecke, K.E. (1985), *Design, planning, scheduling and control problems of flexible manufacturing systems*, Annals of Operations Research 3, 3–12.

Stecke, K.E. (1988), *O.R. applications to flexible manufacturing*, in: Operational Research '87, G.K. Rand (editor), 287–324.

Stecke, K.E. (1989), *Algorithms for efficient planning and operation of a particular FMS*, The International Journal of Flexible Manufacturing Systems 1, 287–324.

Stecke, K.E. and I. Kim (1988), *A study of FMS part type selection approaches for short-term production planning*, The International Journal of Flexible Manufacturing Systems 1, 7–29.

Stecke, K.E. and J.J. Solberg (1981), *Loading and control policies for a flexible manufacturing system*, International Journal of Production Research 19, 481–490.

Suri, R. (1985), *An overview of evaluative models for flexible manufacturing systems*, Annals of Operations Research 3, 13–21.

Suri, R. and C.K. Whitney (1984), *Decision support requirements in flexible manufacturing*, Journal of Manufacturing Systems 3, 61–69.

Tang, C.S. and E.V. Denardo (1988a), *Models arising from a flexible manufacturing machine, part I: minimization of the number of tool switches*, Operations Research 36, 767–777.

Tang, C.S. and E.V. Denardo (1988b), *Models arising from a flexible manufacturing machine, part II: minimization of the number of switching instants*, Operations Research 36, 778–784.

Vasko, F.J. and F.E. Wolf (1988), *Solving large set covering problems on a personal computer*, Computers and Operations Research 15, 115–121.

Ventura, J.A., F.F. Chen and M.S. Leonard (1988), *Loading tools to machines in flexible manufacturing systems*, Computers and Industrial Engineering 15, 223–230.

Vliet, M. van, and L.N. van Wassenhove (1989), *Operational research techniques for analyzing flexible manufacturing systems*, Research Memorandum series, No. Ti-1989/16, Tinbergen Institute, Erasmus University Rotterdam, Rotterdam.

Volgenant, T. and R. Jonker (1982), *A branch and bound algorithm for the symmetric traveling salesman problem based on the 1-tree relaxation*, European Journal of Operational Research 9, 83–89.

Warnecke, H.-J. and R. Steinhilper (1985), *Flexible Manufacturing Systems*, IFS Publications, Springer-Verlag, Berlin.

Werra, D. de, and M. Widmer (1990), *Loading problems with tool management in FMSs: a few integer programming models*, The International Journal of Flexible Manufacturing Systems 3, 71–82.

Whitney, C.K. and T.S. Gaul (1985), *Sequential decision procedures for batching and balancing in FMSs*, Annals of Operations Research 3, 301–316.

Widmer, M. (1991), *Job shop scheduling with tooling constraints: a tabu search approach*, Journal of the Operations Research Society 42, 75–82.

Zeestraten, M.J. (1989), *Scheduling flexible manufacturing systems*, Ph.D. Thesis, Delft University of Technology, Delft.

Zijm, W.H.M. (1988), *Flexible manufacturing systems: background, examples and models*, in: Operations Research Proceedings 1988, H. Schellhaas et al. (editors), Springer-Verlag, Heidelberg, 142–161.

Lecture Notes in Economics and Mathematical Systems

For information about Vols. 1–234
please contact your bookseller or Springer-Verlag

Vol. 273: Large-Scale Modelling and Interactive Decision Analysis. Proceedings, 1985. Edited by G. Fandel, M. Grauer, A. Kurzhanski and A.P. Wierzbicki. VII, 363 pages. 1986.

Vol. 274: W.K. Klein Haneveld, Duality in Stochastic Linear and Dynamic Programming. VII, 295 pages. 1986.

Vol. 275: Competition, Instability, and Nonlinear Cycles. Proceedings, 1985. Edited by W. Semmler. XII, 340 pages. 1986.

Vol. 276: M.R. Baye, D.A. Black, Consumer Behavior, Cost of Living Measures, and the Income Tax. VII, 119 pages. 1986.

Vol. 277: Studies in Austrian Capital Theory, Investment and Time. Edited by M. Faber. VI, 317 pages. 1986.

Vol. 278: W.E. Diewert, The Measurement of the Economic Benefits of Infrastructure Services. V, 202 pages. 1986.

Vol. 279: H.-J. Büttler, G. Frei and B. Schips, Estimation of Disequilibrium Modes. VI, 114 pages. 1986.

Vol. 280: H.T. Lau, Combinatorial Heuristic Algorithms with FORTRAN. VII, 126 pages. 1986.

Vol. 281: Ch.-L. Hwang, M.-J. Lin, Group Decision Making under Multiple Criteria. XI, 400 pages. 1987.

Vol. 282: K. Schittkowski, More Test Examples for Nonlinear Programming Codes. V, 261 pages. 1987.

Vol. 283: G. Gabisch, H.-W. Lorenz, Business Cycle Theory. VII, 229 pages. 1987.

Vol. 284: H. Lütkepohl, Forecasting Aggregated Vector ARMA Processes. X, 323 pages. 1987.

Vol. 285: Toward Interactive and Intelligent Decision Support Systems. Volume 1. Proceedings, 1986. Edited by Y. Sawaragi, K. Inoue and H. Nakayama. XII, 445 pages. 1987.

Vol. 286: Toward Interactive and Intelligent Decision Support Systems. Volume 2. Proceedings, 1986. Edited by Y. Sawaragi, K. Inoue and H. Nakayama. XII, 450 pages. 1987.

Vol. 287: Dynamical Systems. Proceedings, 1985. Edited by A.B. Kurzhanski and K. Sigmund. VI, 215 pages. 1987.

Vol. 288: G.D. Rudebusch, The Estimation of Macroeconomic Disequilibrium Models with Regime Classification Information. VII,128 pages. 1987.

Vol. 289: B.R. Meijboom, Planning in Decentralized Firms. X, 168 pages. 1987.

Vol. 290: D.A. Carlson, A. Haurie, Infinite Horizon Optimal Control. XI, 254 pages. 1987.

Vol. 291: N. Takahashi, Design of Adaptive Organizations. VI, 140 pages. 1987.

Vol. 292: I. Tchijov, L. Tomaszewicz (Eds.), Input-Output Modeling. Proceedings, 1985. VI, 195 pages. 1987.

Vol. 293: D. Batten, J. Casti, B. Johansson (Eds.), Economic Evolution and Structural Adjustment. Proceedings, 1985. VI, 382 pages.

Vol. 294: J. Jahn, W. Knabs (Eds.), Recent Advances and Historical Development of Vector Optimization. VII, 405 pages. 1987.

Vol. 295. H. Meister, The Purification Problem for Constrained Games with Incomplete Information. X, 127 pages. 1987.

Vol. 296: A. Börsch-Supan, Econometric Analysis of Discrete Choice. VIII, 211 pages. 1987.

Vol. 297: V. Fedorov, H. Läuter (Eds.), Model-Oriented Data Analysis. Proceedings, 1987. VI, 239 pages. 1988.

Vol. 298: S.H. Chew, Q. Zheng, Integral Global Optimization. VII, 179 pages. 1988.

Vol. 299: K. Marti, Descent Directions and Efficient Solutions in Discretely Distributed Stochastic Programs. XIV, 178 pages. 1988.

Vol. 300: U. Derigs, Programming in Networks and Graphs. XI, 315 pages. 1988.

Vol. 301: J. Kacprzyk, M. Roubens (Eds.), Non-Conventional Preference Relations in Decision Making. VII, 155 pages. 1988.

Vol. 302: H.A. Eiselt, G. Pederzoli (Eds.), Advances in Optimization and Control. Proceedings, 1986. VIII, 372 pages. 1988.

Vol. 303: F.X. Diebold, Empirical Modeling of Exchange Rate Dynamics. VII, 143 pages. 1988.

Vol. 304: A. Kurzhanski, K. Neumann, D. Pallaschke (Eds.), Optimization, Parallel Processing and Applications. Proceedings, 1987. VI, 292 pages. 1988.

Vol. 305: G.-J.C.Th. van Schijndel, Dynamic Firm and Investor Behaviour under Progressive Personal Taxation. X, 215 pages.1988.

Vol. 306: Ch. Klein, A Static Microeconomic Model of Pure Competition. VIII, 139 pages. 1988.

Vol. 307: T.K. Dijkstra (Ed.), On Model Uncertainty and its Statistical Implications. VII, 138 pages. 1988.

Vol. 308: J.R. Daduna, A. Wren (Eds.), Computer-Aided Transit Scheduling. VIII, 339 pages. 1988.

Vol. 309: G. Ricci, K. Velupillai (Eds.), Growth Cycles and Multisectoral Economics: the Goodwin Tradition. III, 126 pages. 1988.

Vol. 310: J. Kacprzyk, M. Fedrizzi (Eds.), Combining Fuzzy Imprecision with Probabilistic Uncertainty in Decision Making. IX, 399 pages. 1988.

Vol. 311: R. Färe, Fundamentals of Production Theory. IX, 163 pages. 1988.

Vol. 312: J. Krishnakumar, Estimation of Simultaneous Equation Models with Error Components Structure. X, 357 pages. 1988.

Vol. 313: W. Jammernegg, Sequential Binary Investment Decisions. VI, 156 pages. 1988.

Vol. 314: R. Tietz, W. Albers, R. Selten (Eds.), Bounded Rational Behavior in Experimental Games and Markets. VI, 368 pages. 1988.

Vol. 315: I. Orishimo, G.J.D. Hewings, P. Nijkamp (Eds), Information Technology: Social and Spatial Perspectives. Proceedings 1986. VI, 268 pages. 1988.

Vol. 316: R.L. Basmann, D.J. Slottje, K. Hayes, J.D. Johnson, D.J. Molina, The Generalized Fechner-Thurstone Direct Utility Function and Some of its Uses. VIII, 159 pages. 1988.

Vol. 317: L. Bianco, A. La Bella (Eds.), Freight Transport Planning and Logistics. Proceedings, 1987. X, 568 pages. 1988.